The Taiping Heavenly Kingdom

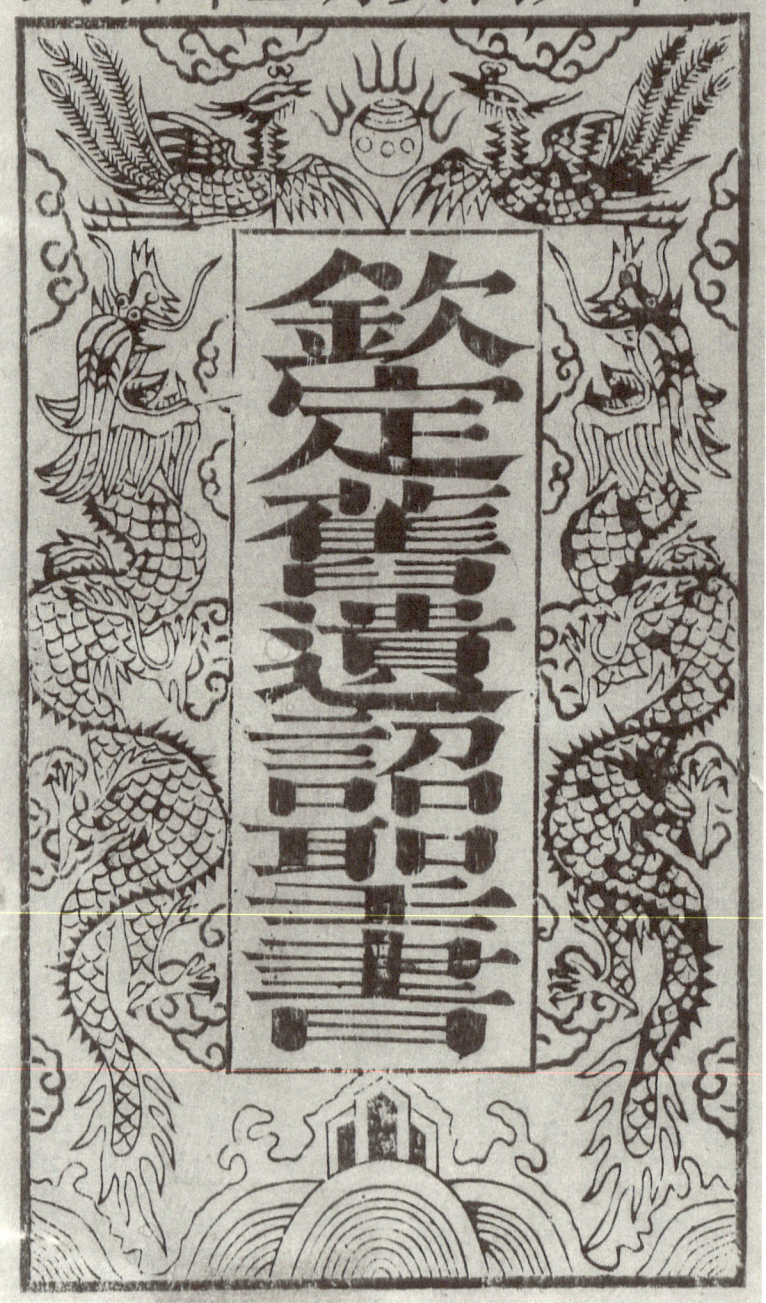

The Taiping Heavenly Kingdom

Rebellion and the Blasphemy of Empire

THOMAS H. REILLY

A China Program Book

UNIVERSITY OF WASHINGTON PRESS

Seattle and London

This publication was supported in part by the China Studies Program, a division of the Henry M. Jackson School of International Studies at the University of Washington. Additional support was provided by the Donald R. Ellegood International Publications Endowment.

© 2004 by the University of Washington Press
Designed by Pamela Canell
First paperback edition © 2014 by the University of Washington Press
Printed and bound in the United States of America
18 17 16 15 14   5 4 3 2 1

All rights reserved. No part of this publication may be reproduced or transmitted in any form or by any means, electronic or mechanical, including photocopy, recording, or any information storage or retrieval system, without permission in writing from the publisher.

University of Washington Press
PO Box 50096, Seattle, WA 98145, USA
www.washington.edu/uwpress

Library of Congress Cataloging-in-Publication Data
Reilly, Thomas H., 1954–
  The Taiping heavenly kingdom : rebellion and the blasphemy of empire / Thomas H. Reilly.—1st ed.
    p. cm.
  Includes bibliographical references.
  ISBN 978-0-295-99372-0 (pbk : alk. paper)
  1. China—History—Taiping Rebellion, 1850–1864—Religious aspects. 2. Christianity—China—Influence. I. Title.
DS759.4.R45R44 2004   951'.034—dc22   2004005244

The paper used in this publication is acid-free and meets the minimum requirements of American National Standard for Information Sciences—Permanence of Paper for Printed Library Materials. ANSI Z39.48–1984. ∞

Frontispiece: Cover of the Taiping *Royally Authorized Old Testament* (Qinding Jiuyizhao Shengshu). Although the cover is dated 1853, the use of the term *Qinding* in the title is documented only for the years following 1860. Courtesy of the British Library.

To the Chinese Church

Contents

Acknowledgments ix

Introduction 3

1 / The Early Catholic Search for the Name of God   19

2 / The Protestant Bible and the Birth of the Taiping Christian Movement   54

3 / The Taiping Challenge to Empire   78

4 / Worship and Witness in the Taiping Heavenly Kingdom   117

5 / The Taiping Legacy and Missionary Christianity   150

Notes   173

Glossary   209

Bibliography   213

Index   225

Acknowledgments

This book has been a long time in the making, and the people who have contributed to its completion constitute an extensive list. I would like to acknowledge those contributions here.

The topic of the Taiping Rebellion first caught my attention during a short missionary appointment in Taiwan in the mid-1980s. Toward the end of my time there, I was asked to teach a class on the relationship of Christianity to Chinese culture, and I referred to the Taiping movement to help illustrate some of the abiding issues concerning that relationship.

For the few years I was living in Taiwan, a number of individuals and groups aided the development of my thinking about these issues. First on the list are two churches in Taipei, the Village Two Church and the Song Shan Church. The members, elders, and pastors of these churches inspired me with their efforts to shape Christianity into a Chinese religion, and I can never be thankful enough for the many times I was invited to share a meal with them. Several individuals outside of these churches were instrumental in developing and testing my thinking about Taiping and Chinese Christianity, including Rev. Kuo Ming-chang, Rev. Daniel Hung, Ms. Zhu Tianwen and the Sansan Cultural Group which met in her home, and Dr. David Guoduan Zhou. A number of missionary friends contributed to my thinking about these issues and helped me, too, with more practical matters, and they include Dave and Linda Ludwig, Dennis and Claudia Brice, and Phil and Anne Towner.

My first formal study of the Taiping Rebellion began in a class taught by Dr. Cynthia Brokaw during a post-baccalaureate year at the University of Oregon in the spring of 1989. It was largely due to her recommendation that I began graduate study the following year at the University of Washington, where I had the good fortune to study under Dr. Kent Guy. In his Modern China graduate seminar, I completed a paper on the Taiping that became the nucleus of my dissertation. From the start, Dr. Guy encouraged my study of the Taiping, believing that what I was discovering about the Taiping was something unique and important. Throughout my years at the UW, he set high standards for me and the rest of his students, and at the same time worked tirelessly to enable us to meet his standards. A better teacher, I have not had.

I am also thankful to Dr. Mary O'Neil at the University of Washington, who patiently worked with me as I thought through topics related to Christianity and politics, and church and state, in the course of my study of Reformation Europe. She pointed out the connection between the war against images (idols) and the struggle against monarchy in the Reformation, which proved to be a pivotal point in my understanding of the political motivations of the Taiping movement.

When the time came for me to undertake research for my dissertation, several individuals and institutions contributed to its successful completion. During the several months of my work in China, Professor Mao Jiaqi of Nanjing University graciously introduced me to various experts on the Taiping movement. He recommended me to Dr. Jiang Tao of the Chinese Academy of Social Sciences, who in turn introduced me to Beijing's Ming-Qing Imperial archive and who helped me with logistical problems as well. Both of these men generously gave of their time in helping me to explore my topic and find ways to better approach it. The Hong Kong University library and the Fu-jen University library in Taiwan also assisted me in my research. Upon returning to the United States, I visited Yale Divinity School's Day Missions Library where, due to the capable instruction of Ms. Martha Smalley, I was able to survey years of missionary journals in a short two-week period. This was then followed by a brief stint in Harvard-Yenching Library's collection of Chinese Protestant missionary literature.

For my time in China, funding for research leading to this publication was provided by the Research Enablement Program, a grant program for mission scholarship supported by the Pew Charitable Trusts, Philadelphia, Pennsylvania, and administered by the Overseas Ministries Study Center,

New Haven, Connecticut. A Pacific Cultural Foundation subsidy helped me complete the writing of the dissertation.

Since I have been teaching at Pepperdine University, I have been aided in my research in part by the Dean's Fund. Those funds supported a very productive week at the University of San Francisco's Ricci Institute, made possible by the friendly and talented staff there. Mr. Mark Mir of the institute acquainted me with several reference works for the study of early Chinese Catholicism. Here in Malibu, Dr. David Baird, Dr. Connie Fulmer, Dr. Darlene Rivas, and Dr. Glenn Webb have always been supportive of my work. Glenn Webb especially has shouldered the heavy administrative burden of the Asian Studies program during these years in order to give me the time I needed to work on the manuscript. He and Carol Webb are my models for Asian Studies teachers, in love with Asia and selflessly serving their students. Dr. Dan Bays, now of Calvin College, commented on an earlier form of the manuscript and has been an encouraging voice along the way. My church family has offered many a prayer for the project's success.

The University of Washington Press has done a wonderful work, especially in the person of Lorri Hagman. She has guided this project to its completion with efficiency, professionalism, and a welcome dose of graciousness. Tammy Ditmore did a splendid job creating the index. One outside reader in particular, whose identity I still do not know, was particularly helpful in his or her comments. Because of the comments and criticisms of Dr. Kent Guy, Dr. Mary O'Neil, Dr. Dan Bays, and this anonymous reviewer, the manuscript is all the stronger. I am grateful that they took my work so seriously and were so generous in the time they gave to the task.

Finally, I must thank my wife, Mei-na, and my son, John Patrick, for sustaining me through the long and sometimes discouraging process of researching and writing this manuscript: my wife with her sense of perspective and my son with his sense of humor.

The Taiping Heavenly Kingdom

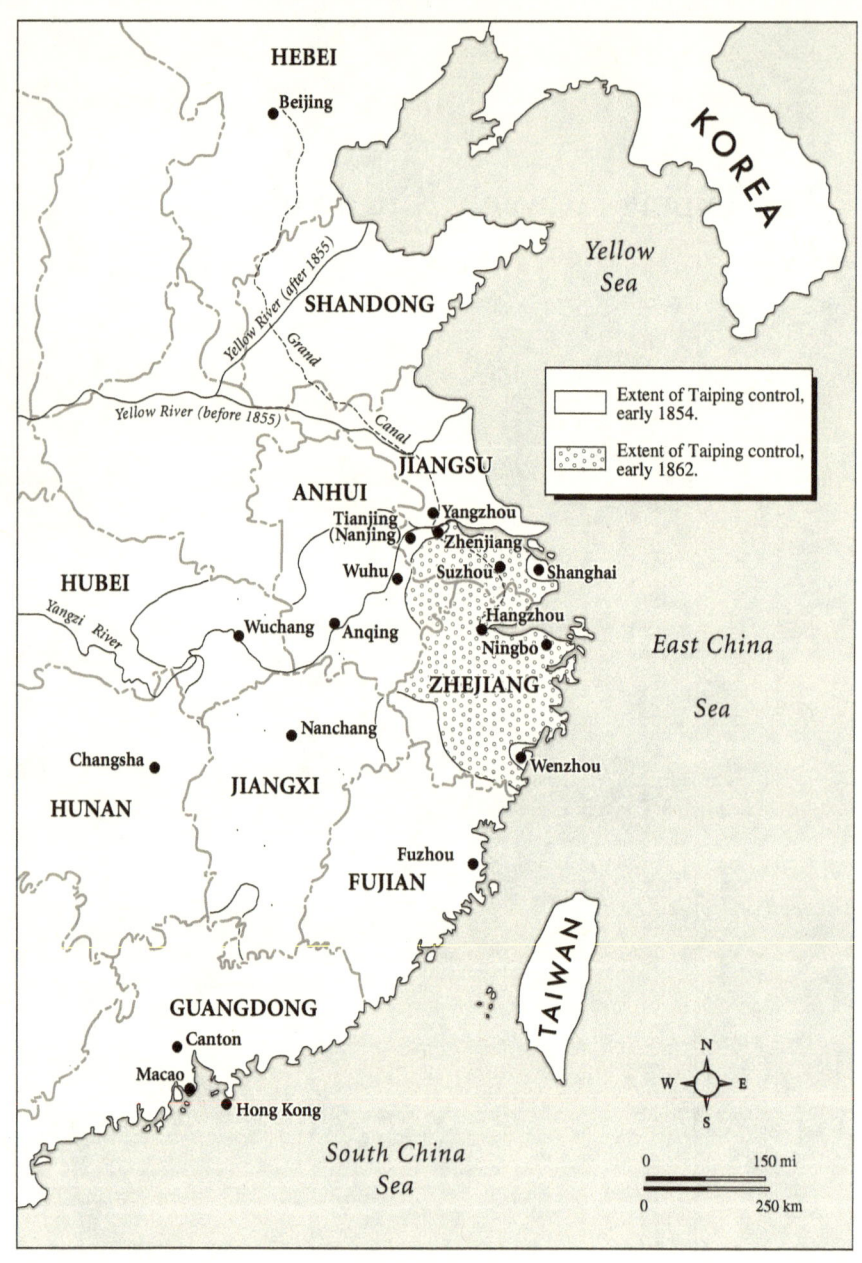

Areas occupied by the Taiping Heavenly Kingdom.

Introduction

The subject of this study is the Taiping Rebellion, a nineteenth-century Chinese uprising, and the religious creed that animated it. Over the thirteen-year course of the insurrection, from 1851 to 1864, twenty million people lost their lives, and Qing imperial and Taiping rebel armies fought in and over almost every province of the Chinese empire. Imperial forces finally managed to suppress the rebellion, but at a high cost: the Manchu rulers acquiesced to changes in the political and social order that eventually resulted in the end of their dynasty and, more consequentially, in the fall of the traditional empire.

Scholars have assembled a list of factors to explain why the Taiping rebels failed in their immediate bid to topple the emperor. Many have placed the alien character of the Taiping faith at the top of the list. Inspired by Christian teachings, the core of the Taiping creed focused on the belief that Shangdi (Sovereign on High), the high god of classical China, had chosen the Taiping leader, Hong Xiuquan (1814–1864), to establish his Heavenly Kingdom on earth. Does admitting that this faith was new and that it was inspired by Christianity oblige us at the same time to declare that it was alien? And who are we saying found it alien?

The Taiping rebel creed may have repelled certain groups, particularly those that wielded power in the established system, such as the gentry. A rebellion, like a revolution, is not a dinner party, after all. But the Taiping faith did not repel the common people. For if it is proposed that the common people found the Taiping creed strange and unfamiliar, we must ask how were the Taiping rebels able to mount their rebellion in the first place, recruiting multitudes of followers in their sweep through inland provinces?[1]

Perhaps the rebel ideology was a factor in the movement's initial success among the common people as well as a factor in its eventual defeat. In this study, I am interested in understanding what in the Taiping creed initially appealed to the common people. How was the Taiping movement able to generate more interest, recruit more followers, and sponsor more radical social changes than even the earlier native White Lotus and Eight Trigram sectarian rebellions?

Previous scholarship on this topic has failed to emphasize that when the Taiping religion left Hong Xiuquan's hands, it was no longer a Western religion, a foreign creed. The Taiping faith, albeit kindled by Anglo-American Protestantism, developed into a dynamic new Chinese religion, one whose conception of the title and position of the sovereign deity challenged the legitimacy of the imperial order. Hong Xiuquan presented this new religion, Taiping Christianity, as a revival and a restoration of the ancient classical faith in Shangdi. This was the substance of the Taiping appeal.

In accordance with their faith in Shangdi, the Taiping rebels denounced the divine pretensions of the imperial title Huangdi. Huangdi is the term that the ruler of the Qin dynasty (221–206 B.C.E.) chose as his title after he had conquered all the kingdoms of the classical era and unified China under his control. Westerners translate this title as "emperor." Yet the *di* syllable is written with the same character in both Shangdi and Huangdi, and it can be translated as either "god" or "emperor."

In a similar fashion, the Taiping condemned the sacral nature of the imperial office. The imperial title and office were blasphemous usurpations of Shangdi's title and position, and the rebels called instead for a restoration of the classical system of kingship alongside the worship of Shangdi.

Previous rebellions had declared their contemporary dynasties corrupt and therefore in need of renewal; the Taiping, by contrast, declared the long-standing imperial order blasphemous and in need of replacement. In the Taiping movement and religion we witness a new development in Chinese history: a radical change in popular thought regarding the authority of the emperor and the legitimacy of the imperial order. The Taiping was the first movement to advocate not just the removal of the then-ruling emperor or the end of one particular dynasty but, along with this, the abolition of the entire imperial system and the institution of a whole new religious and political order.

The Taiping movement, then, was not based on the traditional appeal of a sectarian rebellion. On the contrary, the Taiping leaders did not see themselves as sectarians or rebels. They related their faith more to the native Chinese classical religious tradition than to popular forms of sectarianism.[2] Their purpose was to lead a revolution in the older sense of the English term, which signified a return to an earlier time. Hong Xiuquan and his Taiping followers believed that with the advent of the Qin dynasty and the founding of the empire, Chinese culture had taken the wrong turn, as it was the ruler of this dynasty who first took the title of Huangdi. A more fitting term than "rebellion" or "revolution" would be "restoration," for the leaders of the Taiping movement wanted to restore the religious and political order of the classical past, the order that existed prior to the founding of the empire.

Restoration of the classical political order was important to the Taiping mission, but restoration of the classical religious order drove the movement. Religion was at the heart of the Taiping movement, and Taiping culture was the physical expression of these religious beliefs. The Taiping would have regarded their movement as a failure if all they had achieved were political goals, for Hong Xiuquan's greater ambition was to remake all of Chinese culture according to his vision of a restored worship of Shangdi. This intended religious transformation would express itself in every dimension of Taiping cultural life: in Taiping political aspirations, historical identity, racial consciousness, economic programs, and even hairstyles. This ambition of the Taiping could be termed a cultural revolution in its attempt to restore all of Chinese culture according to Hong Xiuquan's religious vision.

The Taiping religious vision antedated the call to political rebellion. It was the worship of a new god that demanded the establishment of a new king, not vice versa. The religious movement was not transformed into a political rebellion; the Taiping movement was from start to finish a religious movement. In even their most secular documents, such as the anti-Manchu *Proclamation by Imperial Sanction* (Banxing zhaoshu) or the communalistic *Land System of the Heavenly Dynasty* (Tianchao tianmou zhidu),[3] the Taiping cite religious motives as justification for their actions. One cannot deny the intention of the Taiping to stage a political rebellion. Yet, they did so because this political aim served the larger religious goals of the movement.

SCHOLARSHIP ON THE TAIPING

Some scholars of modern China have been reluctant to affirm the essentially religious character of the Taiping movement, and especially the distinctively Christian character of the movement. This reluctance is due in part to a reaction against the exuberance of some nineteenth-century missionary observers, who saw in the initial stages of the movement the promise of the conversion of the whole of China to Anglo-American Protestantism. But more than that, this reluctance also seems to indicate a resistance against affirming Taiping Christianity as a fully authentic Chinese religion, along with a hesitation in acknowledging Taiping claims concerning religious aspects of the Chinese imperial institution. As a result, little scholarship to this point has acknowledged Taiping Christianity as both a dynamic new Chinese religion seeking to identify with classical tradition and as an authentic expression of Christianity. No study has yet considered the Taiping charges against the sacral nature of the imperial office and the divine associations of the imperial title.

Two of the earliest twentieth-century scholars who dealt with Taiping religion at length were Vincent Shih and Eugene Boardman. In his *The Taiping Ideology: Its Sources, Interpretations and Influences* (1967), Shih treats the Taiping religion as an ideology, with Christianity alternately serving as a unifying force in that ideology and as a tool of the rebels only. He repeats a phrase both in his introduction and conclusion that demonstrates his greater affinity for the latter interpretation. It is a statement that seems counterintuitive to the manner in which people normally come to believe in a faith: "The Taipings were consciously or unconsciously looking for something that would replace the traditional ideology. . . . They were seeking some positive outlook that would enable them to break the hold of the orthodox ideology upon the minds of the people. . . . Just at this moment came

Christianity" (xiii). If indeed the Taiping leaders were searching for a replacement ideology, this suggests that the Taipings' first commitment was to rebellion and that their motives were largely political.

Shih's work is representative of many scholars of his time who were trying to find historical precedents for the Communist revolution. In many cases these scholars, who may not have been Marxist themselves, still reflected a Marxist view of the role of religion in history and society. Even for non-Marxists, the Taiping religion was an ideology of revolution and a tool of the rebels. In this line of interpretation, the core of the movement was a political ideology and not a religion, and political and religious motivations were seen to be mutually exclusive. When Shih does address religion, he assigns it an instrumental role only. He does not acknowledge that the Taiping took their religion seriously.

In his *Christian Influence upon the Ideology of the Taiping Rebellion, 1851–1864* (1952), Boardman does assign a certain priority to the religion in spite of using the term "ideology" in his title. He tends, however, to treat Taiping Christianity as some cheap, foreign copy of the real thing. That real thing would be Anglo-American Protestantism, the same standard by which nineteenth-century Protestant missionaries judged the Taiping religion. Boardman would have commended the man the nineteenth-century missionaries hoped would serve as a model of Christianity for the Taiping, Hong Rengan, the Shield King and former London Missionary Society evangelist. Yet the Shield King was in truth more of an Anglo-Saxon Protestant than a Taiping Christian, and as such was never accepted by the other leaders or the rank and file of the movement, and that rejection again highlights the distinctiveness of Taiping Christianity.

Boardman does not appreciate that distinctiveness. Instead, he discusses each of the different Taiping doctrines and shows how and where they fell short of traditional European Christian formulations. He seems incognizant to the possibility that in some respects Taiping Christians could be more faithful to other, more universal values, such as apostolic Christian standards, than their European cousins. Hong and his followers, for example, exposed European Christian cultural assumptions concerning capitalist economic ideas and also opposed the Enlightenment principle of the division between secular and sacred realms. In Boardman's hands, however, Taiping Christianity was not a dynamic new Chinese religion, but a static Western import only.

A study of the Taiping and their religion that serves as a bridge between the scholarship of the previous generation and that of our own is P. Richard Bohr's unpublished dissertation, "The Politics of Eschatology: Hung Hsiu-ch'uan and the Rise of the Taipings, 1837–1853" (1978). Bohr takes Taiping religion seriously and sees the impetus to revolt as arising out of the same eschatological impulse that provoked revolts among messianic groups in Europe and America. He highlights this integral aspect of Taiping religion, one that was also an important element of Chinese popular religion, but fails to address the even more important restoration of the worship of Shangdi. Indeed, he does not even discuss the distinctive Taiping doctrine of God, which was integral to the restorationist impulse.

Whereas the earlier generation of scholars working on Taiping religion emphasized the Christian character of the Taiping, even while they regarded the rebels as imitation Protestants, more recent scholarship has tended to diminish and, in some cases, dismiss the Christian aspect altogether. These scholars have emphasized the connections between the Taiping religion and its local, popular, and indigenous religious contexts.

Rudolf Wagner in his *Reenacting the Heavenly Vision: The Role of Religion in the Taiping Rebellion* (1987) was the trailblazer in this effort. He placed the religion of the Taiping at the center stage of the action, arguing for the authority of Hong's vision in the formation of the Taiping movement. Hong's vision of the journey to Heaven and the Heavenly Father's court was confirmed by Liang Afa's (1789–1855) tract *Good Words to Admonish the Age* (Quanshi liangyan), the Protestant missionary text that started Hong on his road to rebellion. The tract served to confirm Hong's vision as a divine message from God and a call to revolt, and the vision did the same for the tract.

Of all the interpretations that emphasize local, indigenous connections of the Taiping faith, Wagner's remains the most persuasive. Wagner also most fully acknowledges that the authority of the indigenous religious sources of Taiping religion did not countermand the authority of the other, more specifically Christian sources of Taiping religion. Indeed, his work shows how popular religious elements often (but not always) complemented specifically Christian sources. He describes how, for example, Hong Xiuquan's vision of his journey to Heaven, where he was commissioned by the Heavenly Father to preach to the people and to slay demons, prepared the way for his reading of *Good Words to Admonish the Age*. The tract and Hong's vision fit together as "two halves of a tally," which Wagner tells us was the imperial method for verifying the most important official messages.[4] Wagner could also have mentioned that Hong's vision elevated the Old and New Testaments to the status of books that were "pure and without error."[5] Regarding the relationship of Taiping Christianity and popular religious elements, Wagner demonstrates that in many cases the two religious perspectives were synthesized.

By contrast, in *Resistance, Chaos and Control in China: Taiping Rebels, Taiwanese Ghosts and Tiananmen* (1994), Robert Weller argues that only when Hong's original Christianity had "dissolved" into local Guangxi provincial religious culture were early members of the Society of God Worshippers (Bai Shangdi hui; the earliest form of the Taiping movement) able to divest themselves of Hong's Christian doctrine and thereby win a large following. While the incorporation of local religious elements might help explain how the Taiping were able to initially attract some followers, how could local religion alone have sustained the rebellion as the Taiping moved away from these peripheral areas? How could a religion primarily constituted of elements from Guangxi local culture attract men and women from areas such as Hunan and Hubei?

Of all the popular religious elements, Weller especially highlights the role of spirit possession. This kind of activity in the Taiping movement had been noted by Western observers in the nineteenth century and was used in the court of Western public opinion as evidence of the "depraved and superstitious" character of the rebels. Several of the documents produced by the Taiping and translated by Franz Michael in his 1971 collection of source materials testify to the impact of spirit possession on the movement. His compilation includes volumes 1 and 2 of *Book of Declarations of the Divine Will Made During the Heavenly Father's Descent to Earth* (Tianfu xiafan zhaoshu), a publication that typifies this phenomenon. Professor Wang Qingcheng's discovery of two more Taiping documents, *The Sacred Decree of the*

Heavenly Father (Tianfu shengzhi) and *The Sacred Decree of The Heavenly Elder Brother* (Tianxiong shengzhi), have cast further light on this aspect of the movement.[6] Along with this discovery, more attention has been paid to the Taiping leaders Yang Xiuqing (the "Eastern King," 1822–1856) and Xiao Chaogui (the "Western King"), who served, respectively, as the mediums for the Heavenly Father and the Heavenly Elder Brother.

A similar concern for local religious connections is shown by Barend ter Haar in his 1996 article "China's Inner Demons: The Political Impact of the Demonological Paradigm."[7] He posits the presence of two distinct eschatological paradigms in Chinese popular religion: one primarily messianic and salvationist, heralded by such movements as the White Lotus; the other messianic and demonological. It is the latter paradigm that strongly influenced Taiping religion, especially accounting for its anti-Manchu agenda. While such an agenda certainly was part of the Taiping mission, I would not give it the priority of place that ter Haar grants it, since what distinguished the Taiping Rebellion from all previous rebellions was the movement's stated intention to repudiate not just the Manchu emperors, but the entire imperial system.

These three scholars are correct in pointing out various local, popular religious elements within Taiping religion, but I want to comment on some of the conclusions that they draw from their work. First, Weller and ter Haar seem to believe that the presence of popular religious elements in Taiping religion argues against its Christian character. Yet, the best scholarship on the Taiping, one representative of which is Wagner's study, has recognized that the Taiping followers were drawn to elements in the Christian message that their Chinese background inclined them towards, whether it be spirit possession or the desire to restore the worship of Shangdi. Indeed, as we will see in chapter 3, *The Sacred Decree of the Heavenly Father* and *The Sacred Decree of The Heavenly Elder Brother* speak directly to the issue of the blasphemy of the imperial title.

Moreover, the popular religious elements on which these scholars focused—demonological symbols, visions, and spirit possession—are not necessarily alien to the Christian message, and are present in the gospels of the New Testament. While these phenomena may not have been a prominent part of Anglo-American Protestantism, Taiping practices did not contradict the teachings of early Christianity.

The most problematic aspect of this approach to Taiping religion, especially as it is represented in Weller and ter Haar, is its distortion of the character of the movement. Chinese and Western observers of the time most commented on the distinctively Christian aspects of the rebel religion. Taiping soldiers were expected to memorize the Ten Commandments, to attend worship services where they prayed to Shangdi as the Heavenly Father and sang their version of the traditional Christian doxology, and to attack and destroy religious statuary regarded as idolatrous. The Taiping called themselves the Society of God Worshippers and then the Taiping Heavenly Kingdom. All of these elements illustrate the uniquely Christian character of the movement.

In my view, these scholars have emphasized what is marginal and have marginalized what should be emphasized. It is almost as though the Taiping adherence to Christian ideas was of little significance for the rebellion. The student of Taiping history is left to wonder why, if elements of popular religion were as dominant an influence on the movement as these scholars suggest, earlier rebellions sparked by these same ideas did not result in an even greater impact than that of the Taiping. Yet the White Lotus and especially the Eight Trigram rebellions, to name two of the most prominent, can be characterized only as local and short-lived. Neither of these movements demonstrated the kind of creative impulse and constructive energy that the Taiping displayed.

Close readings of the local religious context do help explain how certain elements, such as spirit possession, became so influential in the movement. These same studies, however, virtually ignore what the Taiping themselves deemed the most important element of their movement: their desire to restore the worship of Shangdi. The most significant and influential Taiping documents are infused with distinctively Christian ideas and notions. The Taiping published the Old and New Testaments widely, and also such works as *Land System of the Heavenly Dynasty* and *Book of Heavenly Commandments* (Tiantiao shu). These same texts also dominate lists of royally sanctioned works, lists that were published regularly by the Taiping.

The texts included on these lists are available today, and each is strongly Christian.[8] Significantly, not only are the recently discovered works by Wang Qingcheng absent from these lists, but even Liang Afa's work does not merit a place. If the Taiping permitted only these explicitly Christian texts to be published, should we not likewise consider these texts as most authoritative for understanding the character of the movement? These same texts and publications are commented on by both foreign and Chinese observer alike, and the Christian aspect of the movement accounts for the captivation of early Western observers of the Taiping. Missionaries and diplomats expected the presence of popular religious elements in a Chinese movement such as the Taiping, but where, they wanted to know, did these Christian elements come from, and how was it that they played such a prominent role?

In each of two general surveys of the rebellion, Jen Yu-wen's *The Taiping Revolutionary Movement* (1973) and the more recent *God's Chinese Son: The Taiping Heavenly Kingdom of Hong Xiuquan* (1996) by Jonathan Spence, the Taiping religion is accorded a prominent place. Jen Yu-wen is an enthusiastic booster of Taiping Christianity in theory,[9] and he praises the Taiping for their fidelity to one God and for their practices of worship and prayer. But in many ways he tends to view the Christianity of the Taiping as a copy of modern Protestantism. He does not emphasize the distinctiveness of Taiping Christianity or address what specific role Christianity played in sparking the rebellion.

Spence, in a fashion similar to Bohr, stresses the apocalyptic elements of the Taiping faith. He makes use of the accounts discovered by Wang Qingcheng and various Christian publications of the Taiping. Spence has written a vivid and moving narrative account, with a dramatic focus on the person of Hong Xiuquan.

These works leave room for a study such as mine, which seeks to construct a wider religious and ideological context for the Taiping and to explore some of these same texts with an eye to their challenge to the imperial system.

None of the studies surveyed above affirms Taiping Christianity as a distinct new form of Christianity or Chinese religion. An earlier generation treated Taiping Christianity as a warmed-over Protestantism; the current generation tends to dismiss the Christian dimension of Taiping religion altogether. Not one of these studies, for example, explores the implications of the Taiping name for God or discusses Hong's struggle with the title of Christ, and how that title fit with the Taiping faith in Shangdi. While not the most orthodox formulation—he saw himself as the younger brother of Jesus—Hong's solution was a triumph of theological insight for which he receives no praise or even recognition. These works have failed to recognize and affirm that the Taiping religion was not 90 percent Anglo-American Protestant and 10 percent Chinese popular religion, or vice versa. Taiping religion was something new: fully Christian, albeit with Chinese popular religious elements; fully Chinese, albeit inspired by Anglo-American Protestantism. These elements all played a part in the creation of Taiping Christianity, but the creation transcended the sum total of the parts.

The most serious of my criticisms of the above studies, however, whether a monograph on Taiping religion or a general history of the rebellion, is that not one of them discusses Taiping religion in the context of Hong's indictment of the blasphemous character of the imperial institution. Inasmuch as the Taiping rebels can contribute to our understanding of Christianity and Chinese religion, what they discovered about the religious claims and dimensions of traditional Chinese imperial culture may be their most significant legacy.

A NEW VIEW OF THE TAIPING

Hong's religion was different precisely because it did not accept the position or role of the emperor. Taiping Christianity directly challenged and opposed the emperor and the imperial office, and with it, the imperial cultural system as well. In the Taiping understanding, the emperor had usurped the office and blasphemed the title of Shangdi. Because the Taiping attacked the emperor and mounted a rebellion, scholars have thereby wrongly conceived of the movement as just another political rebellion; but Hong's rationale for targeting the imperial office focused on the religious and cultural aspects of the institution, not primarily its political aspect. His crusade began by targeting the temples of the city gods along with an attack on the magistrate's yamen. Indeed, as we shall see later, Hong first publicly proclaimed himself Heavenly King in a temple, in a poem he inscribed on the temple wall.[10] While similar in certain respects to earlier sectarian revolts, then, the Taiping movement was radically different at its core. The Taiping sought to destroy the political office of emperor, the Confucian cultural apparatus, and the hierarchical society that supported it, and to build on these ruins a revived classical religious culture.

The first chapter of this study of the Taiping Christian movement looks at the career and achievements of Matteo Ricci (1552–1610), the successful early Catholic missionary to China, and examines the translation of European Catholicism into the Heavenly Lord sect or teaching (*Tianzhu jiao*, the name by which Catholicism is known in China). Catholic catechisms, especially Ricci's own, along with early Catholic ritual guides, document his very distinctive early missionary approach to the Chinese.

Ricci was the pioneer of a method that was later followed by some Protestant missionaries and which proved to be so influential with the Taiping. The Jesuit missionary identified Christianity with the religion of China's early classical period, and he was the first Westerner to refer to the Christian God using the name of Shangdi (decisions made during the Rites Controversy of the early eighteenth century would later disallow the use of this term). Along with the name of the high god of China's classical religion, the Jesuits would also borrow the classical idea of Heaven's rule over mankind. The challenge for the Catholics, as it would be for the Protestants who followed them, was how they would apply this Christian identification with the classical religion to the contemporary situation.

The Jesuits applied this idea to the traditional paradigm of the Three Teachings (that is, Confucianism, Daoism, and Buddhism; during the Ming dynasty [1368–1644] especially, there was an attempt, encouraged by such emperors as Ming Taizu, to create a more syncretic religious culture). The Catholic missionaries spoke of Christianity as completing Confucianism—providing the Confucian school a religious basis rooted in the classical religion—and displacing Buddhism. In this sense, then, Ricci was able to identify with Chinese culture. Yet his religion does not ultimately correspond with the traditional cultural paradigm. In some places it fit into the Confucianism he intended to complete, and in other places it suited the Buddhism he intended to displace. Catholicism, however, corresponded with the Three Teachings well enough that it did not challenge the traditional imperial order; it did not require any kind of radical paradigm shift.

This lack of correspondence to any one Chinese teaching did not hurt Catholicism's popular appeal. As time passed, however, and the religion became more identifiable with the translation of its doctrines and rituals, Confucian scholars increasingly associated Catholicism with Buddhism, the catchall category Confucians set up for all beliefs that did not fit elsewhere. The decision to name the Catholic God "Lord of Heaven" (Tianzhu), and not "Sovereign on High" (Shangdi), facilitated this response. As a consequence, Ricci's aspirations for associating Christianity with the classical religion were not realized. The Heavenly Lord Sect would instead in 1724 be designated a Chinese heterodox sect, and this created problems—and opportunities—of another kind.

The arrival of Protestant missionaries in China at the beginning of the nineteenth century—well over two hundred years after Catholic missionaries had arrived in China and almost a hundred years since Catholicism was declared a heterodox sect—comprises the second chapter of this book. Protestants also attempted to identify with the classical religion and were more successful in doing so at one especially critical point: the naming of God. But the Protestants still were unable to break through the imperial religious order and connect with Chinese culture and society in any new and novel fashion.

It was Hong Xiuquan, whose imaginative mind adopted the central idea of identifying with the classical religion, who created a new paradigm for Chinese thought and culture. This is the subject of chapter 3 of my study. Not only was Hong not bound by the constraints imposed on Ricci, but he was positively enabled by the circumstances in which he found himself. The Protestant contribution to his efforts was considerable. In addition to translating the word "God" and other terms, the missionaries also passed on to Hong a good dose of Protestant iconoclasm, which helped him reconceptualize the Chinese religious landscape. In Hong's understanding, the emperor had established himself as an idol to be worshipped ahead of Shangdi, thereby eliciting the wrath of both Shangdi and the Taiping.

Hong introduced a paradigm to replace that of the Three Teachings: he posited a dualism between the traditional imperial order and the Taiping-revived classical order. In effect, he replaced the Three Teachings with the two orders, which opposed rather than complemented each other. Hong presented his Christian-inspired creed as an alternative to Confucianism, not a completion of it. He presented his faith as a more orthodox and faithful heir of the ancient classical religion than the Master's teachings themselves. Hong opposed the imperial system, which the Confucians supported, as inimical to the classical religion.

This examination of the Taiping religious creed looks at three of the central tenets of the faith and explores the Taiping interpretation of these concepts. A wide range of Taiping documents, together with missionary literature, including some of the earliest Chinese-language Protestant Bibles and catechisms, provides an extensive and in-depth analysis of Taiping beliefs.

Complementing this study of the Taiping creed, chapter 4 examines the practice of the creed, focusing especially on the actions of iconoclasm and desacralization in Taiping-occupied China. These actions were aimed at destroying the imperial institution and image. In describing the depth and breadth of the impact of Taiping religious practice, this analysis relies mostly on accounts of Qing and Western observers.

The fifth and final chapter of this study analyzes the impact of the Taiping Christian movement on the Heavenly Lord sect, first looking at how the gentry attempted to identify the Taiping with the Heavenly Lord sectarians so as to deny the original contributions of the Taiping. On the one hand, the gentry characterized the Taiping Rebellion as an ordinary sectarian rebellion, thereby salvaging the traditional way of conceptualizing Chinese political thought and covering up how the Taiping had exposed the imperial order as antagonistic to the classical order. On the other hand, the gentry, by identifying the Taiping rebels with Catholicism, stigmatized Chinese Catholicism as a perverse and heterodox doctrine. This part of the study examines a gentry-produced anti-Catholic publication that documents this campaign. The last part of the chapter analyzes various postbellum Catholic and Protestant catechisms and literature, searching for ways in which the Taiping movement affected how missionaries understood and presented their teachings.

This interpretation of the Taiping movement seeks to understand the Taiping religion not primarily in the context of a traditional peasant rebellion or as a new sect competing with the established teachings of Confucianism, Daoism, and Buddhism. It attempts instead to understand Taiping Christianity in the context of Chinese religion as defined by Hong Xiuquan. For Hong and his followers, the Chinese religious context was dominated by the cultural orthodoxy of the realm, which involved the sacred character of the imperial office and the divine associations of the imperial title.

Beyond establishing the fundamentally Christian character of the Taiping Heavenly Kingdom, this study of the Taiping Christian movement is important for at least two reasons. First, the Taiping movement uncovered the religious nature of the imperial institution, and this has significance for the 1911 Revolution, an event that was much more radical than it is generally credited as being. For if the emperor was the religious symbol that the Taiping depicted, removing him did not just signal a mundane political change, a mere shifting of chairs on the political dais, but a deep and transforming ideological revolution as well.

Second, this examination of the Taiping experience helps us make sense of religious changes that are occurring in China today. These changes are especially evident in the countryside, where the revival of traditional religions and the birth of new faiths is taking place, including the rise of a Chinese Christianity. Influential studies on Christianity and China that have appeared over the years have contended that a fundamental hostility exists between Christianity and Chinese culture.[11] This conclusion is difficult to sustain in view of what happened during the era of Taiping China and what is happening in China today. My hope is that a more nuanced perspective can be considered, one that acknowledges a certain divergence between Roman Catholic, American Southern Baptist, or even Russian Orthodox cultures and Chinese culture, but that leaves room for the development of a dynamic new culture created by religious movements such as Taiping Christianity. In this book, I make a case for this new Chinese Christianity and the fundamentally Christian nature of the whole Taiping movement.

In their creation of a vibrant new Chinese Christianity; in their understanding of the sacral character of the imperial office, image, and title, and the relationship of all these to imperial culture as a whole; in their consequent efforts to destroy the institution of empire and smash the image of the emperor; and finally, in their conceiving of a modern religious, cultural, and political order that could be continuous with the past but could also create a new present, the Taiping made an original and historically significant contribution to Chinese history. The Taiping faith transformed to some extent how all Chinese people understood their religion, the imperial office and title, and the entire traditional imperial and Confucian order.

1
The Early Catholic Search for the Name of God

The history of the faith that inspired the Taiping must begin with the work of Matteo Ricci and the early Jesuit missionaries to China. Their contribution is rightly called seminal, for it was the Jesuits who initiated the approach that proved so influential with Hong Xiuquan and the Taiping movement: they identified Christianity with the classical religion of China.

Jesuit efforts to portray Christianity in terms of the classical religion initially were persuasive to a number of the Confucian literati. Ricci spoke of his efforts in two ways: of returning to an "original Confucianism" and of "completing Confucianism." Believing that Confucianism needed a transcendental faith to complete its ethical teachings, Ricci argued that Christianity served as a more suitable basis for Confucianism than Buddhism, since Christianity was closer in character to the transcendental religion of Heaven, which was originally featured in the Five Classics. This collection of five books (*Book of History, Book of Songs, Book of Changes, The Spring and Autumn Annals*, and the *Record of Rites*) from the Zhou dynasty (1040?–256 B.C.E.) was edited and compiled by the Confucian school and served as Confucianism's transcendental basis. Incongruous as it may seem, Ricci presented Christianity as a way for the Chinese to return to their ancient faith.

This was Ricci's strategy. However, by choosing to present Christianity as a complementary aspect of the classical religion and not as some new, foreign religion, Ricci failed to challenge the dominant paradigm of the Three Teachings (Confucianism, Daoism, and Buddhism). Instead he worked within the paradigm, and so in effect sanctioned it. Since he at first identified with and supported Confucianism, this approach won Christianity a share in the laurels of orthodoxy. But as time went on, and as the Confucian elite learned more about the metaphysical character of Christian doctrine and the redemptive and salvationist nature of its religious rituals, they came to define the religion in terms of the only transcendental religion they knew: Buddhism.[1]

This perception of Buddhist affinity was all the more justified in their view because the language and concepts the Jesuits employed in the translation of Catholic doctrine and rituals had largely been borrowed from Buddhism. If the language of Buddhism could so easily be used to translate these doctrines and rituals, how did Catholicism distinguish itself from the Indian religion? Some of these questions must have influenced Emperor Yongzheng (r. 1723–35), for when he decreed in his elaboration of his father's *Sacred Edict* (a compilation of Confucian exhortations delivered to the people in twice monthly village lectures) that all religious associations outside of Confucianism were but varying shades of heterodoxy, Christianity was similarly categorized and proscribed. Thus, the Jesuit strategy in targeting the Confucian elite can be said to have ultimately failed.

Nevertheless, contrary to how several studies of Christianity in China have portrayed the events, the history of early Chinese Christianity did not end with the proscription of the faith in 1724. The era of the imperial proscription was as important to the development of Chinese Christianity as was the era of Matteo Ricci and the early Jesuits. For it was during these years of persecution following the imperial decree that Chinese Catholicism developed into what, to all appearances, can be called an indigenous Chinese sect: the Heavenly Lord sect (or teaching).[2] So while the Jesuit strategy may have failed, the overall Catholic mission to create a Chinese Christianity can be characterized as a success.

Employing the word "indigenous" to describe a religion whose origins lay outside China may seem somewhat anomalous, but highlighting the developments that took place during the period of early Chinese Catholicism helps explain the use of the term. This chapter first examines early Jesuit efforts at translating Christianity into the Chinese idiom and then looks briefly at the experience of the Heavenly Lord sect during the era of proscription and in the period surrounding the Opium War of 1839 to 1842.

By the time of the Opium War and the treaties concluding that war, the Heavenly Lord sect had become indistinguishable in some of its language and in several of its rituals and practices from other ordinary Chinese sects. Because of this, Catholicism did not seem unfamiliar to the people; indeed the challenge for the Catholic missionaries, especially during the years of proscription, was to distinguish their sect from all the other heterodox sects and to clearly differentiate the name of the Christian God from the names of other deities. The missionaries attempted to draw a distinction between themselves and Buddhist sectarians especially in their beliefs and doctrines. They still attempted, however, to associate these doctrines with the classical religion even while they used Buddhist terminology to articulate these beliefs.

The Heavenly Lord sect was a religion that did not quite fit the sectarian mold. It could be identified with ancient classical religion or with Buddhist sectarianism. How it fit both the orthodox classical and heterodox sectarian molds is important for understanding the later appeal of the Taiping.

THE STRATEGY OF MATTEO RICCI

Matteo Ricci arrived in China in 1583. While he was not the first Jesuit to reach the shores of the Middle Kingdom, he is still regarded as the pioneer of the mission, as he was responsible for initiating the approach followed by all successive Jesuit missionaries. Ricci and the early Jesuits sought to create a Chinese Christianity.

Their most notable contribution to the development of a Chinese Christianity was the translation of Christian apologetic literature, doctrinal teaching, and liturgy into Chinese. The Jesuits were able to translate into authentic Chinese the most fundamental Christian concepts, save two of the most important, the terms for God and Christ. The following discussion of names, terms, and titles used in the translation of Christianity serves as an important introduction to the issues faced by the Jesuits and also lays the foundation for examining these same issues when they are later addressed by Protestant missionaries and the Taiping.

What is God's name? This was the most controversial question in the translation process. The controversy over the translation of the term for God was part of the Rites Controversy, which erupted a century after Ricci's death but was already an issue during Ricci's time. Pope Clement XI in 1704 ruled out the use of the term Shangdi in the same decree in which he ruled against Christian participation in Confucian rites.[3] Matteo Ricci had used the term Shangdi with much success in his teachings, but even as early as 1628, some missionaries expressed their reservations about the use of the term.[4] There was no controversy, however, over the Chinese term for Christ, Jilisidu, often shortened to Jidu, largely because it was not a translation but a transliteration of the Latin term for Christ, Christus. Every other concept—including Holy Spirit, devil, angel, holy, sin, heaven, and hell—was successfully translated into an authentically Chinese term.

This "term question," which is discussed more fully in chapter 3, was intimately connected to Ricci's presentation of Christianity as a more faithful completion of Confucianism than that offered by Buddhism or effected by the Neo-Confucianism of Zhu Xi,[5] who in the twelfth century combined Buddhist and Daoist metaphysics with Confucian ethics. David Mungello describes this effort:

> Several Jesuit missionaries, including Frs. Ruggieri, Ricci, and Valignano, made the decision to blend Christianity with Confucianism rather than Buddhism. This decision followed an unsuccessful experiment in adopting the clothing and spiritual role of the Buddhist monks, and thereafter the Jesuits did not turn back from their decision to identify in dress, thinking, and social status with the Confucian literati. . . . In 1612 the eminent scholar-official . . . Xu Guangqi expressed this plan in the form of a short, memorable phrase of the type of which the literati were so fond. In the preface to a work on Western hydraulics, Xu wrote that Christianity should "supplement Confucianism and displace Buddhism" (*buru yifo*).[6]

This was the central achievement of the Jesuits, and it has been singularly, more often solely, celebrated.[7]

In completing Confucianism, Father Ricci did not have in mind supplementing the Neo-Confucianism of the time. He believed Zhu Xi's synthesis had led Chinese away from the classical religion. He sought instead to supplement what he referred to as "original Confucianism."[8] By this, he meant the Confucianism of Confucius. Even more, he wanted to go back to the sources of Confucianism, the Five Classics, rather than the writings of the philosopher himself.

Western scholarship has been captivated by the story of Ricci setting aside the Buddhist vestments he first donned in coming to China and clothing himself with Confucian robes, taking this episode as the interpretive key for understanding what the Jesuits meant in their stated purpose of complementing Confucianism and displacing Buddhism. Such a view is supported especially by the Jesuit apologetic works most Western scholars have used in their analysis of the impact of the Jesuit mission. These highly philosophical works, the most well known of which is Matteo Ricci's *The True Meaning of the Lord of Heaven* (Tianzhu shiyi), targeted a Confucian literati audience.

A perusal of Father Ricci's apologia clearly reveals his strategy of completing Confucianism by identifying with the classical religion and displacing Buddhism. The Jesuit apologist structured his discussion of the Catholic religion in three basic parts. In the first part he addressed questions concerning the nature and identity of God. Ricci described his God as the creator and ruler of the universe and identified Him with the deity of the Chinese classics, Shangdi. In referring to God, Ricci most frequently used the terms Shangdi (Sovereign on High) and Tianzhu (Lord of Heaven), and he used these titles interchangeably. He also used other terms, such as Tiandi (Sovereign of Heaven) and Shangzunzhe (Supremely Honored One).[9] In the early years of the mission, one hundred years prior to Pope Clement XI's final ruling, there was a slight but not exclusive preference for Tianzhu. Ricci certainly attempted to link the names Tianzhu and Shangdi, evidently believing that this association would overcome the inadequacies of using either term separately.

At more than one point, Ricci very directly equated the deity that the Jesuits spoke of as the Lord of Heaven with Shangdi, the god whom the ancient Chinese worshipped in the classics. In a chapter titled "Mistaken Views about the Lord of Heaven," Ricci took on Neo-Confucian ideas of principle and the Supreme Ultimate. After dealing with what he described as Zhu Xi's mistaken views, he laid out the correct views of the Lord of Heaven. Ricci leads off by stating, "He who is called the Lord of Heaven in my humble country is He who is called Shang-ti [i.e., Shangdi; the English translation of this text uses the Wade-Giles romanization] in Chinese." A few sentences later, he asserts more boldly, "Our Lord of Heaven is the Shang-ti mentioned in the ancient canonical writings [as the following texts show],"[10] and he lists on the following two pages several different texts that support his statement. Included among these is a reference from the Book of Songs (sometimes called the Book of Odes): "The Arm of King Wu was full of strength; Irresistible was his ardor. Greatly illustrious were Ch'eng and K'ang, Kinged by the Sovereign-on-High." He follows several of these classical quotations with this concluding statement, "Having leafed through a great number of ancient books, it is quite clear to me that Shang-ti and the Lord of Heaven are different only in name."[11] Hong Xiuquan would not need to add to Ricci's explanation, as the name of Hong's God and the name of the classical high God were one and the same.

The earliest converts to Catholicism strongly endorsed Ricci's views. The identification of Shangdi with the Christian God appealed to the Confucian elite, and much has been written about their support of the Jesuit strategy. Most of the studies that examine the impact of early Catholic missionaries focus on the response among the highest-level elite, especially the three pillars of the Chinese church: Xu Guangqi, Li Zhizao, and Yang Tingyun. Xu (1562–1633), the Ming dynasty grand secretary, is credited with articulating the four-character phrase *buru yifo* (complete Confucianism, displace Buddhism), which summarized the strategy. In his writing about this topic, Erik Zürcher quotes Yang Tingyun, who states that since Catholicism has not been affected by the superstitions of Buddhism, "it can be practiced in such a way that [their doctrine] and our Confucianism mutually support each other."[12]

These ideas filtered down to the local elite and gentry as well. Nicolas Standaert has written of one member of the local elite, Yan Mo, who composed a treatise, *A Study of God and Heaven* (Ditian kao), in the late seventeenth century on the issue of the name of God, demonstrating that the debate was not limited to just the highest profile of converts. Yan Mo argued for the greater use of the term Sovereign on High rather than Lord of Heaven. Of the three parts of his treatise, the middle section lists some fifty-nine quotations from the classics, documenting the similarity he found between the Christian God and the classical deity Shangdi.[13]

Erik Zürcher discusses a document he discovered that also attests to the reach of the Jesuit strategy. In this document we have the testimony of a local magistrate. A prefect, ruling in Shanxi province in the summer of 1635, issued a proclamation that used Jesuit ideas (he even refers to a Jesuit missionary by name) to bolster his campaign against sectarians.[14] The official accuses Buddhism and Daoism of deluding the people and leading them away from their proper service to Heaven. Here he refers to Heaven as a personalized deity, after the teachings of the Jesuits. One final bit of evidence that the appeal of the Jesuit teaching concerning Heaven and Shangdi reached far beyond the confines of the top elite comes from the naming of a church in Jinan as the Completing Confucianism Hall (Bu Ru Tang).[15]

Most Western scholars who have studied the Jesuit mission strategy have examined the supplementing of Confucianism and have paid less attention to the displacement of Buddhism. How did the Jesuit missionaries conceive of this aspect of their evangelical task? While Ricci, in *The True Meaning of the Lord of Heaven,* may have left his preference for the terms for God intentionally vague, his antagonism towards any kind of Buddhist or Daoist understanding of God was not at all veiled. Following his discussion of the Lord of Heaven as creator and ruler of the universe, Ricci mounted an attack on what he regarded as mistaken notions concerning God and his relation to the creation. Ricci declared that the *wu* (nonbeing) of Daoist thought and the *kong* (emptiness) of Buddhist thought were concepts "totally at variance with the doctrine concerning the Lord of Heaven."[16] He also seeks to correct the Neo-Confucian idea of the Supreme Ultimate (Taiji) as the "reality which produced heaven and earth."[17] He appeals to the classics for support: "Although I arrived in China late in life and discovered that the superior men of ancient times worshipped and revered the Sovereign-on-High, of Heaven and Earth, but I have never heard of them paying respect to the Supreme Ultimate. If the Supreme Ultimate is the Sovereign on High and ancestor of all things, why did not the sages of ancient times say so?"[18] Indeed, the most ancient classics did not mention such a concept.

Ricci was particularly relentless in his attacks on Buddhism in those sections where he discussed the nature of spiritual beings and the human soul, especially in a section where he refuted the idea that God, creation, and humanity were an indistinguishable unity. "The Buddha failed to understand himself, so how could he understand the Lord of Heaven; but, happening to be possessed of some talent, and having been given a task to perform, he became boastful and arrogant, and recklessly and with no inhibitions whatsoever, considered himself to be as worthy of honor as the Lord of Heaven.... Arrogance is the enemy of virtue. The moment an arrogant thought is conjured up in our minds, all our conduct is corrupted."[19] In his refutation of the Buddhist doctrine of reincarnation, Ricci is even more hostile. He first asserts that this doctrine was really obtained from Pythagoras and spread to India, where at the time this doctrine reached India, a prince by the name of Sakyamuni had thoughts of beginning a new faith:

> Sakyamuni happened to be planning to establish a new religion in India. He accepted the theory of reincarnation and added to it the teaching concerning the Six Directions, together with a hundred other lies, editing it all to form books which he called canonical writings. Many years later some Chinese went to India and transmitted the Buddhist religion to China. There is no genuine record of the history of this religion in which one can put one's faith, or any real principle upon which one can rely. India is a small place, and is not considered to be a nation of the highest standing. It lacks the arts of civilization and has no standards of moral conduct to bequeath to posterity. The histories of many countries are totally ignorant of its existence. Could such a country adequately serve as a model for the whole world?[20]

THE CHRISTIAN MESSAGE IN BUDDHIST DRESS

Ricci's antagonism to Buddhism can be misleading. While he was conducting his campaigns against Buddhist doctrine, he and his Jesuit colleagues were at the same time plundering Buddhist dictionaries and pillaging Buddhist lexicons, stealing some of the religion's most valuable treasures in order to translate their Christian message. The Jesuits appropriated Buddhist vocabulary, concepts, and language for their own missionary purposes. What is thus striking about the Jesuit translation effort is how much of the language employed by the missionary fathers was infused with the spirit of the Indian religion. On the other hand, the terms that most directly connected Ricci's work to a Confucian ethos, particularly Shangdi and Tian (Heaven), became the very ones that were later forbidden by the pope. And it is not surprising that Tianzhu, the term that was finally selected as the most appropriate for translating the name of the deity, was of a Buddhist provenance.

Ricci and his Jesuit colleagues may have reassured themselves that they could still maintain their connection to Confucianism in spite of these translation decisions. And the connections are maintained. The missionaries continued to support Confucian ideas of the authority of the Five Classics, and even notions of orthodoxy. They continued to identify with Confucian scholars and to distance themselves from Buddhist monks. They continued to risk papal wrath in their defense of Christians participating in the Confucian rites. Nonetheless, these translation decisions at the least would have made their support of Confucian positions more problematic.

Beyond the weakening of the connections to Confucianism that these translation efforts effected, there is the attendant strengthening of the ties to Buddhism. Indeed, the possible risks of spiritual pollution posed by Christians participating in Confucian rites seem mild when compared with the dangers posed by this cultural and linguistic borrowing. Even when the Jesuit fathers did not borrow a word directly from the Buddhist lexicon, they did so indirectly, combing the popular religious vocabularies for their translations.

But could they have done otherwise? Buddhism itself was a translated doctrine, and in the first centuries of its penetration into China, Buddhist missionaries had mined the Chinese common religious lexicon for their own translations. Arthur F. Wright comments on the Han dynasty (202 B.C.E.–220 C.E.) Buddhist translation experience:

> In these early efforts—in oral discourse, written translation, and exegesis— to present Buddhist ideas in Chinese language and metaphor, there was

necessarily a heavy reliance on the terms and concepts of indigenous traditions. Buddhism had somehow to be "translated" into terms that Chinese could understand. The terms of Neo-Taoism were the most appropriate for attempting to render the transcendental notions of Buddhism.

Wright then lists several examples of such terms appropriated by Buddhist monks, including *dao* ("the way"; used for translating the Buddhist term *dharma* and sometimes used for translating "enlightenment"); *zhenren* (Daoist: "immortal"; used for translating the Buddhist word *arhat*, "fully enlightened one"); and *wuwei* (the Daoist idea of "non-activity"; used to translated the Buddhist term *nirvana*).[21] The final result of this translation process was that by the time of the Jesuits, any word with any kind of religious connotation at all would be understood primarily in a Buddhist sense.

Early Catholic missionaries seem to have been just as comfortable as their early Buddhist counterparts in making use of the Chinese common religious lexicon in translating their own doctrine, and maybe even more so.[22] While there were transliterations of geographic terms and biblical personages in Catholic translations, few of the most fundamental Christian doctrines incorporated transliterated concepts. Buddhism, on the other hand, featured several such transliterated terms, even for its cardinal doctrines. Erik Zürcher describes the early process of translating Sanskrit scriptures into Chinese. He notes, for example, how in the early period of the Buddhist mission to China, even the transliteration for Buddha's name itself was not standardized. Rather, there were four different commonly found transcriptions. Three used the same character to represent the initial sound *fu*, with a different character to represent the final sound of the master's name (the literal translations of the transliterated characters for the Buddha's name include *futu*, or "floating map," and *futou*, "floating head"). Only one transliteration used the character with the initial sound *fo*, which is the character that came to represent the Buddha's name.[23] Titles for the different manifestations of the Buddha, such as Shijiamoni, Amita, and Milefo, all favorites of Chinese sectarians, were likewise transliterated.

Early Jesuit missionaries, by contrast, showed little such caution, boldly borrowing from both popular religious and Buddhist lexicons. The words for heaven (*tiantang*) and hell (*diyu*), the latter with its multiple levels and different classes, were the most prominent example of this borrowing.[24] The Buddhists, at the time of their entrance into China, had themselves appropriated these ideas from popular Daoism. At the time of appropriation, these ideas were transformed. So, as Arthur Wright points out, heaven and hell "became in turn places for reward or retribution of accumulated karma."[25] At each stage of appropriation, these ideas become richer and more complex, so that the Buddhist idea of hell included certain Indian ideas of karmic retribution and torment along with the Chinese idea of the netherworld as possessing a bureaucratic structure. In his catechism, Ricci comments on the Catholic use of these ideas, a new stage of appropriation, when he has a Chinese inquirer remark, "If you say there is a Heaven and a Hell to come, then that is Buddhism. We Confucians do not believe this teaching."[26]

The Catholics borrowed several other terms. The word for the devil (*mogui*) was another borrowed term, being a construct based on the Buddhist name for the destroyer or the evil god along with the common Chinese term for ghost, or malevolent spirit. Even the Buddhist term that was finally determined to be most fitting for God, Tianzhu, can refer either to the "Lord of Devas, a title of Indra" as Soothill defines him, or the Lord of the Sixth Heaven of Desire.[27] Thus, as Knud Lundbæk points out, "There was something odd about the term Tianzhu; it simply did not sound right to the Chinese literati. It does not occur in their classical literature, and moreover there is a Buddhist deity with the same name."[28] Perhaps because of its greater obscurity and pliancy, this term was still favored over Shangdi, which was more popularly identified with the classical pagan past and with contemporary Daoist beliefs.

Other terms, while possessing strong religious connotations and used by the Buddhists, were originally drawn from the Chinese secular world.[29] Prominent among these was the word the Jesuits used to translate the term "holy." They employed the Chinese term *sheng*, whose meaning in both secular and religious contexts connotes sagely wisdom more than moral holiness, although *sheng* includes the latter sense to distinguish between, for example, the secular sage and the religious saint. The Jesuits were no pioneers here, as the Buddhists earlier had adopted this same sense of the word for describing their own holy people, places, and things. *Sheng* was also used in a secular sense to denote things imperial, so that the Chinese would refer to the imperial throne as the *shengzuo* (imperial or sacred throne), and an imperial edict was likewise referred to as *shengyu* (sacred words or imperial decree).

Another term that the Catholics took from the secular world, again following the Buddhist example, was *fanzui* (committing a sin or crime). The provenance of the Chinese term was the legal world, where it meant to commit a crime. The religious meaning of committing a sin can be distinguished only by context, for the primary sense of *fanzui* remained a legal one.[30] This distinction between committing a sin and committing a crime may be an example of Western conceptual habits, since we have tended to draw sharper divisions between the secular and sacred worlds than the Chinese were comfortable doing.

By using terms borrowed directly from Buddhist scriptures or from the literature of popular religious Daoism, or indirectly from the Chinese secular (mostly political and legal) world, the Jesuits faced a dilemma. However different the content of the Catholic message was, it still would be strongly associated through its linguistic forms with Buddhist and popular religious beliefs. It needs to be noted, however, that the Catholic missionaries worked to preserve the purity and integrity of their message in the same manner that Buddhist monks refined and matured their translation efforts in an attempt to make their translations more fully and clearly convey distinctively Buddhist ideas.[31]

Translation was not a one-shot effort for Buddhist missionaries; neither would it be so for the Catholics. Arthur Wright's remarks on the Buddhist enterprise are again illuminating for the Catholic enterprise. Wright describes the work of the second generation of Buddhist translators as "emancipating" Buddhist ideas from Daoism. A similar effort was made in Catholicism in that, over time, Catholic translators increasingly made Buddhist terms and concepts their own. Indeed, this was what was happening in the entire debate over the proper name of God, trying out different terms and seeing which could be used and which could not. Nonetheless, in the first few generations of this process, there would have been some confusion as the Catholics began to use Buddhist terminology. Indeed, that confusion is still present in the Chinese religious world, since even Buddhism was never able to fully "emancipate" its teachings from Daoist or other popular religious influences. In China, syncretism, especially at the popular level, was the rule.

TRANSLATING THE TEACHINGS FOR THE PEOPLE

Identification with a more popular religious worldview was evident in the doctrinal literature of the Chinese Catholic mission. Catholic missionaries attempted to set their religion apart from Buddhism by pointing to the distinctive doctrines and teachings of the church, yet that distinctiveness was lost in part when they employed Buddhist terms to translate key Catholic doctrines and teachings.

A good example of how Buddhist-tinged language and concepts affected the presentation of Christian doctrine is in a work produced in 1675, *Catechism of the Holy Religion of the Lord of Heaven* (Tianzhu shengjiao bai wenda, "One hundred questions and answers about the holy teaching of the Lord of Heaven"), by a Belgian Jesuit, Philippe Couplet (1622–1693).[32] That Couplet would see the need for the production and dissemination of this kind of introductory religious literature evidently grew out of his own missionary labors. He served in a number of culturally distinctive and geographically diverse cities in China, including Xi'an, Nanjing, Suzhou, and Songjiang, as well as a number of provincial postings, including Jiangxi, Fujian, Zhejiang, and Huguang (Hubei-Hunan).[33]

Couplet's text reads like a Western catechism. The missionary was mainly concerned about challenges to the doctrine of worshipping one God. For example, when discussing the Trinity, the question put by the catechist reads, "Can these three persons be called three Lords of Heaven?" The answer follows, predictably, "Persons, though three, together, they are one nature; one substance; one Lord of Heaven."[34]

The dispatch with which such a response was delivered tends to misrepresent the seriousness of the challenge posed by polytheism. While Buddhism in its early centuries was not a theistic religion, it became so in China. A number of different gods, responsible for various phenomena, were revered in popular Buddhism, and Couplet's catechism neither helps its audience distinguish between spiritual beings nor appreciates the complexity of the matter. The real confusion over whether the Chinese should be worshipping one God and not multiple gods, however, arises in the discussions which do not specifically address the matter of one God in three persons.

Such issues surface, for example, in a discussion of angels, which are called "heavenly gods" (*tianshen*) (*shen* can be translated as god or spirit, so *tianshen* can also be translated as "heavenly spirits"), and in a discussion of the "Holy Spirit," the third person of the trinity, who was called the "holy god" (or "holy spirit") (*shengshen*). Where did these spirits or gods come from? The most confusing aspect for the Chinese believer would be the fact that the "holy god" is not a distinctly different being from the "heavenly god," even though *shengshen* is identified with Tianzhu. No advice is offered on how or whether these gods should be worshipped alongside the one God, or whether, as the Chinese were accustomed to doing in their native religions, the people should make distinctions in their worship by offering different types of sacrifices to various gods, such as a more valuable sacrifice being offered to a higher god. And there are even more *shen* (god or spirit) than these: the catechism refers, for example, to a guardian heavenly spirit or god. All of a sudden, there is not one god, or three gods, but a whole choir full of gods, a reality not dissimilar from the Chinese popular religious vision of the spiritual world.

Another kind of problem arose in relation to the person and role of Jesus. This problem related to the secular associations of the title of Jesus as well as the religious associations of the imperial office. In the catechism, there is no mention of Jesus' title, Christ. The Jesuits had decided to transliterate this term as Jilisidu rather than translate it. Usually, though, they would substitute another term or phrase that they felt more clearly described Jesus' role. For example, Couplet's catechism raises the query "The Lord of Heaven when he descended to be born was referred to by what title?" The answer is "Jesus. That is to say, the Saviour of the World."

Not much was said about him, though this catechism does discuss Jesus' death on the cross and his ascension, all of which Ricci passed over in his apologetic work *The True Meaning of the Lord of Heaven*. Ricci's apologia deals with Jesus Christ and the Church and its practices for only three to four pages. He does not even mention the crucifixion. This omission was a common practice of the Jesuit fathers, since they believed depicting the Lord of Heaven suffering the death of a criminal would scandalize Confucian scholars. The missionaries were correct in this belief, for it was a prejudice of the Confucians to believe that judgments rendered by the imperial government in this life would be upheld by the court of the rulers of the next world.

In failing to give proper emphasis to Jesus and his crucifixion, Jesuit missionaries may have helped their Chinese audience to better deal with the worship of the one God, but at the same time they missed the opportunity to clearly expose the Chinese tendency to deify the imperial person and role. If it had been translated, the title Christ (the Greek translation of the Hebrew term Messiah) would have more sharply defined the political implications of the mission of Jesus, especially since the Hebrew background of the title (which the Greek translation does not completely capture) refers to one who is anointed to rule as a king. This failure to translate the title Christ, then, may have prevented the Jesuit missionaries from exposing the religious claims of the Chinese emperor and from exploring the role that the emperor served in the Chinese religious world.

It was the religious dimensions of the title of Christ that are the focus of Father Couplet in his *A Catechism of the Holy Religion of the Lord of Heaven*. Ignoring the political implications, however, moved Jesus into a role more closely associated with the Buddha. For example, to the question concerning when this savior will descend again into the world comes this response: "When the world is utterly exhausted, the myriad things will all be consumed by fire. On that day My Lord Jesus from Heaven will suddenly appear and judge the sin [*zui*] of all people."[35] In this catechism the work of Jesus cannot be distinguished materially from the work of the Buddha, who came to save the world and whose role was to oversee the end of one eon and usher in the beginning of the next. Indeed, discussion of a godhead in three persons, even accompanied by a more detailed explanation of what this concept entails, would have made it difficult for the common Chinese neophyte to distinguish between the three Buddhas who ruled over the three ages and the three persons of the one Christian godhead.

TRANSLATING THE RITUALS FOR THE PEOPLE

The association between popular Buddhism and Christianity was pronounced in the ritual language and practices of the early Chinese church much more than in the translated doctrinal literature. Yet none of the major studies of the early efforts of the Jesuits deals with this aspect of the sinification of Christianity.

In 1615, Pope Paul V granted Jesuit missionaries the right to translate the liturgy of the mass and the sacramental rites into Chinese. The work of translation was assigned to one Father Ludovico Buglio, an Italian Jesuit missionary who served in China from his arrival in Macao in 1636 until his death in Beijing in 1682. He completed, amidst heated debate among his missionary colleagues as to the wisdom of such a policy, the translation of the liturgy, the missal, and the breviary, along with a translation of Thomas Aquinas's *Summa Theologiae*, all well before the rulings of Clement XI, which decided the issue of the terms to be employed.[36] Rome in 1615 had initially extended permission to use the Chinese vernacular in the liturgy; however, permission was withdrawn by Pope Innocent XI in 1680. It is unclear from the various studies whether permission was withdrawn only for translating the celebration of the mass or if the ruling also included translation of the sacramental rituals.[37] Even if this decision affected only the celebration of the mass, this still meant that later Catholic missionaries proved to be even more conservative in the work of translation than earlier Catholics and more conservative than Buddhists, early and late. Thus, as the Rites Controversy heated up, missionary timidity replaced earlier evangelical boldness.

Buglio's work on the sacramental rituals reveals a much greater adaptation to Chinese and Buddhist popular religious conceptions than do the Jesuit apologetic treatises. His translation of this ritual manual was intended to provide guidance to missionaries and native priests in conducting various sacramental rites. The title page bears the title of the work in Chinese, *Shengshi lidian* (A manual of ritual holy matters) and in Latin along with Buglio's name; it also lists the date and place of publication as Pekin, 1675. The table of contents shows that the manual covers such Catholic ritual and sacramental events as baptism (*xidi*, "wash of purification"), penance (*tong jie*, "painful begging of pardon"), confirmation (*jianzhen*, "establish and rouse to action"), eucharist (*shengti*, "the holy body"), matrimony (*hunpei*, "to contract or arrange a marriage"), extreme unction (*zhongchuan*, "final transmission"), burial (*zhonghou*, "after the passing"), and exorcism (*chugui*, "casting out ghosts"). The manual also includes the rites for various feast days such as Pentecost, an event that is translated as "the descent of the holy ghost" (*shengshen jianglin*). These translated terms suggest that the Jesuits made the closest contact with Chinese popular religion through the liturgical life of the church.

Beginning with baptism, the manual explains that the effect of the sacramental ritual is to pardon humanity's original and fundamental transgression (*yuanzui*) and to cancel the punishment that the transgression deserves.[38] This explanation is dependent to a large extent on the use of legal terminology. The manual makes clear the importance of baptism; without it, one could not enter the Kingdom of Heaven (Tianguo).[39] Any water that has been blessed and made holy can be used.

At the baptism, these words of institution were to be spoken: "Today, the evil god [or evil spirit; *xieshen*] leaves you, the good god [or good spirit] [comes upon] you."[40] These words may be a bit jarring to modern sensibilities, but Catholic baptismal rites always included this language of exorcism. Other terms used in these formulas were part of the common heritage of Chinese popular religion and were also used by Buddhist believers. Prominent among these was the word *shen*, which, as noted, can be translated as either "god" or "spirit." This word is one of the most fluid terms in the Chinese religious vocabulary. Chinese speak of the different *shen* of people, of people becoming *shen* and so being worshipped, and of the *shen* of animals and various inanimate objects, such as mountains and trees (which, because they possessed *shen*, were obviously animate objects for the Chinese). The Jesuits chose to use this term for their translation of the Western concept "spirit," as in Holy Spirit, but also for the spirit of men and women. They also used it to translate the words for "angel" (*tianshen*, heavenly god), and "evil gods" (or "evil spirits," *xieshen*). It is hard to know if the effect of these terms would have been to supplant or confirm the Chinese religious worldview.

In the final action of the baptismal ritual, the manual instructed the officiating priest to make the sign of the cross on the forehead of the baptized while declaring that he was drawing the holy sign of our Lord and Savior Jesus (Yesu) Christ (Jilisidu). The priest then led a prayer that closed in the name of Jesus and that focused on his apocalyptic role: "Our Lord, Jesus Christ [Jilisidu], who after that day will descend to judge the living and the dead, and, with fire, destroy the world."[41]

After the prayer, the participants were all expected to profess together the Apostles' Creed. The language used in the translation of the creed showed some of the same reluctance exhibited earlier by the Buddhists in translating their own "sacred language." The text of the creed was translated into authentically vernacular Chinese with a few significant exceptions: the titles of the three persons of the Godhead and the term for the church were transliterated from the Latin. Thus the opening line of the text reads, "I believe in one almighty Lord of Heaven [*weiyi quannengzhe Tianzhu*]," but then gives the Chinese transliteration of the Latin term for Father, Badele (Latin, *pater*). So it is also with the part of the creed where the believer confesses his faith in the Son and the Holy Spirit. For the section of the creed that concerns Jesus, the Chinese Christian professes, "I believe in the only *feilue* [transliteration of the Latin *filius*], Yesu [transliteration of Jesus] Jilisidu [transliteration of Christ], our Lord." The confession of faith in the spirit was even more cryptic for the Chinese Catholic, as it reads, "I believe in Sibiliduo Sanduo [transliteration of the Latin Spiritus Sanctus]." These transliterated terms were thus an important component of the Apostles' Creed, which was itself a prominent part of most liturgical celebrations.

More than baptism, the rites concerned with sickness and burial would have been associated with religious matters normally presided over by Buddhist priests. At these occasions there was less dependence on transliterated Latin and more leaning on traditional Chinese religious language. At the last rites, the Catholic priest was to instruct the stricken believer to repeat a prayer that ends this way: "We all anticipate entering your dwelling place, and we look towards the eternal blessings of the Lord, where all who love virtue and enjoy good fortune will enter. We demand that any evil spirits/gods immediately depart and we beseech the heavenly gods/spirits [i.e., "angels"] approach."[42] If such prayers proved less than effective, the priest would be summoned to officiate at the burial rites, where, as the casket was lifted, he would pronounce this benediction: "May the Lord of Heaven and all the saints [*shengren*] relieve and protect. May the Lord of Heaven and all his heavenly spirits/gods welcome [our beloved one], and receive his soul, and bring it before the throne of the Lord of Heaven."[43]

More illustrative of the proximity of Chinese Christianity to Chinese popular religion, Daoist and Buddhist, was the rite of exorcism. The cosmologies of both traditional Catholicism and popular Buddhism included a world inhabited by spirits, malevolent and benevolent. While the Jesuit interpreter of the manual distinguished between such spirits or gods by using adjectives such as heavenly, evil, good, and unclean, the target of the rite of exorcism was a *gui*, which, since this term usually refers in Chinese thinking to a malevolent presence (especially when it is hungry), is probably best translated as demon or ghost rather than spirit. The difference between an evil spirit or god and a *gui*, however, lies beyond the scope of this study.[44]

In the instructions given to the officiating priest, the manual cautions the exorcist to first prepare all the spirit utensils (*shenpin*) for casting out demons. Then he is advised to press his hands against the demon-possessed person; at the same time, the manual warns any of the priest's assistants that even touching the afflicted person will have dire consequences. The priest begins by reading the exorcism classic (*chuguijing*)[45], and the text leads him through the steps involved:

> The demon-possessed person whether he laughs or is silent, speaks of private, secret matters or takes on some strange form [*qiyizhe*], the priest should [steel himself and] not believe his empty words. Rather, the teacher, my Lord the Exorcist, should command the demon not to speak and instead to speedily come out. At all times, he should concentrate on being humble. It is absolutely necessary to the success of the exorcism to remember that demons are only beings created by the Lord of Heaven [Tianzhu]. Also [keep in mind that] there is no benefit in conversing with a demon, there is only harm. By all means do not do so. If after three times, the demon has not come out, do not lose hope and give up. Rather, you should totally trust in the Lord of Heaven, and expend yourself in this effort for many days.

At the end of the session, the priest invites all those attending to join him in prayer:

> Almighty Lord, ... Jesus Christ [Jilisidu]. Formerly you bestowed authority on your followers: our feet could trample on poisonous dragons and pythons, on all the power of the evil demons. This is because your virtue has conquered death. If lightning from the heavens should strike, since I revere your name, I humbly beg you to grant that I, your insignificant servant, whose transgressions are forgiven, might, relying on your grace and ability, be brave and attack this fiercely poisonous dragon. May you together with the Lord of Heaven, the *Badele* [transliteration of the Latin term for "Father"], live and rule forever and ever, Amen.[46]

Beyond the Buddhist-tinged language that the missionaries used, many of the church's doctrines and rituals suggested a connection to Chinese popular religion. This connection had not at first been apparent to the Confucian observers, since these doctrines could be taught and the rituals could be practiced only when a congregation of believers, a church, had been formed. As churches were established and missionaries began to expound Christian doctrinal teachings and practice Christian sacramental rituals, the religion of the Heavenly Lord appeared to the Confucians to more closely mimic popular Buddhist religious doctrines and practices than Confucian teachings and rites. Such was the case especially with missionary practice in the provinces, where the Dominicans and Franciscans eagerly and openly displayed the more supernatural elements of the religion.

JESUIT FAILURE, JESUIT SUCCESS

It is not clear what finally motivated the Emperor Yongzheng in 1724 to declare the Heavenly Lord teaching a heterodox teaching (*xiejiao*). Was it a result of the more oppressive and increasingly rigid intellectual world of Qing China? Was it a result of the literati's growing understanding of the true nature of Christianity and what they regarded as its resemblance to Buddhism? Or was it just the more mundane result of a conflict between the Roman pope and the Chinese emperor as manifest in the papal ruling "Ex Illa Die" in 1715?[47] Each of these factors no doubt played a role in the Emperor Yongzheng's decision, although it is difficult to assess which factor was the more significant.

The literati's changing perception of the Heavenly Lord teaching certainly made it easier for the emperor to render his decision. That the literati had increasingly lost interest in the religion of the Heavenly Lord is noted and lamented by every scholar sympathizing with the Jesuit mission. David Mungello describes the state of the mission immediately prior to the emperor's decree with a palpable sense of loss, yet one wonders about the occasion for his melancholy portrayal since the statistics he cites all point to a vibrant, growing church:

> In terms of numbers, the Hangzhou church in Hinderer's time had not yet declined. In the years from 1718 to 1720 there were more than one thousand Christians in Hangzhou, which is twice as many as the five hundred recorded in the annual letter of 1678–1679. Although Fr. Hinderer was the sole missionary in Hangzhou at this time, he was assisted by thirty catechists who had been trained in the Jesuit college. In his letter of 27 September 1719, Fr. Hinderer gave an accounting of the previous year's progress. Between 1 September 1718 and 1719, Hinderer baptized 228 people.... In addition, Hinderer had heard 1,615 confessions and distributed the host to 1,230 communicants.[48]

Such statistics in a later era would be cited as evidence of the progress of a mission. But this is not how many of the Jesuit sympathizers read these numbers, for the statistics reflected changes in the profile of their converts: "The nature of the converts was changing. Whereas the twenty baptisms of 1678 and 1679 had involved literati like Zhang [a literati whose apologetic work Mungello's study chiefly examines], Hinderer was baptizing people of less distinguished status."[49] In a word, this changing profile represented a failure of the Jesuit mission, not just in its goal of trying to reach the elite classes, but more profoundly in its purpose of representing the faith as a return to an "original Confucianism."

This failure suggests that the debate in Western and Chinese historiography over such terms as "popular" and "elite" religion is not just the product of a Western construct unnaturally imposed on traditional Chinese society. Although there was a commonality in how both the people and the elite related to the spiritual world, divisions in Chinese society are reflected in the failure of the Jesuits' strategy. These divisions proved to be a greater reality for the missionaries than any unity that might have existed.

At the same time, it is important to keep in mind that this was a failure of Jesuit strategy only. The overall Catholic mission was remarkably successful. As the translation enterprise partook of more and more Buddhist-infused language, and as the missionaries conducted more of their Buddhist-suggestive liturgies, the mission, while increasingly alienated from the Confucian elite, drew near to and increasingly identified with the common people.[50] Indeed, it is difficult to unequivocally state whether it was the fact that Catholicism was identifying too closely with Buddhism that caused the strain with the Confucian elite, or whether Catholicism was identifying too closely with the people and their religious beliefs, and what Confucians would have regarded as vulgar superstition, that is most responsible for the rift. One senses that if Catholicism was identifying with a more elite form of Buddhism that the Confucians would have been less repelled by the identification.

Jacques Gernet, in his study *China and the Christian Impact: A Conflict of Cultures,* takes note of these changes in the profile of the Christian convert, and argues that the literati, once they realized the resemblance of Christianity to Buddhism and other heterodox teachings, wanted nothing more to do with the religion. Gernet attempts to show how the Western Christian and the Chinese Confucian discourses were too alien to each other for there to be any real understanding between the two.[51] In his argument, Gernet marshals an army of evidence supporting his perspective. Yet, the accumulation of this evidence also demonstrates that there was a popular embrace of Christianity and a sense of affinity between Chinese popular religion and Christianity.

One reason for the eager popular embrace of Christianity was that it was associated in the people's minds with their Buddhist-inspired religious doctrines and practices. Neophytes often drew inspiration from Buddhist and Daoist literature in envisioning their new life in the Christian faith, as Gernet shows:

> In a text that originated in a Christian community in Quanzhou, in Fujian Province, there is an account of a Chinese Christian called before the "Heavenly Court." After remaining dead for a short while, he is returned to life by virtue of his merits. It is an amusing transposition of the edifying tales of Buddhist and Taoist inspiration about descents into hell. The angels of paradise appear in the role of infernal judges, assessors, ushers and their subordinates, and the bureaucratic atmosphere conveyed is similar to that found in traditional tales. The analogy holds good for many details: the messenger who accompanies the dead man in his visit to the infernal regions and, in this case, to the court of Heaven and the Christian hell, the description of the court of justice, the existence of a register of merits and faults which determines the span of life granted to each man, the importance of pious actions such as adorning places of worship and reciting or copying sacred texts—all meritorious actions highly recommended in Buddhism.[52]

Gernet suggests that the people's interest in the new religion also grew out of their fascination with magic and the miraculous, features prominent in their own popular religion. His text includes account after account of miraculous events reported in missionary writings, especially highlighting the role that sacred images, holy water, relics, and Latin-language prayers played in these events. Describing his findings, Gernet concludes, "The missionaries' accounts are full of cases in which the sick, the possessed and the mad are cured or women in childbirth are delivered thanks to sprinklings of holy water, the application of holy relics, making the sign of the cross, or pronouncing the words, 'Ye-su' and 'Ma-li-ya.' The scenario usually follows the same pattern: only after having vainly tried medicine and Buddhist and Taoist ceremonies of exorcism do the sick turn to the missionaries."[53] It is significant that this resemblance between the Heavenly Lord religion and the Buddhist and Daoist faiths was most apparent in the teachings about heaven and hell and in the rites involved with sickness and death, all moments of crisis about which Confucian doctrine was largely silent.

This resemblance between the faiths led Gernet to argue that these converts were really only apparent conversions, since in most cases the conversion did not amount to a change in mentality. Rather, these newly baptized Christians continued to express their faith in the categories of traditional popular religion. Gernet here stumbles over a contradiction in his analysis. On the one hand, he describes how the Catholic religion was understood in the categories of Chinese popular religion, yet he also tries to make the point that there could not have been any real conversions, since the peasants could hardly have understood "a religion so profoundly alien to the Chinese traditions."[54] He makes this comment after he has demonstrated in fourteen previous pages of comments and anecdotes how profoundly familiar the common people found the Catholic religion. He would maintain, though, that this was only a surface familiarity, a resemblance, and that there were deep differences between the mentalities of the two religions. Is this not begging the question? If indeed those differences made the religion so alien, why did the common people respond to it so familiarly?

A more faithful explanation of these events is that Christianity had begun to resemble—at least on the popular level—a Chinese sect. Whether the missionaries had compromised the Christian message or whether the peasants were just too slow in discerning its alien essence are questions that can never really be answered, since we do not possess documents produced by these early peasant converts.

But such questions may be irrelevant for the purposes of this study. What can be established is that on a popular level, Christianity was not regarded as an alien doctrine in the sense that the peasants kept it at a distance. Rather, in its language and some of its practices, and perhaps even in some of its doctrines, the religion of the Heavenly Lord bore a resemblance to that other alien faith, Buddhism, which had centuries earlier attempted to fill the same transcendent religious void the Heavenly Lord sect was now trying to fill, a void that Confucianism by itself had never succeeded in satisfying. Ricci and his Jesuit followers may have failed in their attempt to persuade the Confucian mandarinate of the identification of their Heavenly Lord with Shangdi, and of their Catholic religion with the classical religion, but they succeeded in creating a Chinese Christianity that appealed to the common people.

PROSCRIPTION AND CHINESE SECTARIANISM

This resemblance between the teaching of the Heavenly Lord religion and Chinese sectarian religion did not escape the notice of the authorities. In 1724, Emperor Yongzheng first declared the teaching of the Heavenly Lord sect to be a heterodox teaching and called for its proscription. Catholicism would be prohibited until 1858, when in the Treaty of Tianjin, Emperor Tongzhi proclaimed the Heavenly Lord religion to be beneficial to society.

The period of proscription has often been overlooked in surveys of early Chinese Catholicism. This is unfortunate, since it was a formative period in the indigenization of the faith. There was, nevertheless, a cost to this indigenization. The cost involved a growing identification with Buddhist sectarianism, and heterodoxy, and the attendant increasing distance from the Confucian classical religion, and orthodoxy, with which the Jesuit missionaries had initially sought to connect. Is this Lord of Heaven just another name for the Sovereign on High, or is this a name designating one of the multiple gods of Chinese popular religion? This same polarity will later frustrate the Taiping religious movement.

Although much scholarly energy has been spent explaining the proscription of the Catholic religion as a matter of fallout from the Rites Controversy, less has been said about how much its resemblance to Chinese sectarianism may have also played a role. Indeed, Emperor Yongzheng's decision in 1724 should be seen in the context of his several actions taken both to extirpate heterodoxy and cultivate orthodoxy, and these actions themselves seen in the larger context of the general nature of his centralist and autocratic rule.[55] J. J. M. DeGroot argued along such a line, pointing out that in the same year Yongzheng made this decision against the Catholic religion, the emperor published a decree against native heresy as well.[56]

Although the Heavenly Lord sect was proscribed during this one-hundred-plus year period, from 1724 to 1858, the religion was not persecuted during the entire period, and even when persecution did break out, it was still largely local and temporary. Standaert's *Handbook of Christianity in China* lists three different periods of persecution: 1746–48, the late 1770s, and 1784–85 (this latter period is characterized as the "sole large-scale persecution").[57]

The Jiaqing period (r. 1796–1820), which falls outside the purview of the *Handbook,* was one of the most trying times for the Heavenly Lord sect. Whereas Emperor Yongzheng had proscribed the practice of the Heavenly Lord religion, seizing church buildings and property (he converted churches into schools, granaries, and even temples) and deporting missionaries, Emperor Jiaqing criminalized the practice of the religion. On July 19, 1811, two years before the Eight Trigram uprising of 1813,[58] the practice of the Heavenly Lord sect was criminalized. This criminal status marked the Heavenly Lord sect from the middle of the Jiaqing reign until the treaty ending the Opium War, that is, from 1811 to 1842.[59] While the intention of this law may have been to nip potential rebellion in the bud, it also is an example of how the regime's conception of its authority mandated the elimination of all religious rivals. Indeed, in the original legislation of 1811, a line states that in opposing the gods and ancestors, Catholic teaching is no different from fomenting rebellion.

This law was at first applied very strictly. The courts shortly thereafter adopted a more tolerant attitude toward the Heavenly Lord sect, regarding it as less heinous than other sects. Cases from the commentary section of the law code suggest that distinctions generally were made between the Catholics and other, more notorious sects. When these distinctions were made, they made reference to behavior and rituals for the purpose of determining rebellious inclinations and rarely referred to doctrine and beliefs. Heavenly Lord sectarians were still characterized as religious criminals, but the wording of the laws suggested that the Board of Punishments expected local officials to discriminate between the different forms of sectarianism, between those with a history of rebellion and those with no such history.

A memorial from the succeeding Daoguang period (r. 1821–50) supports this thesis. In 1831, the governor general of Hubei province responded to a central government directive to investigate the formation of the newly discovered Triad organization. Responding to the court's mandate, Governor General Lu Kun reported that he found no trace of the Triad organization in his area, though he ordered the officials under him to be on the lookout for signs of such activity. He agreed with the censor whose investigation first prompted the report that these secret society bandits, who formed such associations and organized the masses, needed to be severely punished to the full extent of the law.

Yet, in spite of the fact that this governor filed his report amidst calls to conduct an investigation into the activities of this menacing, interprovincial Triad network, in a context fraught with tension, this official still attempted to make distinctions among his religious subjects. These distinctions were based on behavior and practice, and the governor judged between peaceful and rebellious sectarians. Once making these distinctions, he allowed the peaceful sectarians to continue participating in their religion.

Looking back over all the cases dealing with those criminals who practiced religion and who had been charged with banditry, the governor general declared that while there had been at one time many cases of sectarian activity and secret society activity, practices of the kind the emperor described were presently nowhere to be found in his jurisdiction:

> From the time of Jiaqing 18 to Daoguang 9 [that is, 1813 to 1829] those bandits who have practiced religion, but have repented and confessed [to officials], including Liu Yi and others all together amount to nineteen cases. They involve those who traditionally have practiced the Heavenly Lord Sect, the Great Vehicle Sect, the Dragon Flower Sect, the Three Sun Sect, the Niu-Pa Sect, the White Lotus Sect, the Green Tea Sect, and the Purity Sect. All these sects [*jiao*] are vegetarian, chant scriptures, seek blessing and help relieve disaster. There is not one article of their situation which is illegal.[60]

The governor summed up his appraisal of these groups with a focus on their practices, and he makes no distinction between the Heavenly Lord sect and the other Buddhist-oriented sects, either in doctrine or ritual.

This report is somewhat puzzling, if not contradictory, all the same. The official claims that these sectarians have confessed and repented, which would suggest that they gave up the practice of their faith, but then the governor declares that not one aspect of their practice was illegal. Did they confess, and did the governor then find they had nothing to confess? It would seem that this governor interpreted the target of the law criminalizing heterodoxy to be heterodox practices only, and he further limited the practices considered heterodox. He does not seem to think that the law prohibited participation in the sect itself.

This was a general rule, and yet there were also exceptional times and cases. Catholic and other sectarian believers could be treated as harshly as the law allowed. This was especially the case when the emperor called for harsher penalties to display his power and glory, or in the case of local officials, when they felt social stability was being threatened. In general, the officials tended to view the Heavenly Lord sect as a common Chinese sect, heterodox but apparently not as subversive to society as other sects.

THE OPIUM WAR USHERS IN A NEW RELIGIOUS ORDER

This official judgment would be transformed by the arrival of a new wave of Western adventurers. The growing presence of European traders was especially in evidence in the British sponsorship of the opium trade. This tipped the balance of power in the region, and it would upset that balance entirely in the first Opium War, which lasted from 1839 to 1842. This change in the balance of power resulted in a new status for the Heavenly Lord sect, which in turn culminated in changes to the imperial religious order.

The persecution of Heavenly Lord sectarians, like some capricious summer storm, came to a sudden end at this time. This dramatic turn of events lifted the spirits of missionaries working in the provinces. A more optimistic outlook is evident in missionary letters featured in *Annals of the Propagation of the Faith*, the first volume of which was published in 1838, just one year before the outbreak of hostilities between China and Great Britain. This series of reports served the same purpose as its predecessor *Lettres Edifiantes et Curieuses*.[61] Both series were aimed at encouraging a general religious interest in the missions of the church throughout the world, and both tended to concentrate on those areas where the French had a national interest (there were more reports from Quebec than Latin America, for example).

While the initial reports in the *Annals* on the state of the Chinese church were somewhat gloomy, these were submitted with an increasing sense that the tide was turning. Estimates of the total number of Catholics on the eve of the Opium War ranged anywhere from 200,000 to 300,000, with

The Early Catholic Search for the Name of God   47

Latourette settling on a range of 200,00 to 250,000.⁶² *Handbook of Christianity in China* provides more specific estimates, in the range of between 215,000 and 217,000 Catholics.⁶³ These numbers suggest that there was little change in the Christian population during the period of proscription, but that impression would not be wholly accurate, for there was a great deal of growth in Sichuan, even while there were dispiriting setbacks in Jiangnan. Spread throughout the empire, the sectarians were concentrated around Beijing, in Zhejiang (a vicariate apostolic that included Jiangxi and Fujian), Jiangnan, and Sichuan.⁶⁴

The numbers picked up quickly, and exuberant reports of conversions began to be regularly featured in the *Annals* even before the emperor lifted the ban on the practice of the Heavenly Lord sect in 1844. (It, however, would still be classified as a heterodox sect until 1858. Believers could thus practice their Catholic religion but did not enjoy the full protection of legality during these intervening years.) Indeed, in the first issue of this serial, reports dated three and four years before the signing of the treaty already testify to the change of mood, even in spite of sporadic incidents of persecution. That mood was brightest in areas where, a decade or so later, the Taiping would do some of their heaviest recruiting: Hunan, Hubei, Jiangxi, and Jiangsu.

Persecutions still flared up nonetheless. In 1840, a Lazarist missionary by the name of Father Perboyre was captured in Hubei, beaten, tortured, and thrown into prison. Later, the vicar apostolic of Huguang passed on an account of the missionary's execution:

> Father Perboyre was led to death, accompanied by five malefactors, who were beheaded before his eyes . . . before consummating his sacrifice, he [Father Perboyre] knelt down, and remained some time in prayer; his hands being then tied behind his back, he was raised on a cross, after which his throat was cut by the executioner. His agony lasted a long time. After his death, the soldiers divided his clothes among themselves, and his body remained on the gibbet during the remainder of the day and all the following night. It was at midday, on a Friday, that our glorious colleague expired.⁶⁵

The outlines of his martyrdom are perhaps a little too reminiscent of one that took place some eighteen hundred years previous, but that does not diminish the price he paid. This punishment, however, was an exception to the rule. Most missionaries were merely escorted out of the country. That the good father's martyrdom occurred at the time of the struggles with England over the opium trade suggests that the missionary was as much a victim of the consequences of Western imperialism as of Chinese tyranny.

Chinese Christians usually did not suffer such severe punishments either. Yet, in the memorials that make up the law code's commentary, every case indicated that Heavenly Lord sectarians, when called on to do so, apostatized. When they did, their crime of participating in heterodox activity would be pardoned. But these documents have their own spin. Would provincial officials even report cases of peaceful sectarians who did not choose to renounce their heterodox faith? Obstinate and rebellious sectarians were easy to punish; peaceful and devout peasants who refused to renounce their faith would go against type. This is why in some places it was reported that if the Heavenly Lord sectarians did not trample on the cross as a sign of their renouncing the faith, officials would help them, dragging them by force over the cross. At other times, soldiers sometimes would falsify their abjuration, and the judges would go along with the fiction,[66] so as not to punish those whose only crime was meeting together to pray and to chant scriptures.

The Opium War and the signing of the Treaty of Nanjing brought an end to most of these persecutions. Church life returned to some sense of normalcy.[67] Those believers who may have been holding back because of persecution were now emboldened to practice their faith. In December 1842, Christmas was openly celebrated in Nanjing, with a Chinese priest preaching the sermon and a "multitude of neophytes" in attendance (a later report estimates that Christians at the Christmas celebration numbered two thousand). Another missionary singles out Suzhou and Nanjing as boasting considerable congregations.[68] The vicar apostolic of Huguang (incorporating the provinces of Hubei and Hunan) wrote in 1842, "Although my vicariate is not so large as many others, it reckons more than eighteen thousand neophytes, scattered in a hundred different congregations, over a surface more extensive than all of Italy."[69] He was probably comparing the size of his flock to that of the relatively larger Jiangnan church, where the estimate of the Christian population was nearly seventy thousand.[70] In 1846, a Jesuit missionary from Jiangnan wrote that though conversions were not numerous, he himself had baptized about 130 adults in the first half of the year.[71] The Lazarists, who were in charge of a wide range of provinces, reported twenty churches and 12,000 neophytes for Jiangxi, and twenty chapels and 4,500 Christians for the vicariate apostolic of Zhejiang.[72] The missionary explorer L'Abbe Huc reported visiting a village along the Yangzi River where one-third of the inhabitants were Christians, and they celebrated Easter by lighting fireworks and throwing firecrackers.[73]

Britain's initial treaty ending their war with China did not provide for the erecting of churches, but the American treaty with China, signed in 1844, did (article 17). Establishing churches (*libaitang*), hospitals, and cemeteries was allowed, and the French treaty, also signed in 1844, called for the same (article 22), yet these establishments were restricted to the five open treaty ports.[74] The lifting of the ban on Christianity was worked out separately from the treaties, and was effected by an imperial rescript on December 28, 1844. In this decision, the emperor gave permission for the Catholics to practice Christianity. Two years later, on February 20, 1846, the Daoguang emperor issued a decree that provided for the restoration of all church properties confiscated during the years of repression.[75] Neither of these imperial decrees allowed for missionaries to propagate their faith outside the treaty ports. But did this mean they could not travel there for other purposes, such as claiming church property? The missionaries exploited the ambiguity. The impact of the Opium War and the new world order was seen in the inland provinces first in the form of these religious changes and only later in the form of economic and commercial changes. These decrees would later be enshrined in the Beijing Convention of 1860.

THE FRENCH PUSH TOWARD TOLERATION

French Catholic missionaries did not wait for the Convention's authorization. Instead, French officials, acting on the church's behalf, began pressing Catholic claims right after the signing of their treaty in 1844. Qiying was the Manchu official and imperial clansman who handled China's foreign affairs from 1842 to 1848. He was commissioned to broker the Treaty of Nanjing, and he handled these religious negotiations as well. The record of his representing French requests to the imperial throne is contained in *A Complete Account of Our Management of Barbarian Affairs* (Chouban yiwu shimo).[76]

Following Emperor Yongzheng's banning of the Heavenly Lord sect and throughout the years leading up to the Opium War, matters involving the Heavenly Lord sect had been handled in the same way as matters involving other heterodox Chinese sects: by local Chinese officials looking to the Qing law code. While Catholic missionaries continued to serve in the court's Astronomy Bureau and would occasionally intervene on behalf of some hapless missionary in the provinces, they could not have intervened in matters involving Chinese followers of the Heavenly Lord.

This method of handling the Heavenly Lord sect began to change with the Opium War, and was formalized with the Tianjin Treaty of 1858 and the subsequent Beijing Convention of 1860. The years between 1840 and 1860 were a period of transition from the era of proscription, when the Heavenly Lord sect was treated as a common, heterodox Chinese sect, to a period when it began to be treated as a foreign religion, protected by unequal treaties. In fact, in documents related to the Heavenly Lord sect, the epithet of *xiyang* (Western), which was attached only infrequently to the name of the religion during the time of proscription, is at this time more often than not used to designate the faith.

Qiying drafted the memorial that served as the basis for the imperial edict granting religious freedom to the Heavenly Lord sect. The court formally received his memorial on November 11, 1844—shortly after the French treaty was signed on October 24. In Qiying's exchange with the emperor and his Grand Council, government anxiety over the impact of legalizing a heterodox sect is palpable. This exchange provides a window not just into the attitude of the government, but also into the changing status of Catholicism, from that of the heterodox Heavenly Lord sect to protected foreign mission of the French government. In its former status, it threatened the government because of associations with native heterodoxy; it now appeared threatening because of its connections to a foreign enemy.

The request for religious toleration of the Heavenly Lord sect was not Qiying's idea; rather, he responded to a request made by the French emissary Theodose de Lagrene to rescind the ban on Catholic religious activities. In his memorial, Qiying makes clear that the French official tried to force this legislation into reality. He furthermore characterizes the whole manner in which the French representative made his repeated demands as blasphemous (*duqing*).

Part of the explanation for the French representative's brusque behavior was that Lagrene was able to demonstrate a legal basis for his demands. The French emissary had produced a copy of a ruling issued by the Bureau of Rites in 1692, during the thirty-first year of Emperor Kangxi's reign (it was actually a rubbing; the ruling must have been engraved in stone).[77] This ruling was surely a copy of Kangxi's edict, which called for the toleration of Catholicism. When Qiying and his ministers inquired as to who had given him this rubbing, and where it was found, Lagrene told them that it had originally come from China, and that it had been kept as a treasure by some of his countrymen for a long time. Qiying was incredulous, but he reports that after investigating the rubbing, looking at the color of the paper and the style of the characters, he determined that it was not fabricated, especially as he remarked to the emperor that no one in this man's country at that time knew how to write Chinese characters or had developed the technique of engraving characters on stone.

Still, Qiying sought out further information on the background of the Heavenly Lord sect. He reported to the emperor how he was conducting an investigation into the history of the sect, a history he summarized for the Grand Council. He found that the sect indeed had entered China during the Ming dynasty in the person of the Westerner, Li Madou (Matteo Ricci), and that in every province foolish peasants had been tricked into joining it. In this sense, the Manchu official opined, the religion was difficult to tolerate. Nevertheless, in the more than two hundred years that it had been practiced in China, there had not been one incident where it was found responsible for inciting any kind of disturbance. In this way, Qiying argued, it was different from such heterodox sects as the White Lotus, the Eight Trigram, and the White Sun.[78]

In those cases where the Heavenly Lord sectarians had merely been guilty of practicing their religion, the court had required only that they trample on the cross, indicating that they repented their religious practice, and local officials had pardoned them of their crime. That is to say, although the law was severe, the official attitude was tolerant. Besides, Qiying declared, officials had not been so thorough in searching out and prosecuting these cases lately. Because this was the case, there was then no practical difference in the court's present policy between proscribing and not proscribing the sect.

As he advocated this change, Qiying maintained in his memorials that he had strictly refused to assent to the Frenchman's most blasphemous demands, not giving any ground whatsoever. The only matter Qiying decided to allow had to do with the ordinances of the Heavenly Lord religion, that is, that the sectarians be allowed to meet together once a week for worship, at which time they could call upon the likeness of the wooden cross, chant scriptures, and exhort one another to good works. All this seemed to be a necessary obligation and legitimate expression of the religion.

The only problem that the Manchu official could foresee in allowing these practices was that those adhering to the religion were scattered abroad in every province. This gave the official cause for concern, for he believed that if the court were to allow the Heavenly Lord sectarians to gather together in a meeting, then the spreading of corrupt practices and disturbances would increase. Moreover, Qiying noted, in the last few years, the White Lotus, Eight Trigram, and other such sects had repeatedly been sought out and their members punished. Indeed, the Blue Lotus (Qinglian) sect was at that moment being investigated, and its followers were being apprehended. If these sectarians were to hear that the Heavenly Lord sect was to be tried under a new precedent that grants a pardon for their crime, this would result in some of these other sectarians craftily attaching themselves to the Heavenly Lord sect. The court would have to watch out for this kind of unlawful behavior.

The critical aspect of this correspondence was that Qiying was not asking that these sectarian practices be declared legal. Rather, he was seeking only that the crime of heterodoxy be pardoned in the case of the Heavenly Lord sect. The emperor was asked to show his magnanimity—or in the words of the memorial, to display the grace of heaven—in this matter. There was no declaration that the sect was legal, let alone orthodox. That would only come later.

As it turns out, the court did not accede to most of these demands or enforce many of these rulings until compelled to do so under pressure from the Taiping Rebellion and the second Opium War (1856–58). A significant factor in this delay was the swinging of foreign policy away from the appeasement tactics of Qiying and his party. Still, the court did begin to honor its promise to pardon the religious crimes committed by Heavenly Lord sectarians and to allow the reopening of old churches and the establishment of new ones.

It is difficult to know just what impact these decisions had in the countryside and what might account for the rapid increase in the number of Heavenly Lord sectarians in the decade following the Treaty of Nanjing. Were people who were already believers now coming out in the open, or were the White Lotus and other sectarians now seeking a protective umbrella for the practice of their beliefs, or was the increase a result of new conversions?

Whatever the source of these new professions of faith, the quasi-legalization of the Heavenly Lord sect and the opening of churches, especially in the Yangzi River valley, inevitably had an impact on rural China, for by the time of the Taiping, the Heavenly Lord sect had revived and was thriving. In every year following these negotiations between the French and the Manchu Qing, more and more followers joined the sect, and this revival breathed new life into other branches of sectarianism as well. A new religious order was emerging, an order that was indicative of changes in the political landscape, and the Taiping would reap the benefits of these changes.

2

The Protestant Bible and the Birth of the Taiping Christian Movement

Catholic Christianity, for all its long history in China, did not set the spark to the Taiping Rebellion. Chinese gentry and officials during the rebellion attempted to trace the fuse of the rebellion back to the Heavenly Lord sect, but that fuse was laid and lit by Protestant Christians.

At the time of the first Opium War (1839–42), 200,000 to 250,000 Chinese followed the teachings of Catholicism; by contrast, Chinese Protestants amounted to just a handful of believers. The Protestants got off to a very late start in the enterprise of missions. Indeed, the most dramatic contrast between the Protestant and Catholic missionary movements was in the timing of their endeavors. While Catholic missionaries had been working in China since the late 1500s, Protestants first arrived in China only in 1807.

Protestants were not only late arrivals to the Chinese mission scene, they were late arrivals to the entire world of missions. There was no significant Protestant mission effort anywhere until the end of the eighteenth century. The English Baptist William Carey published his *An Enquiry into the Obligations of Christians to Use Means for the Conversion of the Heathen* at this time, during the turbulent tides of the Evangelical Awakening.[1] This religious movement, which arose in the early eighteenth century and endured through the first decades of the nineteenth, affected all the Protestant denominations, particularly those in England and America. It gave birth to the Methodists and other Wesleyan groups as well as to evangelical social crusades, such as the anti-slavery campaigns and temperance societies. This movement also produced the first Protestant missionary societies.

Some Protestant attempts at missions had occurred before this period, notably those mounted by the Moravians, a German Pietist group, which coincidentally profoundly influenced Rev. Karl (Charles) Gützlaff (1803–1851), a missionary who would play a critical role in the birth of the Taiping. But these early attempts were mainly scattered and short-lived. Moreover, church leaders did not feel they had a responsibility to undertake the task of missions. As suggested in Carey's title, the Calvinistic churches of England and America believed that if God wanted such people saved, He would do it himself. John Wesley's (1703–1791) revivalistic efforts would spark a change in this view. The first modern Protestant mission society, the Baptist Missionary Society, was formed in 1792, immediately after Carey published his appeal. The London Missionary Society was formed in 1795 and was the first mission to send evangelists to China.[2]

While Carey's appeal does mark the beginning of this Protestant missionary endeavor, it can hardly account for the origins of the movement. Many scholars have looked for the origins of the missionary impulse in the imperialistic designs of Britain. Although imperialistic imagination, which often accompanied imperialistic enterprise, did contribute to the movement, it is also widely recognized that the trade barons who were constructing their economic empire often clashed openly with the missionary bishops who were building their ecclesiastical empire.

Dramatic changes coinciding with the loss of the American settlement colonies and the gain of the entire Indian subcontinent were certainly afoot in Britain's idea of empire at the end of the eighteenth century. The progress of the Industrial Revolution further affected the British idea of empire and provided the economic conditions that made the missionary movement possible. Nevertheless, the sponsors of the trading and economic empire did not warm to the zeal of the emerging religious enthusiasts.[3] The British Crown had granted the East India Company the monopolistic right to trade in Asia, and it had become a matter of company policy to prohibit missionary work among native peoples. In fact, William Carey, the English

Baptist who became the first modern Protestant missionary, was forced to launch his evangelical career in a part of India governed by Denmark because of this very policy.

The search for the origins of the Protestant missionary impulse has yet to take into account the response of British evangelicals to political events in France and on the Continent, a factor that probably contributed more than any other to the missionary movement. Millennial visions were a prominent feature of early British Protestantism, and the dates for the founding of all the modern missionary societies correspond to a renewed sense of the imminence of the millennium and the apocalypse that must precede it. The first major missionary societies in Britain were all founded at the time of the French Revolution, at a time when the Catholic Church in France and the order supporting it there were being threatened with destruction. Such events fit neatly into the English Protestant scheme of the end times. Devout Protestant Non-Conformists believed that along with the downfall of the Roman church, another condition for the advent of the millennium was that "the gospel of the kingdom must be preached throughout the whole world . . . and then the end will come."[4] This apocalyptic motive thus more fully accounts for the rise of the missionary movement, especially in its timing, and this understanding of the origins of the movement enables us to more faithfully reconstruct its impact on China and the Taiping.

CHINA'S FIRST PROTESTANT MISSIONARY

What Protestants lacked in experience, they made up for in energy. Robert Morrison (1782–1834) is credited with being the first Protestant missionary to arrive in China. Though a Scotch Presbyterian, he was sent out by the interdenominational London Missionary Society. Morrison landed at Canton in 1807 aboard an American ship, since the policy of the East India Company (which had a monopoly on trade to China and India) remained hostile to missionaries. Soon after his arrival, though, his growing facility in the Chinese language won him a place on the staff of the company as a translator.[5]

The London Missionary Society had assigned Morrison two tasks: translation of the Bible and evangelism. He spent most of his energy immersed in the former task, which was to have a significant consequence for the rise of the Taiping Rebellion. In 1823, sixteen years after arriving in China, Morrison published a complete Chinese Bible.[6] This focus on the priority of the Biblical text so characterizes the Protestant missionary enterprise and is so characteristic of Protestant activity generally, that we tend to overlook its impact. Yet the translated Bible constituted Protestantism's most influential contribution to the Taiping religion. Indeed the translated Bible, more than any other source, including Liang Afa's tract, had the most dramatic impact on the development of the Taiping Rebellion.

Christopher Hill's study of the English Revolution, *The English Bible and the Seventeenth-Century Revolution*, provides a fascinating parallel. While the parallel between the English Revolution and the Taiping Rebellion cannot be applied too strictly, there are strikingly similar characteristics between them, which one would not expect from two movements that sprung from such vastly dissimilar backgrounds. There is a reason for this. Although seventeenth-century England had been Christian for centuries, it had been Protestant only for decades and had had access to the vernacular Bible for an even shorter time. (The Geneva Bible was published, complete with notes, in 1560. The King James version, which came out in 1611, did away with these sometimes revolutionary annotations.) Hill's chapter "The Revolutionary Bible" documents the revolutionary impact that Biblical concepts, themes, and passages had on the course of the revolution. This impact was possible only because of what Hill refers to as the "political and cultural empire of the Bible in seventeenth-century England." He demonstrates the extent of the use of the Biblical idiom in seventeenth-century thought and culture when he indicates that even in such a "nonreligious" work as Hobbes's *Leviathan*, the author includes 657 citations from the Bible.[7] A similar kind of culture developed in the Taiping movement, and the Bible exerted a similar kind of authority for the movement.

Morrison had already broken ground for this translation project before he left England. In London he had acquired a copy of a Catholic translation of the New Testament, which he had discovered at the British Museum. In spite of all the literature that Catholic missionaries had translated—catechisms, liturgies, sacramental manuals, even portions of

Thomas Aquinas's *Summa Theologiae*—no complete translation of the Bible had been attempted. Selected portions of the Bible were, of course, produced, and they were featured in the various catechisms and liturgies. These portions, however, would never have been presented in the original context of Israelite history. Rather, religious teaching was mostly abstracted from its historical and, more importantly, national context. This approach did have its benefits; but it also has its disadvantages, especially in relation to the indigenization of Christianity.

Jean Basset was the translator of this Catholic version of the New Testament. He was a missionary affiliated with the Missions Étrangères de Paris, and was one of the founders of the organization's mission in Sichuan, where he served from 1662 to 1707.[8] Basset's work, the only Catholic translation to this point, was not a complete translation of the New Testament, as it included only a "harmony" of the gospels (in which the four gospels were combined into one account of the life of Jesus), the Acts of the Apostles, Paul's letters, and the first chapter of Hebrews. Basset died before completing the rest of the work, with the result that the apocalyptic book of the Revelation of John was left untranslated into Chinese. An Englishman by the name of John Hodgson had a copy made of Basset's manuscript at Canton in 1737, and he presented it to Sir Hans Sloan Bart, who in turn donated it to the British Museum. So it was that Robert Morrison, engaging a Chinese resident in London, copied the Sloan manuscript, and then brought his own copy—a copy of a copy—to Canton in 1807.[9]

Basset's translation is at once wholly original and totally puzzling. The most intriguing aspect of his work was his translation of the term for God. Basset did not use the term Tianzhu (Lord of Heaven), as mandated by the 1715 papal decree, nor did he use Shangdi (Sovereign on High), the name forbidden by the same decree. Rather, he used Shen (God or Spirit) consistently throughout the harmonized gospel and the epistles.

This translation of God creates a problem. The difficulty in translating the term *shen* is that since there is no capitalization in Chinese, there is no indication that this is a proper noun in the Chinese. With the other Chinese terms for God, Shangdi and Tianzhu, translators can capitalize them in English, as they are more clearly proper terms in the Chinese. Translators who used *shen* usually worked around this problem by referring to this particular god as being either the one and only god or the highest god, and so arrived at a proper name for God. Context also goes a long way to making the meaning clear. I capitalize this term when it is clearly the translator's intention that it refers to a proper name, and when there is some indication of particularity from the context. But the reader should realize that in the Chinese, it is not always clear, even in context, whether this word is referring to one of several gods, or just one particular god.

Why, though, does Basset adopt this anomalous translation for the name of God? One explanation for this decision is that Basset was engaged in his translation before the final papal decree on the name of God was promulgated, and so his choice of this term may have reflected the fluidity of rules guiding the Catholic translation effort prior to the papal decree.[10] Yet it might also be the case that Basset's decision to use the term Shen reflected his personal belief in its appropriateness, a belief that was supported in part by his mission's own doctrinal position. The Missions Étrangères de Paris strictly rejected the Jesuit approach and repudiated any compatibility between Christianity and Confucianism. Such a position was inimical to the use of Shangdi as the name of God, as the Missions Étrangères de Paris would have denied any identification between the Christian God and the Sovereign on High of the Chinese classical past.[11]

Whatever his motivation, Basset's God is Shen. The first chapter of his gospel harmony, for example, taken mostly from the Gospel of John, states that in the beginning was the word (*yen*), and the word was a god (*shen*), and that this word-god was in the embrace of another god (*shen*).[12] Neither of these gods is identified with Tianzhu, and Basset never has recourse throughout his translation to this term. Even accounting for the fact that Basset died before the papal decree was published, it is still strange that he did not employ the term even once in his translation. Not only did he not use what would become the officially mandated term, Tianzhu, but the term he used for translating the one highest God, Shen, does not appear in any other piece of Catholic literature.

Because of his choice of this term for rendering the name of God, Basset was compelled to adopt two other anomalous translations. These are his translations for the terms Holy Spirit and angel. In all the other religious literature produced by the Catholics, the term for the Holy Spirit was consistently translated as Shengshen (Holy God). (Again we encounter a similar problem as with the use of *shen*. When earlier Catholics used this term for angel, *shengshen* would be lowercased. Here, Basset is using the term for Holy Spirit, and so I have capitalized the term. Only the context in Chinese indicates whether to make this a proper or common noun.) Basset, however, again parted company with his Catholic missionary colleagues. He referred to the Holy Spirit as Shengfeng (Holy Wind). In chapter 1 of the gospel harmony, Mary asks how she can bear an heir to the throne of David since she is a virgin; the angel responds that "the Holy Wind will come upon you." The angel later confirms to a skeptical Joseph that it was "the Holy Wind which accomplished this."[13]

Then there is Basset's irregular translation of the term for angel. In all other Catholic literature the term used was *tianshen* (Heavenly god). But since Basset adopted the term Shen to name the highest God, he could hardly refer to choirs of angels as occupying equal status with the high God. Consequently, Basset used two different terms in translating the word angel: *tianshi* (heavenly or imperial messenger—this term was used by the Qing court to designate its messengers) and *shenshi* (divine messenger). So in Basset, the angel who appeared to John the Baptist's father Zechariah was called the Lord's heavenly messenger, while the angel Gabriel who appeared to Mary, bringing her glad tidings, is a divine messenger. And on that starlit Christmas night, when the birth of Jesus was announced to the shepherds, it was a crowd of heavenly messengers who declared to them that peace has come to men of good will.[14] There were no "Heavenly gods" (that is, *tianshen*, the conventional term for angels in all previous Catholic publications) in Basset's constellation of beings.

When the time came for Robert Morrison to produce his own translation of the New Testament, his debt to Basset is heavy, and his borrowing is extensive. Where Basset translated a passage, Morrison followed that translation almost word for word. The only significant change that appears in Morrison's 1813 New Testament translation is that Morrison sometimes uses the term "Messiah" for the term "Christ," where Basset consistently used the term "Christ." All other changes are minor and of no significance.[15] Where there is no Basset passage to follow, even here Morrison, seeking to be consistent in usage, continues to employ the same terminology.

Morrison continues to use Shen for God, Shengfeng for the Holy Spirit, and then his own term, *shenshizhe* (divine messenger), for angel. Morrison had to translate all four gospels, using Basset's gospel harmony as a guide. So, for example, in the passage describing the Annunciation, when Mary asks the angel Gabriel how all this shall come to pass, Morrison translates the angel's (or messenger's; the term used in this passage is simply *shizhe*) response as, "The Holy Wind [Shengfeng] will fall upon you," and the child to be born to her will be called "the son of God" (or, alternatively, the son of a god).[16] On Christmas night the angels (*shenshizhe;* divine messengers) appear as a heavenly army (*tianjun*) rather than as just a crowd of angels, as we saw in Basset's translation, but the army of angels, like the crowd of angels, still renders glory to God (Shen) in the highest.

The accumulated effect is that one could characterize Morrison's Bible as more the work of the Catholic Basset than the Protestant Morrison. Jost Zetzsche spells out the impact of this dependence on Basset: "Morrison's great reliance on Catholic sources, especially the Basset manuscript, had a lasting impact on Protestant terminology, which to the present day is deeply indebted to Catholic terminology."[17] Indeed, this is true. Most of Basset's translations of key theological terms became standard Protestant terms. At the same time, we need to reiterate that Morrison did not borrow from standard Catholic terminology, but from the translation of an idiosyncratic interpreter of Catholic terminology.

THE MESSAGE OF CHINA'S FIRST EVANGELIST

Robert Morrison proved to be quite accomplished in the task of translation that his missionary society had assigned him. In his second task, that of evangelism, he was less successful. His partner in translating the Bible, Rev. William Milne (1785–1822), apparently was more suited to the work of evangelism. It was only after Morrison introduced his Bible printer, Liang Afa, to Milne that Liang converted to Christianity, becoming China's second Protestant and its first ordained evangelist.[18] Liang Afa would be instrumental in bringing the Christian message to the Taiping.

Liang's seemed to be a sincere conversion, although it was after the form of nineteenth-century Anglo-American evangelicalism, which stressed individual salvation from sin over national deliverance from oppression and which entirely overlooked corporate aspects of salvation. It would be this kind of Christianity that Liang Afa, in the pages of his evangelistic pamphlet, would pass onto Hong Xiuquan, the leader of the Taiping.

Most scholars of the Taiping Rebellion have emphasized the kind of Christianity that the Taiping leader first came into contact with in the pages of Liang's nine-volume booklet, *Good Words to Admonish the Age*. Eugene Boardman reminds us that "Protestant missionaries in China were much more what may be termed fundamentalist in their beliefs than are many missionaries in the twentieth century."[19] It is probably more accurate to characterize these missionaries as evangelical in the sense given to this term at the time. The Wesleyan evangelical revival had affected all Protestant denominations in England and America, most of which were originally Calvinist in their theological orientation. Under the influence of this "awakening," the Calvinist churches—Congregational and Presbyterian, and even some Baptist—together with the Anglican (Episcopal) Church, were transformed into a less doctrinaire and more energetic Protestantism.

The early missions to China were almost all of this type, evangelical and Calvinist. The London Missionary Society, which was most influential in these early years, was the primary example of this evangelical and Calvinist temperament.[20] In this context, Rudolf Wagner's description of the kind of missionary who served in China during the early years needs a little adjusting, as he states, "The young men who came to China and who had sometimes 'given themselves' at revivalist meetings to be missionaries . . . were typically not sedate and learned gentlemen, like the later arrival, James Legge, but rather a 'revivalist left' of often bizarre evangelical enthusiasts like the German Gützlaff and the American saddler Issachar Roberts, 'the only missionary from the Mississippi Valley.'"[21] Actually, Gützlaff and Roberts were the exception to the rule; missionaries do not get much more bizarre than they were. But most of the early missionaries were sedate and fairly learned men (and very soon, women)—Protestants did not come more sedate than Congregationalists or Presbyterians, even when they were missionaries.[22] It was, however, the exceptions who made a larger impact on the Taiping.

Indeed, the big exception to this rule was Rev. Karl Gützlaff, who was among the hardiest, most eccentric and unbalanced, and most prolific of the missionary pioneers. Indeed, he was probably too eccentric for most missionaries, as Jessie Lutz and Ray Lutz, and others, have described him.[23] A German by nationality, he was sent out by the Netherlands Missionary Society in 1826. Early on, he left that mission in a disagreement with it over entering China. Afterwards he would retain some relationships with different missions, but he was for the most part independent, supporting himself by working for the British in various capacities, mainly as a secretary and translator. He must have been a man of prodigious energy, since he carried on all his missionary activities while holding a full-time job. He took the lead in handing out Bibles from opium ships, conceived of the term "blitz baptism," and founded the Chinese Union (Hanhui, literally "Han [Chinese] Society"; sometimes also referred to as Fu Hanhui, in which "Fu" refers to "Gospel"[24]), members of which first contacted Hong Xiuquan. Gützlaff also served as mentor for Rev. I. J. Roberts, a Southern Baptist operating independently who first arrived in China in 1837 and who later instructed Hong in the fundamentals of Anglo-American Protestantism.[25] The German missionary's impact on the Taiping far exceeded that of all other mission efforts combined, including that of Robert Morrison.

A glance at some of the titles published by these early missionary pioneers, listed in Wylie's *Memorials of Protestant Missionaries to the Chinese*, reveals the focus of their missionary calling. Other than his translation of the Bible, Robert Morrison published eleven works in Chinese, including: *A True and Summary Statement of the Divine Doctrine, An Outline of Old Testament History, Daily and Evening Prayers,* and a geography primer, *Tour of the World*.[26] In addition to his multiple translations of the Bible, Gützlaff composed some 59 works in Chinese, including such titles as *History of England, Doctrine of Redemption, Precious Words of Jesus, God* (that is, Shangdi) *the Lord of All, Outlines of Political Economy,* and *Abandoning Depravity and Returning to Righteousness*.[27]

The dominant emphasis in these lists is on Christian doctrine, interpreted rather narrowly. Where there is an occasional glance cast in the direction of a more secular subject, the titles suggest that a division is drawn between the sacred and the secular: the title *Outlines of Political Economy*, for example, does not suggest that this was a peculiarly Christian view of political economy. Indeed, a pattern emerges in this listing that formalizes a division between the secular and the sacred spheres of life, a pattern that was the legacy of the separate spheres claimed by the Enlightenment and Evangelicalism, respectively. This division influences the entire approach of these missionaries in their presentation of Christianity to the Chinese.[28] It is a division that was, of course, unnatural to the Chinese understanding of reality, and that Hong Xiuquan in large part overcame in his efforts to complete the process of the indigenization of Christianity.

This very division is reflected in Liang Afa's *Good Words to Admonish the Age*, the work through which the Taiping future king, Hong Xiuquan, first learned about Christianity. Liang went out of his way to exclude any discussion of economic, political, or social consequences for the religious ideas he explained, in effect polarizing the world of religion and the world of government and society. He accomplished this, for the most part, through his selection of the Bible passages that appeared in his work. He chose passages that emphasized Protestant themes of individual, as opposed to national or social, salvation. So while the language of Liang's tract was the work of the idiosyncratic Catholic Basset, the selection of gospel themes and passages was the work of Morrison and Liang. Making it an even more Protestant effort was the fact that Liang's tract was nothing but a collection of Morrison's translated scripture, mostly appearing without any commentary or explanation of the contents, making a discussion of matters outside a narrowly conceived religious sphere unnecessary.[29]

The first booklet of *Good Words* begins with a translation of Genesis 3 and a brief description of the Fall of Mankind, beginning not with the Hebrew account of Creation and the physical world that God created and blessed as good, but instead beginning with law, transgression, and judgment—all prominent themes in the succeeding pages. The most fearsome condemnation was reserved for idolaters. The idol of every group in society is condemned: the gods of merchants, peasants, and even seamstresses would all fail.[30] There is then a sudden shift to the Sermon on the Mount, with no transition offered. The first booklet ends with no account of who Jesus was, where he came from, or how he died.

The second booklet contains some of the more familiar evangelical passages from the Bible, including John 3:1–21, and an introduction to Jesus as the "Savior of the World."[31] The third and fourth volumes contain a series of translated passages for which there is some commentary, one of these passages being the creation account from Genesis 1. Volume 5 contains another series of evangelical passages, such as this verse from Matthew 16:26: "What shall it profit a man to gain the whole world and lose his soul?" Volume 6 features another string of translated Bible chapters along with a short description of Liang's life, in which he highlights the suffering he endured during his incarceration in 1834 for his tract-distributing activity (this is one of the rare extra-biblical set of remarks in the work).[32] Following this, there is the first real appearance of apocalyptic literature, a translation from the book of Revelation, chapter 22, where the throne of God is set up beside the river of life.[33] Volumes 7 and 8 take us back to the content of previous volumes, as does the ninth and final volume, which ends with a discussion of the Last Judgment.

Significantly, in Liang's profuse quoting of scripture, he included little from the Old Testament and no passages from the historical books; he referred only briefly to the experience of Israel delivered from Egypt; he did not list the Ten Commandments, though he did refer to Moses and did mention some of the individual commandments (given the prominent role of the decalogue in the Taiping movement, this is a significant omission); he referred to the Jews, but he did not discuss their special role as "God's chosen people"; and he dedicated only a few verses to the history of the kingdom of Israel. In short, he provided an abundance of allusions to an otherworldly, individual salvation, but only meager mention of a this-worldly, historical, national salvation (indeed, his arrangement of the biblical selections violates the historical arrangement in the Bible itself). If Hong Xiuquan was going to establish his Heavenly kingdom on earth, he would need much more ideological support for this endeavor than that provided in the pages of this series of booklets.

Liang Afa composed his book of tracts after he had been ordained as an evangelist. He was evidently a zealous preacher, as he conducted repeated forays into the southern Chinese countryside from his base in Canton even before the celebrated tours made by Gützlaff's Chinese Union, which began sending out evangelists only in 1844. MacGillivray writes of these missions, "Kew A-gong, a convert of Liang A-fa, in 1830, in company with Liang A-fa, itinerated 250 miles into the interior of China, following in the train of one of the public examiners. They thus had free access to the young literati at every examination center, and distributed upwards of 7,000 tracts on the most important subjects."[34] Hong Xiuquan's birthplace, Huaxian, was located within thirty miles of Canton.

THE WORD COMES TO HONG XIUQUAN

Hong Xiuquan, the future Taiping Heavenly King, was born in 1814 into a poor peasant family of the Hakka ethnic minority. He showed some academic promise as a child, and so at the age of seven was sent to school to begin the arduous task of preparing for the Confucian-based civil service exams. In 1836, Hong took the exam in Canton. While there, he listened to some preaching and received a copy of *Good Words*.[35] Comforting words for Hong were what he needed at the time, for he wound up failing the exam. In 1837, after failing the exam again, he collapsed into a delirious state in which he envisioned himself ascending to Heaven, where he met his Heavenly Father and his elder brother, Jesus. His Heavenly Father is described as being clothed in a black-dragon robe and dignified by a long golden beard. He appoints Hong to slay demons and to assume the imperial throne.

Recovering from his illness, Hong went back to his former way of life. Even though he exhibited a noticeable change in his demeanor, during the next few years, he did not show any dramatic change in his behavior. After taking and failing the exam in 1843 for what would be the final time, he returned to his position of schoolteacher in a village near his home. It was at this time, some six years after his vision, that his cousin pointed out to Hong the correspondence between his earlier vision and the contents of *Good Words*. Believing that this teaching was sent from heaven, Hong and his cousin repented of their idolatrous ways and then baptized themselves. Another cousin, Hong Rengan (1822–1864), who later would be appointed "Shield King," and a fellow teacher, Feng Yunshan, followed them into the waters of baptism. They immediately set out together preaching the new message in their home province of Guangdong and in the neighboring province of Guangxi.

In the fall of 1844, Hong returned to Huaxian, his home village, while his disciples continued to propagate the new faith among scattered Hakka communities, the ethnic group to which Hong and his disciples belonged, in Guangxi. For the next two years Hong took up his teaching duties again, composing poetry and writing religious discourses in his leisure time. In 1847, he was contacted by some evangelists in the employ of Rev. I. J. Roberts, and was invited to study under the missionary in Canton.[36] After spending two months under Roberts's tutelage, Hong took a short trip back to Thistle Mountain in Guangxi, where he discovered that Feng Yunshan, in his absence, had gathered several thousand Hakka believers into the Society of God Worshippers (Bai Shangdi hui), a combination of religious sect and secret society.

Though he was welcomed as their heavenly ordained leader, Hong did not remain at Thistle Mountain for long. It was only after burying his father in the winter of 1849 that he returned to stay, on a permanent basis, with his newly gathered flock of Shangdi worshippers. While he was absent from Thistle Mountain, other leaders rose to fill prominent roles in the movement. The most influential of these was Yang Xiuqing, the Eastern King, a former coal miner whose position of leadership in the movement was legitimized by a series of prophetic utterances. In the early stages of the movement, all these leaders submitted to Hong's greater authority, a fact that would soon change. In the autumn of 1850, the Society of God Worshippers collided with the local militia, and in January 1851, the society proclaimed the establishment of their Taiping[37] Heavenly Kingdom at Jintian in Guangxi. By 1853, the Taiping had conquered a vast swath of territory in the Yangzi River Valley and had founded their capital at Nanjing, christening it the Heavenly Capital.

THE BIBLE AND THE TAIPING

The critical years for the movement were those from 1847 to 1850, when the Society of God Worshippers was transformed from what seemed to be purely a religious movement into an obvious political rebellion. Adumbrations of this direction had been part of Hong's visions from the start, so to speak of his religious movement as having no political overtones would be misleading. After awakening from his original vision in 1837, for example, Hong announced to his father that "the venerable old man has commanded that all men should turn to me, and all treasure flow to me."[38] His imperial ambitions were more evident in a conversation he had with his sister, which was recorded in the account of his visionary journey, *Taiping Heavenly Chronicle* (Taiping tianri): "His elder sister, Hong Xinying, came to see him. The sovereign said, 'Sister, I am the Taiping Son of Heaven.' With his own hand he wrote the four words Taiping Tianzi [that is, the Taiping Son of Heaven] for his sister to see."[39]

Still, the only violent actions taken by Hong and his followers at this early stage were attacks on "demons" and their representations in various statues and clay figures (i.e., idols).[40] These actions themselves were not inconsequential; they struck at the established religious and political orders, since many of these representations were approved by the imperial authorities.[41] Nonetheless, nothing inherent in Hong's original vision itself demanded anything more than this kind of iconoclasm. Something happened during these early years, however, which took the movement beyond smashing statues.[42] The decisive event in these critical years was Hong's reception and reading of the Bible. His reading the Bible led Hong Xiuquan to see and make manifest the political implications of his religious faith.

Hong was introduced to various passages of the Bible in Liang Afa's tract—indeed, the tract was but a compilation of selected Bible passages—and yet, as pointed out above, these passages had been abstracted from their historical and national context. Moreover, the selections emphasized a view of salvation that was more individualistic than corporate. *Good Words* also did not contain those passages of the Bible that most compelled Hong to take up arms against the Manchus. Finally, while the issue of idolatry is frequently raised, that of misusing or blaspheming the name of Shangdi is never raised in Liang Afa's text. Nonetheless, the fact that Liang's tract, for the most part, translated portions of the Bible did prepare the future Taiping king for his reception of the Bible. Indeed, the religious authority that Liang's tract had for Hong would be transferred to the materials that constituted Liang's tract, that is, to the Bible itself.

Hong may have been introduced to the Bible in its complete form through the evangelistic work of Gützlaff's Chinese Union, which was formed in 1844 and which had adopted Liang Afa's missionary strategy. The Reverend Gützlaff recruited recent Chinese converts and trained them to preach the Christian message throughout the countryside, in areas where European missionaries could not venture. The membership of the Union grew dramatically during these years, exploding from thirty-seven evangelists in 1844 to 1,800 members by 1849. The Union had been especially active in Guangxi, having established six different stations in the province by 1846.[43] But after Gützlaff's death in 1851, the Union was disbanded in the midst of allegations of misconduct and duplicity.[44] While Gützlaff's efforts were widely ridiculed and he had been exposed to some degree of censure, most missionaries accused him more of irresponsibility than of outright deceit. Even Rev. Theodore Hamberg, a missionary with the Basel Mission serving in China from 1847 until his death in 1854 and who had been personally recruited by Gützlaff for the work of the Chinese Union, but now was the person who initiated the case against the Union, acknowledged that there were still some members who were upright and that the Union had been able to achieve some of its goals. Jessie Lutz and R. Ray Lutz have found in their research that several men who became prominent leaders in the Hakka church had first come to their faith through the help of the Chinese Union.[45]

It had been Gützlaff's express purpose to carry the Bible itself, not just tracts, into the Chinese interior. This strategy was laid out even before the opening of the treaty ports, as he revealed in his *Journal of Three Voyages Along the Coast of China in 1831, 1832, and 1833*. In this book, he discussed what he envisioned as the best method for evangelizing the Chinese populace: "The translation and circulation of the Holy Scriptures, the composition and distribution of tracts, with occasional oral addresses to the people, are the means he [the Christian missionary] would employ to propagate the Gospel of Christ."[46] William Canton noted that the British and Foreign Bible Society had, as late as 1847, awarded the Chinese Union the sum of one hundred pounds, which provided the band of evangelists with four thousand New Testaments, one hundred Old Testaments, and six hundred copies of the Book of Psalms.[47]

Whether Gützlaff was able to fulfill his purpose in the particular case of Hong Xiuquan and his band of followers is difficult to determine. Yet we can make a case for believing that Gützlaff's band of evangelists established contact. The proximity of Hong's village to Canton suggests opportunity. Also, a few references point to a level of awareness of the Union's activities among the Society of God Worshippers. Hong Rengan, the future Shield King and number two man in the Taiping Kingdom, in describing the Taiping Heavenly King's background, related how "in the chia-ch'en year [1844]; he [Hong] heard that some foreign brothers were propagating the Gospel and establishing churches."[48] How did Hong hear about these activities if not through such contacts as the Union? Moreover, Chinese evangelists connected to Gützlaff's colleague, Rev. I. J. Roberts, sought out Hong and invited him to Canton. Some kind of relationship must have already been established for this invitation to have been accepted. Finally, even the Society of God Worshippers, the name first taken by Hong and his followers, suggests a connection to the Chinese Union, since missionaries with the Basel Mission, one of the first big supporters of Gützlaff and the Union, referred to converts who were not yet baptized as "God worshippers."[49]

Prescott Clarke makes the case for a connection between members of the Chinese Union and the early core of the Society of God Worshippers. Clarke lists the large number of reports from Taiping soldiers who claimed to have had a Chinese Union background. These reports were submitted by a wide range of Western contacts, including Capt. E. G. Fishbourne of the *Hermes*, the first foreign ship to visit Nanjing; the British consul Lord Elgin; and several missionaries. Even more persuasively, he points out that the two missionaries who had the earliest exposure to the Taiping were closely associated with the Chinese Union, namely Rev. I. J. Roberts and Rev. Theodore Hamberg. As Clarke puts it, "In the same vein it might be asked why Hong Rengan came to Hamberg in 1852 rather than to another missionary."[50] The obvious answer is that he came because of Hamberg's connections to Gützlaff and the Chinese Union. Even more intriguing is Clarke's suggestion that it may have been bands of Chinese Union members who were responsible for the gathering of so many converts in Guangxi, the same converts who embraced Hong as their Heavenly King when he arrived at Thistle Mountain.[51] Clarke thus presents strong circumstantial evidence for his contention that connections existed between the Chinese Union and the Society of God Worshippers. Because of these connections, it can be assumed that early Taiping followers did encounter the Bible.

One of the most important documents for supporting an early date for such an encounter is the *Taiping Imperial Declaration* (Taiping zhaoshu), believed to have been composed by the Taiping between 1844 and 1845. The document refers to the "foreigners' sacred scriptures" once and to the foreigners' "Old Testament" (*Jiuyi zhaoshu;* here the Chinese for "testament" is the same as that for "imperial declaration") twice.[52] Yet Liang Afa in *Good Words* never refers to the Old or New Testament. Rather he refers to the Bible as an entire book; it is the *sheng jing*.[53] And in *Taiping Imperial Declaration,* Hong does not refer to Liang Afa's tract as the source of his knowledge of God and salvation. His authority is the Old Testament. For example, Hong refers to Noah and the flood, a topic covered by Liang Afa, but the authority he quotes is the Old Testament. All of this suggests a familiarity with the Bible, especially as an Old Testament and a New Testament, which extended beyond that contained in *Good Words*.

Direct support for Taiping exposure to the Bible is available, but only for a later date: it is an established fact that during his sojourn in Canton in 1847, Hong studied the Bible under the American Baptist missionary I. J. Roberts. Indeed, it would be hard to imagine any Protestant missionary of the time, especially one whose mentor was Gützlaff, not giving the Bible the dominant place in the curriculum. We are not left to imagination. The *Taiping Heavenly Chronicle* states that while Hong was at Roberts's chapel, "The Sovereign read the Old Testament and the New Testament long and carefully."[54] Upon reading these books, Hong realized they were the same texts that his Heavenly Father had mentioned in his original vision as being the two classes of books that were "pure and without error." Roberts corroborated Hong's exposure to the Bible in an article in *Putnam's Magazine* in which he told readers that "Hung, sow-tsuen, and his convert and cousin, Hung-Jin, having heard that the foreign missionary ... was preaching the true doctrine in Canton, they determined, early in 1847, to come to our chapel and study the scriptures." Upon reaching the chapel, Hong joined the Bible class, where he was "committing [to memory] and reciting the scriptures, and receiving instructions for two hours daily with the class."55

Hong's response indicates that until his visit to Roberts's chapel, he had not seen the entire Bible. It may be that in addition to the passages in Liang's tract, he had seen only some other Bible portions until this point. It may be that he had read chapters of the Old Testament prior to arriving in Canton (Hong refers only to the Old Testament in *Taiping Imperial Declaration*) and that Roberts's Bible class provided the first occasion for Hong to study the Bible in its full and complete form. Indeed, if Hong and his followers had seen the Old Testament earlier, separately from the New Testament, this would also go a long way in explaining the character of their movement, which was described as being more influenced by Old Testament religion than New Testament.

In any case, when Hong left Canton for Thistle Mountain, he was carrying a complete Bible, Old and New Testaments, under his arm. Reverend Roberts confirms that following a misunderstanding, Hong left Canton and returned to his home village after two months of instruction. The Taiping leader's cousin, Hong Rengan, reminisced about those early days of the movement when "he [Hong Xiuquan] met with Feng Yunshan and others of his intimate friends, when they made an appointment, upon what hill they would assemble the following day. Siu-tshuen here used to converse with his followers, and friends about the congregation in Guangxi. He also occasionally read some portion of the Old or New Testament, which he had received during his stay in Canton."56 Roberts, too, referred to Hong's practice of reading and talking about the Bible, as did Augustus Lindley, a foreigner who fought alongside the Taiping for the last four years of the rebellion. Lindley commented that after Hong's return from Canton to Thistle Mountain, he "replaced their former books with copies of the Bible he had brought from Canton; reserving only such parts [of their former books] as were part of the New Testament."57

The testimony of these participants, combined with the appearance of new concepts and assorted themes not previously prominent in Taiping literature, leads to the conclusion that it is not only certain that Hong read the Bible in its full Old and New Testament context, but that he brought back a copy to share with his followers at Thistle Mountain.

THE AUTHORIZED TAIPING VERSION OF THE BIBLE

Critical for appreciating the impact that the Bible had on Hong and his followers is an understanding of two fundamental matters: the version of the Bible adopted by the Taiping and the attitude of the Taiping towards the Bible.

All witnesses of the rebellion unanimously agree that the Bible the Taipings adopted as the royally sanctioned version and which received their imprimatur was one of the earlier translations executed by Gützlaff. Captain Fishbourne of the British vessel the *Hermes* reported, "The French war-steamer Cassini visited some months after us, and she brought down a reprint of Genesis, of Exodus, and a portion of the New Testament, consisting of St. Matthew's Gospel, printed almost verbatim from the version of Gutzlaff."[58] The American missionary E. C. Bridgman, when he visited Nanjing aboard the American vessel *Susquehannah* the following year, 1854, supported this view: "They have in their possession probably the entire Bible, both the Old and New Testaments, and are publishing what is known as 'Gutzlaff's version' of the same."[59] There is no dissenting voice raised against this testimony.[60]

The replacement of the Morrison version with the Gützlaff version is important, since Hong Xiuquan was exposed to Morrison's version of the Bible in the pages of Liang's tract. In order to understand the impact of this new version of the Bible on the Taiping movement, we need to return to the history of Bible translation.

Robert Morrison had completed his translation of the entire Bible in 1823. Among the missionaries who felt that his translation was too wooden was Dr. Walter H. Medhurst (1796–1857) of the London Missionary Society, who complained that "the style adopted in the present version of the scriptures is far from being idiomatic, the translators having sometimes used too many characters, and employed inverted and unusual phrases, by which the sense is obscured."[61] Medhurst thereupon spearheaded efforts to produce a new, more fluent translation.

The London Missionary Society veteran invited Gützlaff to cooperate with him in producing a revised version of the Morrison translation. The sober Medhurst asking the spontaneous and expressive Gützlaff to help him with this project was an odd coupling. But the relationship worked nevertheless. Medhurst completed his revision of the New Testament in 1837, and Gützlaff his revision of the Old Testament in 1838. This was the translation that was distributed by the Chinese Union.[62] Neither Medhurst nor Gützlaff was satisfied with the end product. Gützlaff revised Medhurst's New Testament revision in 1847 and his own Old Testament revision in 1855.[63] The Bible the Taipings adopted was the version for which Gützlaff was solely responsible for the Old Testament and Medhurst principally responsible for the New Testament.

Missionaries were successful in passing onto the Taiping their reverence for the sacred scriptures. This is the testimony of observers as varied as Captain Fishbourne; Rev. Charles Taylor, an early Methodist missionary; and even the British consul Thomas T. Meadows, who, though skeptical of the Christian character of many aspects of the movement, could still say, "He [Hong] appears to have, once for all, taken the Bible as the highest standard of truth, and to have accepted everything new that he therein finds."[64] The energy the Taiping leadership spent on publishing the Bible further testifies to their respect for the Bible. Fully four hundred men in Nanjing were said to be employed at this task.[65] The entire New Testament was published, but the Taiping only published part of the Old Testament. They only published the first Five Books of Moses, and then Joshua and Judges (they did, however, possess copies of the complete text). This is hard to explain, especially given the tremendous impact the Old Testament had on the movement, but the decision to go with an abbreviated version of the Old Testament may have been based largely on economic feasibility. The Taiping not only distributed these texts to their chapels, where on the Sabbath the people would go to hear the expounding on the "holy book," but they also distributed the testaments broadly and indiscriminately throughout Taiping territory.[66] All this news delighted the missionary observers.

This Taiping respect for the Bible did not always take a form that delighted Protestant observers, however, for the Taiping were inspired to improve the text. They sponsored both revisions and additions to the text. An example of the latter change was the commentary Hong added to the margins of the biblical text.[67]

Hong introduced four different types of changes, the first two of which were minor and insignificant. The first was the correction of genuine mistakes, such as editing an inaccurately written character (at Genesis 19:23, the character *zhao,* meaning "to shine," was printed with the wrong radical, making the meaning "to show"), and the adoption of clearer and smoother translations. A second type of alteration was the replacement of taboo characters with more acceptable alternatives, especially as these appeared in transliterations of names and places. For example, the first of the two characters used by Gützlaff to transliterate the name Jesse in Matthew 1:5 was the same character used to transliterate Jesus' name. So Hong merely substituted a different character with the same sound *ye.*

A third type of correction, the alteration of content according to Taiping theology and moral tenets, was more consequential. Thus, certain people never died in the Taiping version of the Bible, but instead ascended to heaven (Abraham's son, Ishmael, for example, in Genesis 25:17). Nor did God's chosen ones drink wine any longer, as did Isaac at Genesis 27:25. Nor did fathers-in-law have sexual relations with their daughters-in-law, as Judah did to provide an heir for his deceased son and his wife in accordance with the Jewish law—Hong completely altered this story (Genesis 38:16–26).[68] This story in its original form probably violated every vestige of Confucian ethic remaining in Hong's being as well as his newly acquired Christian morality. In deleting the more offensive elements, Hong obviously felt that he was purging the holy writings of some unholy accretions.

A final type of correction rectified titles and addresses. For example, the personal "I" (*wo*) was substituted with the imperial "I" (*zhen*), and the common "say" (*yu*) was replaced with the imperial "decree" (*yu*) when referring to Jesus and Shangdi.[69] Also, for some reason Hong demoted King David to the rank of marquis (Matthew 1:6). These changes, except in a very few instances, such as the account of Judah and his daughter-in-law, did not affect the meaning of the text. In every instance, however, the alterations showed that the Taiping sought to enhance the sanctity and the moral authority of their scriptures.

Some scholars have maintained that the attitude of the Taiping toward the Bible was no different from their attitude to their other "scriptures." Such an opinion is certainly justified when considering the *Book of Heavenly*

Decrees and Proclamations, also known as the "True Testament," the document that narrates and describes Hong's vision of the Heavenly Father. But to go as far as does Rudolf Wagner, who at some points seems to argue for the sacredness of every Taiping publication, including such works as *The Pilgrim's Progress,* is unwarranted.[70] To suggest that the Taiping regarded all these documents as of equal value is grossly inaccurate. It is telling that none of the pietistic tomes, including *The Pilgrim's Progress* and, much more significantly, *Good Words to Admonish the Age,* made it onto the Taiping list of officially sanctioned works,[71] much less were accorded the respect reserved for the Bible and the "True Testament."

An explanation for the Taiping's high regard for the Bible can be found in the prominent place Liang Afa carved out for it in his writings and in the position given it in Hong's vision. As we have seen, Liang's *Good Words* was composed mainly of Bible selections, and Liang appealed to the Bible for his every pronouncement. This authoritative place was confirmed in Hong's vision. That vision as recorded in the *Taiping Heavenly Chronicle* reads:

> The Heavenly Father, the Supreme Lord and Great God, ordered that three classes of books be put out and indicated this to the Sovereign, saying, "This class of books consists of the records which have been transmitted from that former time when I descended into the world, performing miracles and instituting the commandments. These books are pure and without error. And the books of the second class [that is, the New Testament; in Gützlaff's translation as with most other translations, the Old and the New Testaments were published as two separate books] are the accounts which have been transmitted from the time when your Elder Brother, Christ, descended into the world, performing miracles, sacrificing his life for the remission of sins, and doing other deeds. These books also are pure and without error. But the books of the other class are those transmitted from Confucius . . . these books contain extremely numerous errors and faults, so that you were harmed by studying them.[72]

Later, when Hong visited Rev. I. J. Roberts in Canton, he discovered (or, for the first time saw fully) that the first two classes of books were the

Old and New Testaments. Thus the scene was set for the Bible to wield a strong influence on the development of the Taiping movement. The potential was there: they had received the Bible before the rebellious intentions of the movement had crystallized. The Bible, more than *Good Words*, was to propel Hong Xiuquan's transformation of his Society of God Worshippers from a religious movement with political overtones into a full-fledged political rebellion.

3

The Taiping Challenge to Empire

Foreign Protestant missionaries and native Chinese evangelists carried the seed of their Chinese-language religious literature into the fertile sectarian soils of inland Guangdong and Guangxi, sowing its message among the poor and the dispossessed. That seed took root in the heart of Hong Xiuquan. The future Taiping king translated this translated Christian message more authentically into the idiom of traditional Chinese history and culture. The end product of this process of translation and indigenization was the religion of the Taiping, a religion inspired by Protestant Christianity yet so shaped by Chinese traditions that the Taiping leaders successfully represented it as a restoration of the religion of the Chinese classical era.

The main sources of this translated message were Liang Afa's tract *Good Words to Admonish the Age* and Rev. Charles (Karl) Gützlaff's version of the Bible. The Gützlaff Bible played a much more influential role in this indigenization process than did Liang Afa's tract. Liang's tract, which usually receives more emphasis than it deserves, did sow the religious seeds of Hong's original vision, but it was Hong's reading of the Bible that shaped the form and direction taken by the developing Taiping movement.

From his reading of the Bible, Hong was exposed to a view of the relationship between religion and culture that differed from that in Liang Afa's tract. *Good Words to Admonish the Age* was very much a Protestant work, made up mostly of biblical passages that emphasized an individualistic and culturally disembodied salvation. While certainly a foreign work of literature, the Gützlaff Bible, by contrast, presented salvation in its historical development and as an integrated religious, cultural, social, and political whole. In the Old Testament particularly, the Taiping could read of a deity who punished nations that did evil and who rewarded those that did good, all the while being concerned about cultural matters such as music, food, and marriage customs, all matters taking place within the history of a specific people. This connection between religion and its cultural expression was reestablished by the Bible itself in its entirety of Old and New Testaments. The Bible restored the connection between cult and culture that Liang's tract had torn asunder.

Seeing religion in its historical and cultural context had as much to do with the transformation of Hong's emerging faith as did any of its specific doctrines or concepts. This is not to diminish the contribution of these concepts. On the contrary, three of these concepts, especially one that was unique to the Gützlaff translation, contributed dramatically to the transformation of the emerging faith. Christian ideas were translated into the Chinese language by missionaries who were not oblivious to the implications of these translations. Hong and the Taiping received these ideas and shaped them according to the Taiping's own religious vision and to Chinese cultural traditions, thereby completing the process of the translation and indigenization of Christianity. This process culminated in Hong's presentation of his religion as a revival of the religion of the classical era and in his denunciation of the emperor and the imperial system as a blasphemy of the same classical religion. This presentation in large part accounted for the Taiping's enthusiastic popular appeal and constituted the basis for the rebellion.

The revolutionary nature of some of the terms employed by Gützlaff and other translators would not be apparent to casual Western readers of the Bible. But in an imperial Chinese cultural context, in which the emperor accorded to his person and his throne a sacred status and in which he served as a religious, political, and cultural symbol, the terms exploded with a revolutionary impact. The three most explosive terms and ideas that most distinctively define Taiping religious identity and most perspicuously open a window into the Taiping soul were: the name of God, which will receive most of our attention because of its particular connection to the charge of blasphemy; the title of Christ; and the theological construct of the kingdom of Heaven.

THE MISSIONARIES TRANSLATE THE NAME OF GOD

By far the most incendiary term in the translation process was one unique to the Bible version of Gützlaff and Dr. Walter H. Medhurst of the London Missionary Society. This version used Shangdi (Sovereign on High) for the name of God. Indeed, this term and the contexts in which it was featured was largely responsible for the formation of the Taiping movement and the basis of its appeal.

The term Shangdi was initially employed by Matteo Ricci and other early Jesuit missionaries until its use was forbidden by Pope Clement XI in 1715 in his papal bull "Ex Illa Die."[1] The bull enforced a statement issued by the Roman Inquisition that forbade the use of Shangdi and Tian (Heaven) in referring to God, while approving the more innocuous and historically neutral term Tianzhu (Lord of Heaven) as an appropriate substitute.

The first Protestant translators, Robert Morrison and Joshua Marshman (a missionary working in India who also produced a Chinese translation of the Bible), learned from the experiences of their Catholic forerunners and initially refrained from employing the term Shangdi. Morrison, following the lead of Jean Basset, translated God with the term *shen* (god or spirit). In the profusion of passages that Liang Afa quoted directly from Morrison's Bible,[2] Liang used mostly the terms Shen (since Liang uses this term to designate a particular god, I capitalize it; the reader should be aware, however, that there is no such indicator in Chinese) and Shentian Shangdi (the God of Heaven, Shangdi), Shentian (God, or gods, of Heaven), and less frequently, Tian Shangdi (Heavenly Sovereign on High) to translate the name of God. In *Good Words*, Liang had invoked the name Shangdi used alone very rarely.[3]

While Morrison favored the use of Shen, Gützlaff in his translation preferred to use Shangdi alone for the name of God, and less frequently Huang Shangdi (Supreme Sovereign on High) and Shangzhu (High Lord). Genesis 1:1 in the Gützlaff version reads, "Yuanshi, Shangdi" (In the beginning, Shangdi), and Genesis 1:3 reads, "Shangdi yue guang" (Shangdi said light), whereas Genesis 2:4 and 4:1, 4 refers to "Shangzhu, Huang Shangdi" (High Lord, Supreme Sovereign on High) and "Huang Shangdi" (Supreme

Shangdi or Supreme Sovereign on High), respectively. All of these terms, but especially Shangzhu and Huang Shangdi, were associated with the imperial title.[4]

With a flotsam of translations (there were several by this point) floating on a tempestuous Chinese religious sea, Western missionaries gathered in Hong Kong in 1843, following the opening of the treaty ports (and which, coincidentally, was the year that Hong first perused Liang's tract), and began to set down a plan for a unified translation of the Bible. The plan called for the apportioning of the Bible among the missionaries resident at the five different treaty ports. Once a draft of the apportioned section of the Bible was completed at one port, it would be sent to the other ports for evaluation.

When the evaluation process was finished, each port's representatives appointed delegates who assembled at Shanghai in 1847 to undertake the final revision. As the delegates began preparing the final draft of the translation, it was immediately apparent that the committee had become polarized over what came to be known as the "term question," and the proper term to be used for translating the name of God became the central focus of a great debate.[5]

The debate took place in an open forum: in the pages of *The Chinese Repository*, a treaty port newspaper published in Canton. From 1843 to 1851 the newspaper was inundated with articles arguing for one term for God or the other.[6] On the surface, most of these articles seemed to narrowly address religious issues, but it was only in the missionary's mind that such an issue could be limited to a religious definition, especially in China. Regardless of how firmly the writers attempted to fix the channels of the issue, the discussion had a tendency to spill over the most strongly constructed categories.

The debate was a virtual continuation of the Catholic debate some two centuries earlier. It was acrimonious at times, especially as it intensified between the chief protagonists: Rev. William Boone, who served in China from 1840 until his death in 1864 as a missionary bishop of the American Episcopal Church and who endorsed the use of the term Shen; and Dr. Walter Medhurst, erstwhile colleague of Gützlaff in the translation of what became the Taiping Bible, who advocated using the term Shangdi. While sometimes heated, the debate was always impressive, an imposing monument to the breadth of learning these men commanded, with the argument shifting from Roman history to Hebrew grammar and then back to the Chinese classics often in the space of a single journal article.

The contours of the debate were determined by two concerns. The Shen advocates emphasized the need to follow the apostolic precedent in searching for the proper term for signifying the deity. Boone and his allies liked the term Shen because it seemed to better fit with the apostolic example as seen in the New Testament of translating the name of God from the Greek *theos* (god or God, depending on the preceding article). The apostles, though, were not pioneers in using this Greek term. They were merely following the lead of the translators of the Hebrew scriptures into Greek in the pre-Christian translation known as the Septuagint. (The name for this translation is derived from a story about seventy elders originally assembled to translate the Hebrew Pentateuch, the first five books of the Old Testament, into Greek.) In that translation, Jewish translators favored the term *theos* in their Greek translation for the Hebrew term for God, Elohim.

This apostolic model became for Boone and his colleagues the sole criterion for judging the suitability of the term for God. The apostles did not use the name Zeus, the high god of the Greeks, for referring to the God of the Hebrews. Rather, they designated the common generic sense of deity in using *theos*.[7] In the Chinese context, they thus argued that missionaries should also use the generic term for the deity. As Boone explained,

> The following considerations have convinced us, that, in such a case, the generic name for God should be used; and that the use of the name of the chief Deity of any polytheistic nation to render Elohim would be totally inadmissible.
>
> 1. Elohim, in the Old Testament, is not a proper term of the true God, but is a generic term, applied to heathen Deities as well as to Jehovah. It must, therefore, be rendered by a generic term and not a proper name.
>
> 2. In using the generic name for God, under the circumstances we are considering, a translator follows the example of the inspired men, who wrote in the Greek and Latin languages. The Greeks and the Romans were polytheists: the inspired writers of the New Testament, and the Apostles who

preached the gospel to the Greeks and Romans, were precisely in the same circumstances which we are now seeking for a general rule to guide us in our inquiries. The question, then, how did they act under these circumstances, is one of great interest to us. It is well known that the Septuagint translators used *theos* [in the original version of this statement, the Greek letters were used] and not Zeus to render Elohim into Greek; and that the Apostles used the same term in the New Testament. The same course was pursued at Rome; the generic name was preferred to the name of the chief Deity; Deus was used, not Jupiter. If then a translator, engaged in rendering the Sacred Scriptures into the language of a polytheistic people, desires to follow the example of inspired men, he must employ the generic name for God used by them, and not the name of the chief Deity.[8]

Conversely, in using the term Shangdi, Boone objected that missionaries would unwittingly be promoting the worship of a pagan god.

Medhurst responded to this approach with an argument taken from the context of Chinese culture. The apostles, he argued, did not adopt the term *theos* unconstructed. They added the singular nominative article to it, so that in the New Testament the name of God is always "(the) God." Yet there was no such grammatical tool available in the Chinese context. Instead, translators always had to fall back on putting together strings of attributions to convey their meaning of the one God, most simply designated by the form "One True God" (*weiyi zhen shen*).

Medhurst contended that the word for God had to convey to the Chinese the sense of unrivaled majesty that the Christian God possesses. This sense, he felt, was not captured by the term *shen*. Medhurst reasoned that in the Chinese classical texts, the term *shen* denoted the generic name for a god and did not evoke the respect and awe due to the highest God. In his words, "Its simple and original meaning is that of spiritual and invisible beings in general, but always of an inferior order."[9] Medhurst objected to the use of the term *shen* because it could and did signify everything from the spirit of a waterfall to the deification of a dog. Moreover, he pointed out that *shen* is often paired with the word *gui* (ghost) and frequently with a malevolent ghost or demon, which demonstrates that both terms refer to lower-level spiritual beings and not at all to higher-level beings.

The London Missionary Society veteran then returned to the Chinese cultural context and proposed using the name Shangdi for God. He favored the term both because it had a classical Chinese pedigree and because it referred to one who properly occupied the highest position of all the gods in the Chinese world. In fact, Medhurst argued that, in a sense, the Chinese were not polytheists at all. While they recognized the existence of a plurality of spiritual beings, they nonetheless accorded Shangdi only the highest honor. In this line of thinking, he cited the work of a seventeenth-century Greek scholar, Ralph Cudworth:

> Cudworth thinks that the Greeks were both monotheists and polytheists at the same time; that is, understanding the word *theos*, combined in the two terms, in different senses. In the first as conveying what he calls the natural idea of God, viz, an All-perfect Being, the Ruler of the Universe, and the other [sense of the term *theos*] as alluding to certain supposed invisible intelligences, who were the objects of religious worship, but subordinate to the one Supreme. What Cudworth pleads for in behalf of the Greeks may be allowed to the Chinese: and they may be considered as monotheists, because they believe in one Supreme God, the Author and Ruler of all. Much will depend, however, on the sense in which we understand the word.[10]

This is similar to the approach that the Catholic missionaries had adopted. The Lord of Heaven ruled over a vast host of lesser spiritual beings, whose titles were rendered into Chinese by combining different attributes with the generic name for deity: *tianshen* (angel; literally, Heavenly god), *shengshen* (Holy Spirit; literally, holy god), and *xieshen* (evil spirit or evil god). Medhurst was not always so imaginative in his presentations as here. His comments, however, do reveal what he took to be the critical issue. While the Greek word *theos* could refer both to the highest deity and to the plurality of deities, the Chinese word *shen* referred only to the latter. Therefore, the apostolic example could not be followed in this situation, since the Greek case was not truly parallel to the Chinese.

Most of the debate involved the quoting of outside authorities. Each side enlisted the support of both Chinese classical texts and missionary precedent, resulting in a virtual learned symposium on the classical Chinese understanding and use of the terms for representing deity.[11]

Among Chinese authorities, of primary importance were the Chinese classics. Medhurst most vigorously waged this part of the debate, since his argument for the use of Shangdi was predicated on what this term meant in the Chinese context. The discussions were extensive. For example, in one discussion, he quotes from *The Book of History, The Book of Songs, The Great Learning, The Doctrine of the Mean*, and Mencius in order to bolster his argument. He tried to show how Chinese classical writings attributed to Shangdi all those characteristics that Christians attribute to their high God: the deity was responsible for the production and formation of all things; he was called the lord and governor of Heaven; and he enjoyed the sacrifice and worship accorded to the highest deity.

Another attribute assigned to Shangdi was that he issued divine decrees in accordance with the classical idea of the mandate of Heaven. By this mandate, Heaven regulated the affairs of nations and evaluated the rule of kings. Medhurst cited *The Book of History:*

> In the Shoo-king 6th book, 4th section, it is said that "Wan and Woo were able to receive the correct decree from Shang-te [i.e., Shangdi] while high Heaven accorded with their principles, and conferred upon them universal rule".... In the Shoo-king, 4th book, section 9, "The eleven men who aided Woo-wang [King Wu] were able to trace out and understand the decree of Shang-te," which decree is called by the Commentator, "the decree of Heaven."[12]

It was not only Medhurst who saw Shangdi as the highest god of the Chinese pantheon. The English missionary often referred to various Chinese commentators' interpretations and explanations of specific texts, as when he writes, "In the Shoo-king, 5th book, 5th section, the Commentator says, 'when reference is made to the protecting influence which overshadows mankind, the word Heaven is used, and when the reference is to the Lord of all, the word De [that is, Di] is employed.'"[13] Medhurst emerged victorious in this part of the debate because he was able to demonstrate that although the

Greek *theos* ruled the world and lesser spiritual beings, the Chinese *shen* did not; that role in the Chinese context was reserved for Shangdi.

Medhurst and Boone also appealed to various missionary authorities. They reached as far back as possible, even referring to the Nestorian missionaries and citing the terms inscribed on the Nestorian monument, erected during the Tang dynasty (618–907), in their argument. The inscriptions were more of a boon to Medhurst than to Boone. The term for God employed in the inscriptions is "True Lord" (Zhenzhu), and the term for angel was "god of Heaven" (*shentian*),[14] which showed that the Nestorians interpreted the Chinese *shen* as beings of a different, lower order than the supreme God.

After all the pages of textual parry and thrust, however, the debate was at an impasse. If the Chinese cultural context was taken more seriously, Medhurst seemed to win. But if the apostolic example was taken more seriously, then Boone seemed to win. The debate became so protracted and deadlocked at one point that Medhurst, in frustration, suggested that a compromise be adopted: transliterate the English name for God into Chinese.[15] Fortunately, his suggestion was not taken seriously.

This debate then began to spill over into channels outside the narrowly religious. The first was political. In 1848, coincident with the rising politicization of the Taiping, of which the missionary community was at this point unaware, scattered references in *The Chinese Repository* addressed the political dimensions of using the term Shangdi. Indeed, such associations were the basis for Boone's more heated objections to using the term. The American missionary referred to the definitions provided by various Chinese dictionaries, including the Kangxi dictionary and assorted French Catholic dictionaries, and found that "all the dictionaries, both native and foreign, give Judge, or Ruler, as the meaning of Ti [Di] whilst they give no intimation of its being the appellative name of God."[16] More disturbing, the writer felt, was its rendering in certain specific contexts: "We give a few additional texts of Scripture to show how subversive of civil government, the use of this word [Di] to render Elohim [the Hebrew term for God in the Old Testament] would prove. 'I am the Lord and there is none else; there is no God beside me.' (Isaiah 45:5) What would be thought of the English translator who would use the term king as that whereby to render Elohim, into English, in the passages quoted above."[17] Three months later, another writer warned the readers of *The Chinese Repository* of the same danger: "Another objection to Te [Di], is, that it has been used from the highest antiquity, and still is, the title given to the ruler of China."[18] Use of the term Shangdi in just these contexts was indeed to result in these very consequences.

In a particularly astute article, Medhurst responded to this charge by pointing out the difficulty in the Chinese context of separating the religious issue from the political. He began his defense of his use of the term Shangdi by summarizing the charge: "Another objection to Te, is, that it has been used from the highest antiquity, and still is, the title given to the ruler of China."[19] Medhurst did not deny this; on the contrary, he built his defense on the very truth of it.

Surveying the history of the imperial title, he analyzed the divine pretensions associated with it. Medhurst noted that five individuals in the mythic, ancient age had received the title of Di. These were the so-called Five Emperors (Wu Di). In the earliest historical period, however, until the time of the first emperor of the Qin dynasty (221–206 B.C.E.), China's rulers had been called *wang* (usually translated as "kings"). It was this Qin emperor who "arrogated to himself" the title *huangdi* (traditionally translated into English as "emperor," but which can be literally translated as "glorious or supreme ruler," or "glorious or supreme god"). Insofar as the political title *huangdi* came after the religious term Shangdi, Medhurst suggested, the Qin ruler took this title with its divine associations in order to elevate the title and person of the ruler. This interpretation of Chinese history, especially highlighting the blasphemous sin of the first emperor, was also held by early Catholic missionaries and their converts.

The English missionary likened the Chinese practice of elevating emperors to the ancient Roman practice of calling Roman emperors *theoi* (gods) and regularly offering sacrifices to them. At death these same Roman emperors were often honored with an apotheosis (a ceremony whereby the emperor was raised to a divine status). After the apotheosis, priests served these deceased emperors by rendering worship to them. The Chinese emperors cultivated similar associations with divinity. Indeed, Medhurst noted that the addition of the attributive *huang* did not necessarily imply a title higher than that of Shangdi, and he also pointed out that the title of Di alone was used only for deceased emperors. While an emperor was alive, titles such as *huangshang* (illustrious superior) and *shengzhu* (sagacious, or holy, lord), along with *huangdi*, were regularly employed in referring to him. Finally, Medhurst cited ceremonies surrounding the imperial court such as the kowtow and the burning of incense to fortify this analogy to the Roman practice.

Medhurst thus not only refused to deny the charge that the term Shangdi was associated with the imperial title, he provided evidence to further substantiate the charge. He argued, however, that such charges should make his missionary colleagues all the more supportive of the term, since the Chinese emperors, like the Roman emperors of the early Christian era, used the title blasphemously, attempting to usurp the position of God himself. The missionary concluded:

> The resemblance between the deification of emperors practiced by the Romans, and that current among the Chinese, holds good in another respect, that it prevailed in both nations, until the Gospel came among them; and as the practice, and all the superstitions connected with it gave way before the influence of Christianity in the days of Constantine, may we not hope that the same result will follow the propagation of the Gospel in China in these latter days.[20]

Hong Xiuquan and the Taiping would read their history in the same way, and this interpretation would lead them to rise up against their blasphemous rulers.

While Boone objected to using the term Shangdi because of these political associations, even he was not inclined to disassociate the term for God from all political connotations. For example, both Boone and Medhurst attempted to identify the deity worshipped in the imperial religion with the Christian God. In fact, one of Boone's proofs that the term *shen* could designate a being worthy of the highest worship involved a reference to the god of Heaven (*Tian zhi shen*), who was worshipped by the emperor at the winter solstice. In his effort to show the greater worthiness of the term Shangdi, Medhurst also referred to the practice of imperial worship:

At the great sacrifices offered by the rulers of the present dynasty, at the period of the winter solstice, an altar is erected at the southern side of the capital, of a round form, three stories high, the top of which, or the principal place of honor, is intended for the shrine of Shang-te, or Te; having the shrines of the Imperial ancestors arranged on the right and left hand, while those of the attendant Shins . . . are placed on the second story, and are honored with medium sacrifices.[21]

He also noted in another volume that in the *Zhouli* (Rites of Zhou), the ruler was to put on more "felicitous robes" when sacrificing to Shangdi, and he was to remove these same robes when he worshipped the *shen* hills and rivers. He quotes a Chinese commentator's remarks on the reasons for the different dress code: "he [the ruler] did not dare to gratify those who were inferior, by putting on the most honourable dress."[22]

Missionaries soon discovered that naming the Christian deity after Shangdi also compelled them to address an even more fundamental matter, that of the cultural and historical heritage of the people who worshipped Shangdi. Medhurst did not explicitly address until fairly late in the discussion the question of whether he was claiming that the Chinese had worshiped the one true God at one time and then later fell away from Him. Those using the term Shangdi would have answered this question in the affirmative: yes, the Chinese did at one point worship the true God (i.e., the God of the Old and New Testaments). The missionary scholar James Legge, for example, believed this, which is why in his authoritative translations of the Chinese classics he so unapologetically inserted the term God in his every translation of Shangdi. This understanding was the basis for Hong's own reevaluation of his cultural heritage.

Medhurst repeated one refrain throughout his argument that indicated his support for this view. He made a series of references to God "as the Chinese knew him." He very intentionally did this, since he maintained that amidst all of what would be considered by the Christian church as false worship, he believed that in the person of Shangdi, the Chinese had been worshipping the true (i.e., Christian) God. In this, he followed the example of Matteo Ricci, who also equated the two divine beings.[23] As Medhurst expressed it in one of several comments on the subject, "We therefore conclude that by Te the Chinese mean the Supreme God, so far as they are acquainted with him." The seasoned missionary backed up this conclusion in a footnote that referenced the apostle Paul's discussion of human knowledge of God in the Book of Romans, a reference that led Medhurst to remark, "That something of God is ascertainable by pagans, may be argued from the statement of the Apostle Paul in Rom. 1:20:—'The invisible things of Him, from the creation of the world, are clearly seen, being understood by the things that are made, even his eternal power and godhead.'"[24]

For Medhurst, then, Heaven was not just China's Heaven, but Europe's as well. He thus affirmed the essential worthiness of every culture, along with that culture's history, and that such a culture could always be redemptively reclaimed.[25] Such a position is a fascinating one for an English missionary to be taking, since a more severe stance on the corruption of Chinese culture would have made Britain's imperialistic objectives in China easier to justify. This reminds us once again that the missionary and the mercantile enterprises were not always, if they were at all, of one piece.

Rev. William Boone and his supporters would have none of this. In stark contrast to Medhurst, Boone maintained that the Shangdi of the classics was a pagan god, and Chinese culture had been deprived of the light of all revelation from the dawn of its history. This culture and its history were incapable of redemption; the missionaries had begun with a tabula rasa. As one letter to the editor of *The Chinese Repository* distilled the issue, "I would further suggest that if you answer that Shang-ti is identical with Jehovah, you must maintain that the Chinese know and have known, independently of revelation, the true God for thousands of years, for they have unquestionably known Shang-ti for that length of time."[26] Boone set up his position on this issue: "But we are not contending that Shin [Shen] means a true God, or was ever used by the Chinese to designate such a Being as the one described above. On the contrary, we are full persuaded they have no knowledge of a self-existent, eternal, almighty Being, who created heaven and earth."[27]

This cultural aspect of the controversy was summed up in a July 1848 article in which the editor weighed in on the side of Boone in evaluating the import of Medhurst's assertion:

Now, without doing violence to language, we must admit that Dr. Medhurst believes that the Chinese, ancient and modern, do know and worship the one only living and true God—not some imaginary Divinity—but the same Being whom he and all Christendom worship ... when he speaks of the Supreme Being as far as the Chinese knew him, it seems to be evident that he means to affirm that the Chinese do know the true God.[28]

Medhurst responded in the affirmative that the Chinese had known and had worshipped the true God, Shangdi, though they had done so imperfectly, a position similar to that which the Jesuits had taken centuries before.

In the end there was a stalemate. Medhurst had won some arguments, Boone others, but the decision on the debate as a whole was a draw. Those on the side of Medhurst maintained that only the term Shangdi conveyed the sense of the supreme position and governorship that the biblical idea of God purposed to express. Those on the side of Boone continued to favor *shen* because of the apostolic example where the generic terms for god, the Hebrew term Elohim and the Greek term *theos*, were employed to translate the name for God in the Old and New Testaments. The debate ended in *The Chinese Repository* and in the Shanghai "Delegates" translation committee without having broken through this impasse. Each mission and Bible society decided for itself which term seemed most appropriate, and so two different translations of the Bible, one featuring Shangdi and the other *shen*, were published, a practice that continues to the present day. At the same time, this decision in large part also brought to an end discussions concerning the relationship of Christianity to Chinese imperial culture—at least among the missionaries.

HONG XIUQUAN HALLOWS THE NAME OF SHANGDI

Dr. Walter H. Medhurst's understanding of God won over Hong Xiuquan. Though he was not in the audience of the delegates, he benefited from Gützlaff and Medhurst's decision to translate the term for God with the name Shangdi. The repercussions of this term soon became evident in the integrated Chinese worlds of religion, politics, and culture, repercussions that were already anticipated in the missionary debates. In a real sense the missionaries and the Taiping were living in the same world; they were not speaking past each other. Both sides recognized the nature and implications of using this term to translate the name of God, even though the Taiping would take the implications to a far deeper level than the missionaries envisioned.

Hong probably first encountered this name for God in Liang Afa's tract *Good Words to Admonish the Age*. Liang only rarely favored the term Shangdi, though he did employ it frequently in the construct "the God of Heaven, Shangdi" (Shentian Shangdi). Hong might have also heard the term on the lips of those evangelists connected to Gützlaff's Chinese Union and probably from some of their Old Testament selections, which more frequently used the name Shangdi. More importantly, the selections also used the name Huang Shangdi (Supreme Sovereign on High), employing two characters from the imperial title. Hong already indicated his preference for God's name when he called the group of his followers the Society of God Worshippers or Bai Shangdi hui. Thus, already prior to his sojourn at the Reverend Roberts's chapel in Canton in 1847, the future Heavenly King was exposed to the term Shangdi, and he may have been considering even at this point the possible blasphemous implications of the imperial title.

In his two months in Canton, he intensively studied both the Gützlaff Bible and the Ten Commandments. Increasing familiarity with the third commandment ("Thou shalt not take name of the Lord thy God in vain"—in Gützlaff's Bible, God would be rendered as "Shangdi") would have further validated his growing conviction about the gravity of the offense of the imperial title. After his return from Canton, his doubts about the imperial title would have been strengthened even more by what he believed was Jesus' own voice speaking through Xiao Chaogui, the Taiping Western King. Hong Xiuquan now had reason to launch his rebellion: because the imperial title blasphemed the name of Shangdi, he needed to punish the emperor for this most grievous crime (sin) and for leading all the people of China into that same sin. This fundamental indictment would be published throughout Taiping-controlled territory in broadsides calling for the execution of the one who bore this blasphemous title.

While Hong Xiuquan certainly attempted to wield the authority of an emperor, and he boasted of his own connections to divinity, he always made it clear that only the Father could be called Di, and that he was only to be called a king—a Heavenly King, yes, but only a king. As he instructed his Heavenly soldiers, "Henceforth, all soldiers and officers may address me as Sovereign [or, "lord"; the term is *zhu*], and that is all; it is not appropriate to call me Supreme, lest you should offend the Heavenly Father."[29] Although Hong imitated the emperor in some of his practices, in the title he took for himself and in the system of collegial kingship his followers established (with Eastern, Western, and all kinds of kings) he demonstrated that he sought to create something new in his Taiping movement. Although their system of kingship was one of the more distinctive features of the Taiping, scholars have all but overlooked its ideological significance.

Hong's objective, then, was not just to rebel against this one emperor, but rather to topple the entire imperial institution. As he put it in the *Three Character Classic* (Sanzijing), the rulers of the classical period all honored Shangdi and revered heaven. It was only in the Qin dynasty that the ruler arrogated to himself the name of Huangdi, and so "All were deluded by the devil, those two thousand years."[30] This view of imperial history permeates all the major Taiping documents. As the *Taiping Imperial Declaration* (Taiping zhaoshu) emphasizes, it was from the time of the Qin dynasty and the Han dynasty (202 B.C.E.–220 C.E.) that China began straying from the path of righteousness, and each succeeding emperor only added to the weight of that sin. When the Song emperors ascended the throne, they committed one of the most egregious sins yet: they changed the name of Shangdi.

> When Hui of Sung appeared, he changed the appellation of the Supreme Sovereign on High [Huang Shangdi] to the Great Jade Emperor, God of the Golden Palace of the Luminous Heaven. Now to say that he dwelt in the golden palace of the luminous heaven was not so much amiss; but to call him the Great Jade Emperor is indeed the worst kind of blasphemy against the Great God. The Supreme Sovereign on High being the universal Father of all creatures under heaven, how can man change his venerable name?[31]

The Taiping attacked not just the ruling Qing; Hong Xiuquan and his followers held all the emperors from the Qin dynasty down to the Qing dynasty (1644–1911) responsible for blasphemy, the spread of idolatry, and the general corruption of culture. This was the rationale, the ideological justification, for the Taiping Rebellion.

As we have seen, Gützlaff and Medhurst used the term Shangdi throughout their translation, and not infrequently referred to God as Huang Shangdi (Supreme Sovereign on High), the formal title of the emperor. Hong condemned the entire imperial identification with the classical Sovereign on High in these words:

> The Great God is the only emperor [*di*]. The monarchs of this world may be called kings [*wang*] and that is all; but how can they be permitted to encroach a hair's breadth upon this? Even Jesus the Savior, God's Crown Prince [Huang Shangdi Taizi], is only called our Lord. In heaven above and earth below, among men, who is greater than Jesus? Even Jesus was not called emperor [*di*]; who then dares assume the designation of emperor [*di*]? One who does so only demonstrates his blasphemous presumptions, bringing down upon himself the eternal punishment of hell.[32]

This warning, issued before Hong visited Canton,[33] was not the only time that the Taiping published these charges against the emperor before the rebellion was launched.

In the documents discovered by Professor Wang Qingcheng, in the records of those who spoke as mediums for Jesus and the Heavenly Father, Xiao Chaogui, the Western King, and Yang Xiuqing, the Eastern King, this same charge appears. Jesus, the Heavenly Elder Brother, descends to earth in November of 1848 and speaks through the person of the Western King, Xiao Chaogui, saying:

> The Heavenly Elder Brother Jidu [the shortened and more frequently used term for Christ] issued a decree to the Heavenly King saying, "Hong Xiuquan, Little Brother, all your Heavenly Soldiers and Heavenly Generals when cutting off the demons' heads should look to and receive the Heavenly Father, the High Lord's, the Supreme God's [Huang Shangdi] mandate, the

Salvation Lord Christ's [Jidu] mandate and the Heavenly King's mandate and the rest of the rulers' mandates. But you must call yourself only a king; you should not call yourself Di. Your Heavenly Father alone is Di. The Heavenly King answered: I will follow the Heavenly Elder Brother's command.... Only the Heavenly Father shall be called Di. Outside of the Heavenly Father, no one should be called Di.[34]

This same concern for sanctifying the name of Di is repeated in the annotations Hong made in the margins of the Taiping Bible. This challenge was addressed to only one person, the one who had dared assume the designation Di: the present ruler, Emperor Xianfeng.

Because, at the most fundamental level, Hong's view of the worship of Shangdi meant that no other god could be worshipped, his movement began in iconoclasm and continued thus until the very end. Hong's early missionary tours were highly iconoclastic; temples were defaced and statues (idols) smashed.[35] Initially, he and his followers mostly attacked statues and temples that Confucians themselves condemned as morally corrupt. Later, the Taiping would condemn and attack all statues and temples, whether approved by Confucians or not.

In 1847, after studying the Bible with Rev. I. J. Roberts in Canton and upon his return to Guangxi, the *Taiping Heavenly Chronicle* (Taiping tianri) records that Hong's first action was to enter a temple, the Temple of the Nine Demons, and write on the wall of the temple a poem he composed. In that poem he publicly announced that he was the Heavenly King. He had previously declared that he was the Son of Heaven, and the title of Heavenly King had earlier been given to him, but it was only in the Temple of the Nine Demons, after having studied the Bible with Reverend Roberts some three years prior to the rising at Jintian, that Hong publicly proclaimed his intention to reign as the Heavenly King.

The very next incident that the *Taiping Heavenly Chronicle* records occurs weeks later. Hong attacked an idol in a temple in Xiangzhou. He beat it, referring to it as a demon, and ordered his followers to "dig out the eyes of the demon, cut off his beard, trample its hat, tear its embroidered dragon robe to shreds, turn its body upside down, and break off its arms."[36] The destruction of this idol won Hong equal amounts of fame and notoriety, for the demon that was associated with this idol was a menacing and threatening presence in that area. The Taiping document describes how the demon had dared to pull the district magistrate out of his sedan chair and demanded that a dragon-embroidered robe be presented to him, a robe that signified that he was the real power in the region. In Hong's destruction of this idol, he proved that the Taiping and their God were the new rulers of this land.

That Hong's iconoclasm continued to be an identifying mark of the Taiping movement even to the end of their crusade is evident in this first-hand report on the ruins of Ningbo submitted by Rev. Josiah Cox: "In the temples we entered, the destruction of idols has been unsparing. The god of war and his satillites [sic] lay in scattered fragments about their former shrines; here lay a dishonored image prostrate on its nose. Another lost its head. Others stood with bruised eyes and mouths, and ears and noses missing. Some lay about in dismembered heaps."[37] Hong believed that Jesus' declaration in the gospels about the destruction of Jerusalem's temple contained a prophecy about Hong's own mission—that when he as the Heavenly King ascended the throne of all China, God would help him rebuild the very same temple (presumably in China).[38]

This iconoclasm was motivated by Hong's reading of the Ten Commandments, as Hong stated very clearly in the *Taiping Imperial Declaration:*

> By referring to the Old Testament [Jiuyizhao Shengshu] we learn that in early ages the Supreme God [Huang Shangdi] descended on Mount Sinai and in his own hand he wrote the Ten Commandments on tablets of stone, which he gave to Moses, saying, "I am the High Lord [Shangzhu], the Supreme God; you men of the world must on no account set up images resembling anything in heaven above or on earth below, and bow down and worship them." Now you people of the world who set up images and bow down and worship them are in absolute defiance of the Supreme God's expressed will.... How extremely foolish you are to let your minds be so deceived by the demon![39]

Later in the same document, Hong applauded the iconoclastic efforts of previous emperors, including an emperor at the time of the Six Dynasties

(220–589) who "demolished licentious temples" and commended the iconoclastic work of virtuous officials, such as the Ming official Hai Rui, for condemning idolatrous rites. Hong then summarized his short survey of native iconoclasm with these words: "They did not know that which they destroyed, that which they burned, and that which they reproved certainly ought to have been destroyed, burned or reproved; and that which they did not destroy, did not burn, or did not reprove also ought to have been destroyed, burned or reproved."[40] Throughout this treatise Hong condemns imperial idolatry, and he weaves along with it a condemnation of the imperial title as well. Significantly, Hong had pasted copies of the Heavenly commandments on the doorposts of his family's ancestral shrine in 1844,[41] and in 1847 he hung the commandments in the temple of the idol he destroyed in Xiangzhou.

By 1847, Hong definitely does possess a copy of the Ten Commandments, and the prominence of the commandments in the religion of the Taiping became so distinctive that Western observers comment that the Taiping faith was known among the common people as the "Ten Commandments religion."[42] The Taiping followers' reverence for and submission to the decalogue was seen in their fervent iconoclasm and their reluctance to forge close ties with secret societies, policies which if moderated could have won even more people over to their cause. Such support, nevertheless, came at too high a price for the Taiping.

This reverence for the decalogue, however, was not passed on to the Taiping by Liang Afa. Though he did briefly refer to Moses and the handing down of the Ten Commandments, the Chinese evangelist nowhere provides a full listing, and only indirectly mentions five of the ten.[43] More significantly, Liang did not put them in their historical context—in which Israel was entering into a covenant with Jehovah and the people promised to obey him as their God and ruler—which any version of the Bible would have provided. Liang did pass on to the Taiping, however, the sense that obedience to Shangdi's commands was an essential part of the religion of Shangdi. This is reflected in Hong's earliest poems, in which he exhorts his followers, "Obey the sacred commandments, worship the true God; at death it will be easy to ascend to heaven."[44] Indeed, in all the early accounts, there is a standard three-part formula for following Shangdi: cast off demons, worship the true God, and obey the Heavenly commandments.

Liang Afa's tract was very much a New Testament work (only twelve of the fifty-seven biblical passages directly quoted in *Good Words* are from the Old Testament, and many of these passages are limited to two or three verses). Observers of the Taiping religion often commented that it seemed to be more of an Old Testament religion than a New Testament one, and the Taiping God seemed to act more like the Old Testament God—most significantly by leading the troops to battle—than the New Testament one. With a few qualifications, this seems to have been true; although Hong picked up some of his ideas and themes from Liang Afa, he must have obtained most of his Old Testament ideas from the Old Testament itself.

Obedience to God's specific Ten Commandments was not enjoined upon Hong until he visited the Baptist chapel at Canton. He first studied the decalogue in its covenant-making context there, and he also obtained from Roberts the 1840 Baptist publication of the commandments, which was to serve as the basis for the Taiping version and which became an integral part of their corporate worship.[45] Such prohibitions as "Do not lie" and "Do not kill" would hardly have seemed out of place in a Chinese religious setting, especially since the Buddhists had a list of prohibitions themselves (ten in number, in fact, with the first five applying to laymen and clergy alike). The first four commandments, however—those having to do with other gods, idolatry, honoring the name of Shangdi, and respecting the Sabbath—would have distinguished the Taiping list from others.[46] Thus, not only the grievous evil of blasphemy would have been impressed upon Hong when he first saw the decalogue, but he would have been all the more intensely hostile to idolatry as well.

The Taiping understood the obedience enjoined in these commandments not as adherence to a written code, but as a personal and corporate pledge of loyalty to Shangdi (especially since the first three concerned the honoring of Shangdi). By this oath, Shangdi became the Taiping god, and the Taiping became His people, for Shangdi was the true Di; earthly rulers were only kings. The Ten Commandments were Shangdi's edicts. Exodus 20:1 in the Gützlaff version introduced the decalogue with *Huang Shangdi yu ci zhuyan* ("The Supreme Shangdi decrees these words . . ."). The first commandment as it appears in the standard English translation of the time, the King James version, reads, "I am the Lord thy God . . . Thou shalt have no other gods before me." Gützlaff's Old Testament renders this commandment, *Wu zai benmian chong yishen* ("Do not in front of my face worship strange gods"), whereas the Taiping's *Book of Heavenly Commandments* reads simply and positively, *chongbai Huang Shangdi* ("Worship the Supreme Shangdi").

It was the third commandment that implicated the imperial system in the sin of blasphemy. Gützlaff translated the commandment thus: *Wu ducheng ru Shangzhu Huang Shangdi zhiming fu Huang Shangdi wubuzui wangcheng qimingzhe* ("Do not blaspheme the name of your High Lord the Supreme Shangdi; the Supreme Shangdi will certainly condemn as guilty he who recklessly calls upon his name").[47] The *Book of Heavenly Commandments* followed this translation and added, *buhao wangti Huang Shangdi zhiming* ("It is not good to recklessly speak out the name of the Supreme Shangdi"). The poem that accompanied the *Book of Heavenly Commandments* was particularly revealing: "Our exalted Father is infinitely honorable; those who violate the proper boundary and profane his name seldom come to a good end."[48] *The Chinese Repository* had expressed its misgivings about this translation of the third commandment, fearing these very political repercussions if this translation of God was used. The complaint voiced at the time was that it would be subversive of civil government.

This religious belief in the exclusive worship of Shangdi fostered a conviction about the illegitimacy of the Chinese imperial system. According to Taiping teaching, by adopting the term Huangdi, the emperors had committed blasphemy. Hong singled out the first emperor especially for establishing the precedent. This view, which echoed early Catholic missionary sentiments and Reverend Medhurst's comments on the imperial system as a blasphemous usurping of Shangdi's prerogative, became the Taiping ideological motivation for overthrowing not just the Manchus, but the entire imperial system as it was established by the first Chinese emperor, Qin Shihuangdi (r. 221–210 B.C.E.). The imperial figure represented just one more idol to smash. In this sense, the iconoclastic crusade that began in the temples of Guangxi was intended to reach all the way to Beijing's imperial palace.

The Taiping faith in Shangdi was vitally connected to the culture of the classical period, for that culture featured a political system that honored

Shangdi. This system inspired Hong and his fellow leaders to adopt for themselves the title of kings. Hong fashioned his own title after the original Heavenly King of the Zhou dynasty (1040?–256 B.C.E.). It was the practice during the Zhou dynasty for the king of the central Zhou kingdom to be designated as the "Heavenly King" to distinguish him and his title from the kings of the surrounding states. Hong's purpose, however, was not conservative or reactionary—he was not a slavish proponent of a return to Confucianism. Instead, his intention was to establish his Heavenly Kingdom on the foundations of classical China, and thereby continue its traditions into the present. The kingdom Hong envisioned establishing was intended to return to the point where the emperors had led China astray, only this time China was to take the right path.

This vision of the sweep of Chinese culture and history was very much in agreement with the interpretation proposed by early Catholic missionaries and the Protestant Walter Medhurst. They had argued that the Chinese had worshipped the true (i.e., Christian) God in the classical period and had fallen away from that worship. But the Taiping believed that Hong Xiuquan alone would be able to persuade armies of his countrymen to accept this view of the Chinese past. Hong's own cause was further aided by his interpretation of the role of Jesus, the Christ, in this grand design.

JESUS, THE ANOINTED PRINCE

With all the debate surrounding the translation of God, anyone cognizant of the controversies that engulfed the early Christian church might expect that the debate over the title of Christ would exceed in intensity the debate over the name of God, yet that was not the case. In fact, that debate is conspicuous by its absence: although volumes of articles concerning the name of God were published, the debate in *The Chinese Repository* involving the title of Christ was polished off in a single footnote.

Six major councils in the history of the early Christian church had addressed the nature and, consequently, the title of Jesus—was he Lord and God, or was he just Lord? The most consequential of these early councils, the Nicean, which met in 325 C.E., addressed what is known as the Arian heresy, which taught that Christ was a created being and was not equal with God. Out of the Nicean Council came the foundational creedal formulation that Christ was "begotten, not made," "of one substance with the Father." Debates over the person and work of Christ would continue to dominate church life for the next two centuries, yet in nineteenth-century Chinese missions, not one minor church committee addressed these issues. Such issues may have been decided for the European church, but Christianity had entered a new culture, where old questions would arise anew. The missionary translation of Christ's title would skirt these questions, and so it would be left to the Taiping to figure out for themselves the meaning of the title "Christ."

This neglect of the title of Jesus began not with nineteenth-century Protestant missions, but with Catholic missionaries in the early seventeenth century who first transliterated the title of Christ into Chinese as Jilisidu, a word with no meaning in the Chinese language except that given it by the missionaries.[49] No uneasiness over transliteration was expressed at that time or when Robert Morrison, following Jean Bassett, seemingly naively copied the term into his own translation of the Bible. This is not to say Morrison unthinkingly adopted the designation. He did experiment with using "Jesus the Messiah" in some passages, but still he failed to translate the term, merely transliterating the title as Misaiya (Messiah).

But Morrison's decision seems doubly blameworthy because apostolic writers had rendered the Hebrew term Messiah as the Greek term Christ in the first place: both signified "anointed one" in their respective languages. Among all the Protestant missionaries who followed Morrison, especially those who submitted articles to *The Chinese Repository* demanding that missionaries follow the first-century apostles' lead in using a generic term to translate the term God, one would think some awareness existed of the inconsistency involved in this transliteration of Jesus' title. Following the apostles' lead would have entailed translating the Hebrew title of Messiah into its Chinese equivalent, just as the apostles in their own day had translated the Hebrew title of Messiah into its Greek equivalent (that is, "Christos"). But there was no awareness of this inconsistency or of the unnaturalness of calling Jesus "Jilishidu" (usually given in its shortened form, Jidu), as if the title for Christ was a part of his foreign-sounding name.[50] Why is this?

We cannot return to the nineteenth century to answer this question, but from what Hong Xiuquan concluded, this lack of awareness may have been due to the fact that the only truly appropriate rendering in Chinese for the title of Christ was Taizi (Crown Prince or Heir Apparent). The Greek term meant "anointed one," which referred back to the Old Testament tradition where men were anointed by prophets and priests to serve as kings. The only equivalent in the Chinese context, then, would be Taizi. But in the Chinese context, this title could only be claimed by the son of the emperor.

Liang Afa had refrained from using the shortened title Jidu (Christ) except when quoting directly from Morrison's New Testament. He most frequently used the title Jiuzhu (Salvation Lord) and Jiushizhu (World's Salvation Lord).[51] This title was never imbued, however, with the sense that "savior" could refer to a leader or ruler who would save his people from political oppression. The Old and New Testaments' more holistic image of a savior who both rescues from sin and delivers from oppression was narrowed to the former. At times, however, Liang had no recourse but to use political language to describe the mission of Jesus. He was referred to as a king, which was what the leaders of the Jews accused him of claiming to be, and for that charge the Roman rulers crucified him. Still, he was the King of Judea only.[52] Whereas Liang wrote that God (here, Shentian Shangdi) was the King of Kings, and even more atypically that He was the Emperor of Emperors,[53] Gützlaff's Bible was also more conservative with respect to the title of Christ: Jesus was called Jidu, and the wise men still asked where was he who was born King of the Jewish kingdom?

This failure to translate the meaning of the title of Christ prompted Hong Xiuquan to come up with a term that was in keeping with his own vision and with the role he saw Jesus playing in the New Testament. Of course, it was the relation of God to Jesus and then of God to Hong that most bedeviled Hong. The confusion is understandable, for Hong believed that his own mission was to rule China, as appointed by Shangdi. As ruler of the Chinese, he would assume the title Son of Heaven. But if he was to serve as the Son of Heaven, where did that leave Jesus? Since they were both Sons of Heaven, Hong respectfully identified himself as the younger of these sons. Jesus was his elder brother. Confounding the issue of the role of Jesus was the difficulty the Taiping experienced with the nature of

Jesus. Hong and his followers were devout monotheists: they worshipped only God, the Father, for that was what the first commandment called them to do. Jesus was not God (i.e., Shangdi), but rather, God's son.[54]

One of three titles for Jesus favored by the Taiping was Tianxiong, which is translated by Franz Michael and Chung-li Chang as Heavenly Elder Brother. Hong seems to have derived the title from the traditional title of the Chinese ruler as the Son of Heaven. At the same time it echoes early church debates about Christ being one with God, yet not the same person as God the Father. A second title, Taizi, had a more direct historical referent. This was the title given to the heir apparent, the prince who was appointed as next in line to the throne, or the Crown Prince, which is the virtual Chinese equivalent to the meaning of Messiah in Hebrew and Christ in Greek.[55] A third title conferred upon Jesus, Taixiong, is a bit more problematic, but given its connections to Taizi, seems best rendered as Eldest Prince.

The importance with which Hong regarded these issues is copiously documented in the annotations he inscribed into his revised edition of the Taiping New Testament. Most of these comments involved the working out of his own identity as Son of Heaven in relation to Jesus' identity as the Son of God. Hong made sure to clearly indicate that Jesus was superior— he was the elder brother. Many of the annotations, however, attempted to define Jesus' title according to Jesus' relation to Shangdi and were not concerned with Hong's own claims. The annotation above Matthew 10, for example, proclaims that, "The Eldest Prince [Taixiong] himself gives proof that he is Shangdi's son."[56] In Matthew 16, the apostle Peter confesses that Jesus is the Christ, and here Hong wrote that Jidu (Christ) was God's (Shangdi's) son. At Matthew 17, Hong remarked that Jidu was God's Taizi (Crown Prince). Thus, Tianxiong (Heavenly Elder Brother) is God's son at Matthew 10, Jidu is God's son at Matthew 16, and Jidu is God's Taizi at Matthew 17. It would seem to follow that for Hong the titles Taixiong and Taizi, when applied to Jesus, were equivalent. And there is a logic to his appellations, for it was the eldest son who was normally designated the crown prince. Whether we can subject these annotations to this kind of analysis is something of a moot point, but it is reasonable to conclude that for Hong, Jesus' proper title was Crown Prince.

Hong was very clear about one point: that Christ, the Crown Prince, was not to be equated with Shangdi. They were distinct beings, Father and Son. In comments written above Mark 12:28–34, Hong chastised those Christians who had confused the persons of the Father and the Son. "The Eldest Prince clearly proclaims that there is only one Supreme Lord. Why did later disciples through some error feel that Christ was God [Shangdi]? If that were really true, this would be so: there would be two Gods [Shangdi]. Respect this."[57] Hong's comments above the fifth chapter of I John, where one of the most strongly Trinitarian statements in the Bible is recorded (a passage that is omitted in modern versions), clear up some of the confusion, even while again warning his people about the blasphemy of the imperial title: "Now the Eldest Prince [Taixiong] has descended into the world and issued a sacred directive instructing me, saying 'Xiuquan, my own brother, later on you must not proclaim yourself 'Di.' Our father is 'Di.'"[58]

Hong Xiuquan understood that he in his time and place was appointed by Shangdi, the Father, to serve as ruler over the world from the Taiping kingdom, just as Jesus long before had been appointed to rule over the world from Judea. Hong, as the second son of Shangdi, was next in line after Jesus to rule the universal kingdom. Jesus had ruled in Judea but then was killed. The role of ruling the universal kingdom now was left to Jesus' younger brother.

THE KINGDOM OF HEAVEN DRAWS NEAR

Along with the term Shangdi, the concepts of Heaven and Heaven's rule most radically shaped the developing Taiping movement. As a religious movement, the Taiping faithful were organized as the Society of God Worshippers. By the time the Taiping followers renamed their movement the Taiping Heavenly Kingdom, they were openly declaring political ambitions that were solidly rooted in their religious beliefs. The construct of the kingdom of Heaven is not exclusive to the Medhurst-Gützlaff version of the Bible (it is exclusive, however, to the Gospel of Matthew; in the other three gospels, the designation is "kingdom of God"). As kingdom of Heaven or kingdom of God, the concept's potential political associations are self-evident. Still, it is the kingdom of Heaven that the Taiping

*A battle scene between the Taiping and the imperial army.
(Lindley,* Ti-Ping Tien-Kwoh.)

adopted, again for reasons connected to their vision of a restoration of classical culture.

Medhurst had discussed the intricate dilemmas of translation posed by imperial associations with divinity. He documented his problems with the name of God; he had other, related problems in his translation of the phrase "kingdom of Heaven." But how could this biblical phrase be translated without employing the politically charged terms "kingdom" and "Heaven"? Even the latter term in a Chinese context bore strong political implications. Indeed, whereas in the West an expression such as "kingdom of Heaven" might be interpreted as less politically threatening than the word kingdom used alone, in the Chinese context the compound term could very easily be interpreted as more threatening. This is because of the prominent place accorded the teaching of the mandate of Heaven in traditional Chinese political thought. This doctrine of the mandate of Heaven, first expressed in the classical *Book of History*, was considered the foundation of royal and imperial legitimacy.

Medhurst had pointed out in his discussion of the name of God how the Chinese attributed Heavenly aspects to the imperial person and appurtenances. The Chinese employed such terms as Tianwei (Heavenly seat or throne), Tian'en (Heavenly grace), Tianbing (Heavenly soldiers), and Tianchao (Heavenly court)[59] to describe all things imperial. Nor should it be overlooked that the ruler of China was referred to as Tianzi (Son of Heaven), another title that once again demonstrates that the Chinese were not reluctant to confer religious or sacred attributes upon the emperor.

The political associations of the term for "kingdom" (*guo*) were apparently too evident to Morrison and Liang Afa. In this case, it is not that Gützlaff politicized the religious term "kingdom of Heaven," but that Morrison attempted to spiritualize a political term. Liang introduces the idea of the Heavenly Kingdom when he refers to the Sermon on the Mount, a passage in which Jesus makes repeated mention of this ethereal address, as in, "Blessed are the poor in spirit for theirs is the kingdom of Heaven."[60] But Liang, following Morrison, seems to have preferred the idea of a reign of Heaven (Tianwang) over the more terrestrial feel of a kingdom of Heaven (Tianguo). For example, when Jesus speaks of the kingdom of Heaven at Matthew 5:19, he warns against those who teach the little ones to break the commandments of God. Such people, Liang has Jesus saying, will be the smallest under Heaven's reign—Tianwang (reign of Heaven). In this passage, Gützlaff and others adopted the more natural translation of Tianguo (kingdom of Heaven).[61] Likewise, in the Lord's Prayer, the petitioner in Liang's version prayed that your (God's) reign would come to earth (*er wang jiu zhi*), while Medhurst-Gützlaff and others following them used wording more familiar to Western ears: "thy kingdom come."[62] Even in seeking to avoid political connotations in their translation, the missionaries stumbled into them. It was, nevertheless, "kingdom of Heaven" that became the standard translation for this construct, as there were too many places where using this territorial phrase could not be avoided without seriously distorting the meaning of a passage.

Even choosing to translate the idea of the kingdom of Heaven by the phrase "reign of Heaven" did not allow Liang to keep the political implications of his gospel message at bay, for Tianwang can mean "Heavenly King," the very title that Hong took for himself, a choice that seems to be another product of his creative synthesizing mind.

Heavenly King was the title that the Zhou dynasty kings of the pre-imperial era took for themselves. It was the term of choice in the classic Confucian text *The Spring and Autumn Annals* for the Zhou king in his status as the king appointed by Heaven, as distinguished from the kings of the surrounding states. The introductory chapter of this classic states: "In autumn, in the seventh month, the Heavenly King sent the [sub-] administrator Heuen with a present of [two] carriages and their horses for the funerals of duke Hwuy and [his wife] Chung Tsze."[63] Whether Hong first conceived of the idea of his own title by reading it in Liang's tract and then making the connection to *The Spring and Autumn Annals* or whether the inspiration came from Liang's tract at all is hard to ascertain. Hong may have elected to use the title just because it fit with his program of taking the Zhou dynasty and its institutions as the model for his classical revival. It did not hurt that the title was also favored by the leaders of different society and sectarian movements.[64] The title of Heavenly King fit both Hong's political and cultural ambitions.

Equally problematic for translators and for the subjects of the Heavenly Kingdom was the fact that in traditional Chinese society, only the emperor could worship Heaven. During the period of the Taiping Rebellion, the vulnerability of Beijing's Temple of Heaven (Tiantan; this is the standard translation, but more literally translated it would be "Altar of Heaven") to attack was a concern of the emperor, and he acted to protect this symbol of his legitimacy. In 1853, the year that the Taiping rebels captured Nanjing and renamed it the Heavenly Capital, Emperor Xianfeng (r. 1851–61) issued a decree ordering that an additional hundred soldiers be assigned to guard and patrol the grounds of the Temple of Heaven.[65]

The emperor was even more concerned about his people's perception of the Qing dynasty's mandate to rule. Only two months after the Taiping had captured Nanjing, he issued a very personal and heartfelt apology to the people and to Heaven for not having properly fulfilled the mandate, reminding his subjects that though he had not proven himself totally faithful, he still retained the exclusive right to worship Heaven:

> I, though being a man of little virtue, respectfully received the mandate [to rule] from my father, to cherish and nurture the people of ten thousand directions. I have reverently and with trepidation executed this duty for three years now.
>
> I feel deeply ashamed. I have made many mistakes and committed innumerable grievous errors in my reign. From the autumn of the thirtieth year of the Daoguang emperor [1850] the rebels, those roguish clowns, have been jumping up and down, constantly shifting their troops here and there, so that at the present time, there has been no progress made against them. The generals and the soldiers are exhausted by the constant battle; the common people are embittered by the constant demands for provisioning the army. From Guangdong and Guangxi to Hunan and Hubei, and again to Jiangnan, the demonic stench of the maddened and perverse rebels can now [be] said to be extreme.
>
> I the ruler represent Heaven in shepherding this people. But at the present time, what is the shepherd doing? My people are covered with filth and ashes, and have yet to be restored. And I, this man, am found to be ungrateful for having squandered the grace [of Heaven]. My crimes [*jiu*] are heavy. How can I recover? What words can I say? Thinking these empty thoughts and speaking these meaningless words cannot undo what has been done.
>
> Now at this time of extreme difficulty, I can only sincerely implore: "O Vast Heaven, quickly remove my people's calamity!"
>
> The armies, officials and soldiers alike, together have resolutely determined to bring peace back to the people. We need to encourage and exhort each other to clearly sweep away these rebellious bandits so that we can relieve the people from their distress. This is my determined resolve, and it is how I will repay Heaven's grace, and thereby fulfill and live up to my father's intentions for me.
>
> I recall how from the winter of the *gengxu* year [1850] until now, I have personally offered up the Grand Sacrifice nine times. Every time I arrive at the altar [at the Temple of Heaven complex] for the period of fasting [prior

*Naval battle between the Taiping and Imperial forces.
(Lindley,* Ti-Ping Tien-Kwoh.*)*

to the sacrifice], there is never a moment when my thoughts are not focused on the fact that the rebel bandits remain undefeated. Each time I come for the sacrifice I feel all the more ashamed and terrified. Now on the 7th day of the month, it is again time to prepare for the summer sacrifice [for rain]. Therefore I am recording my transgressions so that I might warn myself.[66]

The confessional tone of this passage is noteworthy. The emperor refers to his mistakes, his errors, even his crimes (although he does not use the term *zui,* meaning "sin" or "crime," the term *jiu* is suggestive of the same sentiment). While this apology is offered up to his father and to Heaven, the emperor was aware of the larger official audience and of the people's wavering faith in Heaven's support of his dynasty's rule. Considering this larger audience, the emperor acknowledged only that he had squandered Heaven's grace, not that he had lost it.

Both Liang Afa and Hong Xiuquan at different points in their writing confronted the problem of the association of Heaven with the imperial cult. One issue for both was that common people who worshiped Heaven would be encroaching on an exclusive imperial right[67] and would thereby be committing a subversive act. Liang Afa had tried to counter such a charge by arguing that the Father of all should be worshipped by all, regardless of whether the position one occupies was noble or mean, thereby making such worship an expression of filial piety.[68]

Hong, too, spoke to this issue, but he did not avoid its politically sensitive nature. Rather, he challenged the emperor's association with Heaven and with the divine, regarding this as just one more example of imperial arrogance. That the worship of Heaven was open to all is clear in Hong's introduction to the Ten Commandments: "Now those whose minds have been deluded by the demons say that only the monarch can worship the Great God. However the Supreme God [Huang Shangdi] is the universal Father of all the mortal world. . . . If you say that monarchs [*junzhang*] alone can worship the Supreme God, we beg to ask you, as for the parents of a family, is it only the eldest son who can be filial and obedient to his parents?"[69] Both of these men treated the matter of worshipping Heaven as a matter of filial piety, an approach with which not even the least Confucian of emperors could argue.

The Taiping concept of the kingdom of Heaven was not exclusively shaped by the classical understanding. Millenarian ideas also contributed to the Taiping understanding. Biblical millenarian themes were supported by similar themes from native Buddhist millenarian teachings.[70] Liang Afa avoided the idea of a millenarian kingdom being established on earth and especially shied away from the Book of Revelation, where such a kingdom is most fully described. In his tract, Liang quotes from the Book of Revelation only once, citing a passage in Revelation 22 in which the river of life is depicted as flowing out from under the throne of God. Liang ignored the preceding passage, Revelation 21, which portrays the descent of the Heavenly City to earth, and many other millenarian passages from the Book of Revelation as well.[71] Liang, reflecting the prevailing view of such matters among nineteenth-century missionaries, coolly avoided all mention of any earthly fulfillment of these promises in the present age. Although ardently expounding on the subject of a future judgment beyond this world, he alluded only briefly to the apocalyptic battles that were to precede the advent of the millennium.

Liang reserved his apocalyptic language for describing the horrors of hell, a topic he returned to again and again in the pages of *Good Words*. His book of pamphlets began with the judgment of Genesis 3, in which Adam and Eve are expelled from Eden, and it ended five hundred pages later with a description of the Last Judgment, when the Salvation Lord, with the help of one billion angels, would gather all the world's people before his throne. At that time, as Liang described it, the angels would open the Book of Good and Evil (*shan e shuzhuan*), and then the heavenly messengers would separate the good people from the evil, the sheep (*mianyang*) from the goats (*shanyang*). The Salvation Lord would commend the sheep at his right hand, for when He was hungry they had given Him something to eat, and when He was naked, they had clothed Him. As a result, they would be rewarded with the kingdom (Liang did not elaborate on this kingdom). But those who had not done thus, the goats on his left, would be cursed and ordered to enter the eternal fire, where they would suffer the flames of a scorching fire (*liehuo*). After the judgment, the end would come when the Salvation Lord commanded the Divine Messengers to use the fire of the Heavenly Father's raging wrath to burn the entire earth.[72]

Hong Xiuquan's conception of the millennial kingdom was more earthly, present, and dynamic than that presented in Liang's tract. He believed in a kingdom that was coming, even now, through the instrumentality of the Taiping host. The dynamic element was certainly present in the Bible, in passages such as the Lord's Prayer (from the King James version): "Thy kingdom come. Thy will be done on earth as it is in Heaven." And, as Hong noted, Jesus introduced his Judean ministry with the proclamation that the kingdom of Heaven is drawing nigh, with the Chinese rendering more closely conveying the idea of movement: *Tianguo jinyi* (the Heavenly kingdom draws near).[73]

Where Liang took only a cursory glance at millenarian and apocalyptic passages, Hong set his gaze on them, enthralled with images such as

*Taiping boats landing in preparation for battle.
(Lindley,* Ti-Ping Tien-Kwoh.*)*

that in Revelation 21, where the New Jerusalem, the Holy City, descends to earth: "The New Jerusalem, the Heavenly capital [Tianjing], is where God and Christ descended into the world, bringing both myself and the Young Monarch to be the sovereigns, establishing the heaven of the Heavenly Court. God's Heaven [Shangdi Tiantang] now exists among men. It is fulfilled. Respect this."[74] In Hong's view of salvation in history, there would be no waiting for heaven in the "sweet by and by"; God's reign on earth commenced with the establishment of the Heavenly Capital.

Apart from Hong's annotations in the Bible that related to the identity of Christ, he most frequently refers in these annotations to this dynamic kingdom. Eugene Boardman, reflecting an older Protestantism's understanding of this doctrine, found Hong's dynamic view deficient: "The phrase 'the kingdom of Heaven' or its alternate 'the kingdom of God' was considered by Hong to refer to his own regime, whereas the sayings of Jesus in the New Testament describe Christ's kingdom as an intangible essence not of this world . . . the 'kingdom' was not a terrestrial conception."[75] Such a view expresses the understanding of the early nineteenth-century missionary community.

Hong's view, in fact, closely approximates the consensus of theologians today. Theologians today emphasize the idea that there is some fulfillment of the future kingdom in the present age. Liberation theology has taken this understanding one step further by proclaiming that the kingdom in its fullness is already present.[76] That this view is not far from Hong's own can be seen in his comments on Matthew 5: "It is the kingdom of Heaven which the Heavenly Father and Heavenly Elder Brother now have descended to establish." He elaborates:

> This one great kingdom of which we speak includes Heaven above and earth below. In Heaven above and on the earth beneath there is the Heavenly Kingdom. Heaven above, earth below is one unity.
>
> Don't mistakenly consider that God the Father's Heavenly Kingdom indicates that Heaven above is the only Heavenly Kingdom. For the Elder Brother prophesied saying that the Heavenly Kingdom is close at hand [Matthew 4:17]. Now the Heavenly Kingdom comes into the world. Presently, the Heavenly Father and the Heavenly Brother have come down into the world to create this Heavenly Kingdom.[77]

This dynamic understanding of the kingdom as represented in the Bible and in Hong's thought is associated with an apocalyptic view of history, with God intervening to judge and to save his people. Such a view of history was present in Chinese traditions as the classical idea of the mandate of Heaven, which envisioned a moral Heaven ruling over the affairs of men. Heaven appointed kings and sovereigns to implement order among humanity, and kingly laws could not with impunity violate this moral order. If a ruler proved morally unsuited to carrying out his task, Heaven would remove the mandate and the ruler.

It is significant that the Taiping document that draws most heavily on this idea of the mandate of Heaven is the *Taiping Heavenly Chronicle* (Taiping tianri). Although *tianri* is translated by Franz Michael as "Heavenly Chronicle," the phrase seems to function more as an apocalyptic allusion to the "Day of the Lord" (Zhu *zhi ri*), the day of the Lord's visitation as described in Matthew 24 and I Thessalonians 5. Both passages were scrutinized and commented on by Hong, and such an interpretation better fits with the content of the *Taiping Heavenly Chronicle*. In this document, the authors, using classical precedent, argue that the Manchus had lost Heaven's mandate through their morally unconscionable rule. Thus the loss of the mandate of Heaven was identified with the biblical idea of the Day of the Lord, the Day of Judgment.

Taiping millenarianism may have been inspired as much by sectarian Buddhist ideas as it was by a naïve reading of the Christian scriptures.[78] The belief in a Buddhist millennium was shared by all Buddhist sects, not just those associated with the sects called White Lotus. Beyond the obvious difference that Christ ruled over the Christian millennium and Sakyamuni over the Buddhist millennium, no major contradictions existed between the Christian and Buddhist visions of the millennial reign. Each religious figure would rule over a new world of peace and harmony.

Why was this particular Taiping millenarianism so successful as compared to earlier varieties, such as that of the White Lotus? One reason is that Taiping millenarianism tapped into the Confucian idea of Heaven's mandate more than did other sects. It was therefore more Chinese, more concerned with historical and national salvation. The Taiping version also emphasized the value of this world over the next. This was millenarianism, but millenarianism with a difference: Shangdi entered history not to end it, but to bring his kingdom into it. This unquestionably also resonated more with the secular Chinese mind than did Buddhist ideas of salvation outside of history.

Hong's vision nevertheless coincided closely with White Lotus millenarian visions in that Hong's kingdom was to be ushered in with a great apocalyptic battle, led by a conquering king. Hong at times saw Jesus as this coming king and at other times saw himself in that role. As he announced in his annotations at Matthew 24 and 25, passages that are deeply colored with apocalyptic language and content, "Now the Elder Brother has come down and is seated on his glorious throne, and all the nations are gathered before his temple. It is fulfilled. Respect this."[79] What had been promised in the Old Testament had been fulfilled in Jesus' kingship; what was prophesied in the New Testament was being fulfilled in Hong's own kingship and in the coming of the Taiping Heavenly Kingdom.

The emotional urgency that evangelical religion associated with the second, more triumphal coming of Christ was now transferred to Hong's own crusade. At Revelation 12, the outcome of the cosmic struggle between the dragon and the angels is a rout in which the devil and his minions are cast down to earth, where they proceed to persecute the holy ones. Again, Hong wrote, "It is fulfilled." At Revelation 19, the battle scene in the final conflict is graphically depicted:

> I saw heaven standing open and there before me was a white horse, whose rider is called Faithful and True. With justice he judges and makes war, and on his head are many crowns. . . . The armies of heaven are following him, riding on white horses. . . . Out of his mouth comes a sharp sword with which to strike down the nations. "He will rule them with an iron scepter." He treads the winepress of the wrath of God almighty.

Hong's only comment appeared at the end of the passage that speaks of the serpents and beast being thrown into the lake of fire. Hong again declared, "It is fulfilled. Respect this."[80]

To establish the Taiping kingdom, the Heavenly army had to fight many such battles, yet they fought assured that Shangdi would lead his holy soldiers to victory. *The Book of Heavenly Decrees and Proclamations* (Tianming zhaozhishu), the "True Testament," recorded that shortly after the announcement of the forming of the Taiping Heavenly Kingdom, Hong exhorted his soldiers to continue their struggle:

> All soldiers and officers throughout the army, both great and small, I earnestly beseech you to obey the Heavenly Commands; and with joy and exultation, with majesty and courage . . . to march forward in a body and

together uphold the principles of the Heavenly Father and Heavenly Elder Brother.[81]

And so the apocalypse began.

The genealogy of Taiping Christianity forms an intricate tree. It was born of a mixed parentage, but too much can be made of its foreign ancestry. Hong Xiuquan's vision fit with Christianity, as Rudolf Wagner has written, like two halves of a tally. But his vision could fit so neatly only because it was joined to a Christianity that had already been changed by its translation into Chinese. Taiping Christianity was born out of Hong's effort to reconcile his religious vision with his own Chinese traditions by using the language and concepts of this translated Christianity.

This faith challenged the legitimacy of the imperial institution and threatened to supplant imperial Chinese culture. The Qing loyalist general Zeng Guofan (1811–1872) was right about this much: the success of the Taiping would have meant the end of traditional Chinese culture—but only *imperial* Chinese culture. Their success would have heralded the beginning of a new Chinese culture that had already begun to transform its traditions through a revival of the ancient religion, a reappraisal of the sacred nature of the imperial office, and a renewed understanding of China's place in the world. We will consider how successful the Taiping were in this transformation, especially in the capacity of their faith to appeal to the people and to create this new beginning, as we turn now from the content of Taiping religion to its practice.

4
Worship and Witness in the Taiping Heavenly Kingdom

The doctrines and teachings of the Taiping shaped their beliefs about the illegitimacy of empire. These same doctrines led them to attack the imperial office and to break down the walls of the empire, establishing in its place the Heavenly Kingdom. A singular inadequacy in the many interpretations of Taiping religion is that they focus almost exclusively on content, paying little attention to practice. Yet only with a knowledge of the religious practice can we properly gauge the full impact of the Taiping faith on its followers and evaluate the repercussions of Taiping teachings on Qing society.

Sources written by people who stood outside the movement—Qing loyalist observers and Western, mostly missionary contacts (neither of whom were indifferent to the outcome of the rebellion)—form a vast treasure house of information on the practice of Taiping religion. What is striking in both hostile and sympathetic accounts is their identification of the Christian aspect of Taiping practice as the movement's most distinctive, defining element. One would expect this to be the case with the Western accounts, given the Westerners' own Christian background, but it is also true for the Chinese observers. Both sets of observers acknowledge borrowings from popular religious sources, with the Qing observers decrying the embrace of Taiping Christianity by those whom they refer to as the "foolish peasants" (*yumin*), but Qing and Western observers alike characterize the movement as Christian overall (the Chinese observers link it with the Heavenly Lord sect). What observers saw in the religion of the Taiping, then, was a form of Christianity influenced in part by Chinese native sectarian traditions.

The Qing loyalists, mostly those who lived in Taiping-administered cities, had a wider exposure to the Taiping faith, but were also more hostile to that faith and hence much more prone to focus on the negative aspects of Taiping practice (at least in their published accounts, most of which appeared after the rebellion had been suppressed). These Qing loyalist accounts are in the form of diaries, letters, and essays composed by lower-level gentry, with one major exception: a reconnaissance report compiled by Zhang Dejian for the Qing loyalist general Zeng Guofan. Zhang based this report on his own experiences, on captured documents, on oral accounts from Qing loyalists who had escaped Taiping rule, and on the testimony of hapless Taiping soldiers who had fallen into the hands of their Manchu enemies.[1]

The Western contacts were more sympathetic, at least in the early stages of the rebellion, and they presented a greater range of opinion, allowing the reader to form a more objective view of the events. Protestant missionaries were generally supportive, Catholic missionaries more equivocal, and English merchants and diplomats more or less contemptuous. Yet these Western contacts' exposure to the everyday customs, rituals, and activities of the people of the Heavenly Kingdom was more limited than that of the Qing observers. Taken together, these observer accounts complement each other and present a reasonably balanced picture of the practice of the Taiping faith.

A PORTRAIT OF THOSE WHO PRACTICED THE FAITH

One of the difficulties in reading these accounts of Taiping religious practice is discerning just who is practicing the faith. A few Qing loyalist accounts, for example, give the impression that only a fanatical few among the Taiping original core voluntarily practiced the religion, while some early missionary accounts convey the sense that every one of the followers is a convert, enthusiastically participating in the full range of religious rituals.

The distinction made between city dwellers and peasants can help describe Taiping religious practitioners. Yet this distinction is somewhat problematic because the Taiping often restricted large parts of their cities, and sometimes entire cities, to exclusive habitation by their soldiers. Such a policy seems to have been dictated by whether the city was secure or was threatened by Qing attack. For example, E. C. Bridgman found Nanjing functioning normally in 1854, only a year after its capture by the Taiping, with everyone having returned to his or her own home. When the London Mission Society missionary Rev. Griffith John (who arrived in China in 1855 and served until his death in 1912) visited Nanjing in November 1860, he found it to be functioning much like a normal city. When he returned in April 1861, everyone but the soldiers had been excluded from living within the city walls.[2] Augustus Lindley remarks that residents of Suzhou had initially been banned from residing in the city, even while there was a brisk trade going on outside the city walls.[3]

Any subject that did reside in a Taiping-controlled city would be expected to comply with Taiping social organization and to participate in Taiping religious practices. Nanjing, for example, was organized according to the Taiping ideal of the twenty-five-member governing unit. Each resident of the city would eat in a communal hall from the rations apportioned out of the sacred granary, and at these meals, all the people were expected to offer up morning and evening prayers.[4] Zhang Dejian reports that Taiping officials checked up on city residents to make sure that they were reciting scriptures and chanting hymns. Their compliance was noted on household registers.[5] Zhang also notes that the rebels distributed a copy of the Ten Commandments to every household in Nanjing and all Taiping-controlled areas.[6]

In the countryside, outside the city walls, expectations were less rigorous. Little energy was directed at organizing the countryside according to the idealized administration established in the cities. Taiping soldiers, nevertheless, still expected the peasants to participate to some degree in the religious life of the kingdom. This participation consisted chiefly in listening attentively to Taiping sermons and offering grain for the sustenance of the Heavenly soldiers. A resident of the Heavenly Capital remarked upon preaching activities outside of the cities. The Taiping instructed the people about the Heavenly Father and the Heavenly Elder Brother and how the Father had beget the kings. They described for the people a rosy future in which they would all be able to enjoy blessings without limit.[7] Another observer speaks of the Taiping army's "propagating religion" throughout the countryside.[8]

The peasants were expected to respond to these messages about the righteousness of the Taiping cause by contributing to the needs of various campaigns. These were not always voluntary contributions. In one of his more partisan comments, Zhang talks about how the Taiping, in preparation for "robbing" the common people of their grain, would first assemble the people of the villages and explain to them how these provisions were to be used to support the mission of the Taiping Heavenly Kingdom. The Taiping would say, "The Heavenly Father created the mountains and the seas. . . . Your family's lands and fields all are what the Heavenly Father bestowed upon you, so that it is reasonable for you to respond by contributing your silver and your grain [to the Kingdom]."[9] Significantly, Zhang does not mention, apart from labeling the Taiping as robbers, any coercion in his description.

Western observers frequently commented on the level of popular support enjoyed by the Taiping. An Italian Franciscan missionary whose order was concentrated in the provinces of Hunan and Hubei filed this report during the early stage of the rebellion: "[The Taiping] everywhere announce themselves as deliverers of their country from the yoke of the Tatars. . . . Those who are desirous of seeing established the Chinese dynasty, applaud these pamphlets vilifying the foreigners [i.e., the Manchus]. This enables the rebels to obtain voluntary subsidies in enormous sums, and affords them the means of increasing their army daily."[10] Rev. Charles Taylor also observed such popular support in his visit to Jinjiang, except that he noted that the peasants did receive some benefit from the exchange.[11] Descriptions of popular support were also submitted by Qing observers. An account from Zhejiang during the waning years of the movement, for example, mentioned how the peasants were offering foodstuffs to the Taiping; again, there was no mention of coercion.[12]

While it is important to qualify these accounts by acknowledging those reports that describe the depredation suffered by the peasants under wave after wave of Taiping and Qing banditry, it is significant that no Western reporter and none of these Qing observers ever comment on the peasants offering foodstuffs to the Qing armies. Qing officials dismissed all such incidents involving the popular appeal of the Taiping as the result of Taiping cunning.

A refrain that appears frequently in these loyalist accounts concerns the Taiping use of sectarian religion to trick the peasants, the "foolish people."[13] This comment was made in Wuchang, Anqing, and Nanjing, and echoed officials' characterizations of those who joined the White Lotus rebellion at the turn of the nineteenth century. This description provokes several questions: Why was the government unable to keep the people from being tricked? According to the Qing view, was any peasant who followed the Taiping a foolish peasant? When did a foolish peasant pass over into the category of rebel? And if the Taiping creed was so alien a faith, how could the Taiping have been so successful in using it to trick the people in the first place?

Another distinction concerning the followers of the faith addresses the geographic diversity of the Taiping followers. While all the soldiers were expected to comply with a stricter standard in the practice of the faith, not all the members of the army were equally zealous. A distinction is often drawn between the ardent devotion of the early Guangxi recruits and the tepid commitment of those followers enlisted from other provinces, but the fact is that the success of the rebellion was as dependent on those followers who joined the movement from other provinces as on the early Guangxi converts.

The march from Yongan through Hunan and Hubei and into Nanjing swelled the ranks of the Taiping army from tens of thousands to over a million, although it is usually the case that long marches result in the decimation, not the augmenting, of recruits. The Heavenly soldiers, while triumphant, did not rack up an unbroken string of victories in Hunan and Hubei, so their rebellion was not assumed to be a success (they never did conquer Changsha, for example). Yet people kept joining them. After the Taiping broke through the wall at Wuchang, one observer in that city estimated the total numbers of the attacking force by province: from Guangdong and Guangxi, there were more than twenty thousand men; and from Hunan and Hubei, that is, from the region in which they were then fighting, there were more than forty thousand.

The number of recruits from these latter two provinces so quickly dominated the army of the Taiping that there were some battalions that were completely made up of "Chu" men, that is, Hubei and Hunan recruits. One observer who had lived under Taiping rule in Nanjing spoke of how some of the cruelest tasks of the regime were performed by bandits from Guangxi and from the two "Hu" (Hunan and Hubei).[14] In just a short time, the holy soldiers from Hubei and Hunan were being referred to as "old brothers," as opposed to the "new brothers" recruited from Nanjing and Jiangnan.[15] After a visit to Nanjing in the early 1860s, Rev. Joseph Edkins (1823–1905), a respected LMS missionary and scholar, gave an eyewitness account of the character of the army guarding Nanjing, finding that even at that late date most soldiers stationed at Nanjing hailed from Huguang: "The most [sic] of the insurgents met here were from the provinces of Hupei [Hubei] and Hunan, in the interior of the country. . . . Many of these, by length of service, have been promoted to important posts, and are only second in influence to the original rebels."[16]

Guangxi men, as one would expect, dominated the upper levels of the Taiping ranks: all of the early kings and nobles were from Guangxi. One Nanjing account, which included a list of the top-ranking officials and a short biographical sketch of each of the leaders,[17] shows that some of the more important posts were given to men from other provinces, especially men from Hubei and Hunan. So while Guangxi men filled the top fifty posts, the middle posts showed a much broader representation. Hubei men, such as the North Palace secretary, Zhang Yuxun, were strongly represented at these middle levels.

Another Qing loyalist and Nanjing resident acknowledges that numbers were hard to come by, but still is able to present some significant figures. After the Taiping established a household registration system in Nanjing, the Heavenly Capital, this member of the Nanjing gentry compiled a list of the provincial origins of the city's residents: men with Guangxi origins numbered 1,500; men from Guangdong, 2,900 (the women from Guangdong and Guangxi totaled 2,500); men from Hunan, 10,000 (and 400 women); men from Hubei, 30,000 (and 25,000 women—why there are this many Hubei women is not explained); men from Anhui province, 3,000 (and 3,000 women); men from other provinces, 2,000; and men from Nanjing and other Jiangsu cities, 55,000; (and 110,000 women).[18] It seems safe to assume from such a list that most of those present in the city from outside Jiangsu province were committed followers of the Taiping movement, which would constitute about 50,000 men and 30,000 women, the total of male followers from outside Jiangsu approximating those from within Jiangsu.

Far more suggestive of the character of the movement is the small percentage of followers who called Guangxi their home—only 1,500 men, or 1.5 percent of the total population of Nanjing. Another observer estimated the composition of the army in one sector of the Heavenly Capital: 900 soldiers from either Guangdong or Guangxi; 10,000 from either Hunan or Hubei; and 30,000 from within Jiangnan.[19] These statistics are similar to those reported above, with the percentage of Guangxi men about the same. Obviously, the religious devotion of the few Guangxi followers could not make up for religious indifference among the many followers who came from the other provinces. If the religious commitment of the movement as a whole was as strong as observers report, that devotion would have to be shared by more than those soldiers from Guangxi, otherwise how could the Taiping Rebellion have succeeded as mightily as it had? These numbers testify once again to the universal appeal of the Taiping message. This was not just a localized religion of a fervent few.

Zhang Dejian includes a military roster that lists the names and provincial origins of a sampling of recruits from one Taiping battalion. Assisting a sergeant (*sima*) by the name of Ji Tianshun, a native of Guangxi province who joined the ranks of the Heavenly army at Jintian, was an assistant sergeant from Hubei. Under these two men were five corporals (*wuchang*) who were themselves in charge of four soldiers. Tan Dafu, only nineteen years old, hailed from Hubei. Under his command were four soldiers: one from Hunan, one from Guangdong, and two from Anhui. Another corporal was also from Hubei. Under his command was a man from Hubei, one from Jiangxi, and two from Jiangnan. A third corporal was born in Jiangnan (Suzhou), and those under his charge include one man from Jiangnan and three from Hubei.[20] Almost all those on this roster were enlisted into the service of the Heavenly Kingdom in the third year of the Kingdom (1853).

It would be helpful if there were more such lists so that we could better evaluate the representativeness of this one. We know only that Zhang himself included this one because he thought it was representative, and since he compiled his report for the purview of Zeng Guofan, we can assume it is a reliable one. What is fascinating about this list and those above, all of which come from the early years of the Taiping Kingdom, is that they demonstrate the tremendous geographic diversity in the movement even in its early years.

The provincial composition changed even more during the movement's final stages. Of the two military rosters extant, a list featuring those retainers who accompanied Chen Kunshu, the Hu Wang or Protector King, dates from the later stage of the rebellion. (Franz Michael and Chung-li Chang state that this list was compiled in September and October of 1863.) Chen, a Guangxi man, had been a subordinate of Li Xiucheng (1823–1864), the Loyal King, but broke off from him in 1862 and shortly afterwards captured the city of Changzhou in Jiangsu province.

Of the more than 1,000 persons on this list, fewer than 500 were described in terms of their provincial origins. The largest contingents were from Anhui (201 men) and Jiangsu (215 men). Their positions ranged from Right Second Propaganda Agent (Li Chenghuai, twenty years old, native of Jiangnan) to firewood boy (Zhang Desheng, twenty-two years old, native of Anhui, who had joined the Taiping in 1858). None of these, except the Protector King himself, was a native of Guangxi.[21]

This portrait of the kinds of men and women who practiced the Taiping faith, from the citizens of the Heavenly Capital and supportive peasants to the hardened Hubei war veterans and Anhui firewood boys, demonstrates the movement's heterogeneous character and broad appeal. But what did these Taiping sectarians practice? What religious rituals and customs did this diverse movement follow?

TAIPING WORSHIP

After the Taiping established their Heavenly Capital, on every sixth day of their week, a flag appeared on the street announcing that the next day was the Sabbath and that subjects and soldiers should make the appropriate preparations for worship.[22]

In preparation for Sabbath worship, the people needed to wash their faces in order to devoutly worship the virtue of the Heavenly Father.[23] During worship services, there was to be no distracting clamor or chat-

A meeting of the Taiping ruling council.
Lindley, Ti-Ping Tien-Kwoh.

tering. As one Taiping regulation stipulates, "At morning worship, when we are worshipping the Heavenly Father, if any official or soldier makes any kind of distracting noise or commotion, that person shall be executed."[24] The same reverential tone was set for each of the daily worship services before each meal, when worshippers chanted hymns and recited prayers.

Zhang Dejian described the rebel Sabbath worship service. Unlike the practice at Chinese temples, he tells us, the Taiping did not use incense in their worship. On a table, they set two oil lamps and usually a vase of flowers, accompanied by three cups of tea, three dishes of various (sacrificial) meats, and three bowls of rice. In the front of the table, they placed a bamboo plank about three feet in length on which was written, "Receiving the

Commands of Heaven" (*feng* Tianling). Behind the table were three chairs for those officiating at the service.

Also unlike the practice at Chinese temples, theirs was a corporate worship. At the beating of a gong, the people gathered for worship. Then they sang (chanted) the doxologies (hymns of praise), and listened to sermons and teachings. One of the officials recorded all the proceedings of the service on a piece of yellow paper (signifying imperial business). At the closing portion of the service, the recorder read what had transpired during the service, and all those in attendance signed their names. The yellow paper was then burned, as a memorial (*zou*) presented to Heaven.[25] Sabbath worship was required of all, but only soldiers and officials were punished—by wearing the cangue and being caned (a thousand strokes)—for nonattendance.[26] This form of worship was universally implemented throughout Taiping China and was followed by all the kings until the fall of Nanjing.[27]

Taiping Sabbath worship consisted of prayer, singing, and preaching. The only partially realized *Land System of the Heavenly Dynasty* enjoined, "In every circle of twenty-five families.... Every Sabbath the corporals must lead the men and women to the church, where the males and females are to sit in separate rows. There they will listen to sermons, sing praises, and offer sacrifices to our Heavenly Father, the Supreme Lord and Great God."[28] These three components of Sabbath worship were also part of the Taiping daily worship as well.

The Taiping prayed at Sabbath worship and at their daily morning and evening meals.[29] The Taiping taught their children to pray kneeling down, saying, "We are grateful to the Heavenly Father, the Highest Lord, the Supreme Shangdi who is in Heaven; let your decree be executed on Earth as in Heaven."[30] American missionary visitors to Suzhou wrote down some of the prayers they heard there, including that recited at daily meals: "Heavenly Father, the Great Shangdi, bless us little ones. Provide us day by day clothes to wear and food to eat. Keep us from calamity and difficulty. Grant that our souls may ascend to Heaven."[31] They prayed to Heaven in any and every circumstance, even when facing execution or a serious illness.[32]

Loyalist observers were particularly derisive about the Taiping instructing their soldiers before going into battle to kneel down and pray "Tianfu kangu" (Heavenly Father, watch over us) before they engaged the enemy.³³ One Taiping regulation governing military discipline read, "All soldiers and officials, when they are going to battle to kill demons [i.e., Manchus], together need to sincerely kneel and seek the Heavenly Father's care and His help in battling and killing demons."³⁴ Rev. Griffith John described the content of their prayers: "The subjects of their prayers are, in the case of those who possess a coarser mould of mind, victory in battle, and a speedy subjugation of 'the hills and rivers.' The more thoughtful pray for forgiveness of sin and the salvation of the soul."³⁵

The second component of Taiping Sabbath and daily worship was the singing of songs and chanting of verse. Singing traditional Christian doxologies (songs of praise) was required training for all Taiping soldiers; the doxologies were probably chanted rather than sung since the term most often used to describe this part of their worship was *song jing* (to chant a scripture or liturgy), though the terms *nian* (recite) and *chang* (sing) were also used. One of the most common of the Taiping songs of praise offered to Shangdi is reminiscent of a standard Protestant doxology: "Praise Shangdi, the Heavenly Holy Father, Praise Jesus [Yesu], the Holy Lord of the world's salvation, praise the Holy Divine Wind [Sheng Shenfeng], the Holy Spirit, praise three persons forming one united true God."³⁶ This song greeted the ears of the Methodist missionary Rev. Charles Taylor morning and evening during his visit to Taiping territory, and was the most frequently recorded song by Western and Qing observers alike.³⁷

In most accounts, several other stanzas were added to this standard doxology. In a shorter rendition the worshippers added, "Praise the great way which is able to save one's life, enjoying blessings without limit; the road to the Heavenly Hall is open; today acknowledge, and repent, and your soul will ascend to Heaven." Another version of the doxology, which added a reference to Jesus as the Crown Prince (Taizi) who descended into the service, ended with a call to the Son of Heaven (Tianzi) to reign for ten thousand years.³⁸ A report from Suzhou states that the singing of the Taiping doxology in that city included twenty-eight verses of four to five characters each.³⁹ Such a lengthy tune suggests that even in the declining years of the Heavenly Kingdom, Taiping religious practice was rich and observance was devout.

Preaching was the third component of the Taiping Sabbath and daily service, usually consisting of reading from the Bible or from one of the Taiping doctrinal texts, which loyalists referred to as "bandit books." The sermon was the main focus of the worship service as it was laid out in the *Land System of the Heavenly Dynasty*. Observers, however, say little about the sermons that took place in worship and instead comment more frequently on those delivered outside the worship halls. Ten days after capturing the city of Wuchang in 1853, for example, the Taiping had all the people of the city gather to listen to their first Taiping sermon, which according to one loyalist was long and "stirred up the foolish people."[40] In Yangzhou, they subjected the city's residents to the same sort of sermon, but it was delivered on the Sabbath.[41] Zhang Dejian writes that the Taiping in the various cities they conquered passed out badges that the people fastened to their waists if they were willing to serve as obedient subjects of the Taiping. Then the soldiers ushered those people to places where they could listen to Taiping leaders preach sermons: "Wherever the Taiping dwelt, they would sound a gong and gather the local people [*baixing*] along with their soldiers, on any day at any time and at any place" to listen to the preaching of sermons.[42]

One element of traditional Christian worship that is missing from the Taiping service is a full celebration of the sacraments. Baptism was celebrated from the early days of the Society of God Worshippers. The *Taiping Heavenly Chronicle* records that Hong Xiuquan, Feng Yunshan, and Hong Rengan all baptized themselves following their coming to faith: "The three men together declared their repentance before the Heavenly Father, the Supreme Lord and Great God [Huang Shangdi], and went together to wash [baptize] themselves in the Shih-chüeh-t'an [a pool or small lake]."[43] Interestingly, this account uses the Baptist word for baptism (*jinxi*), signifying that the converts would be immersed, rather than sprinkled, which was a point of contention among the missionaries. But most accounts suggest that the mode of baptism was irrelevant to the Taiping administration, and it even seems that by the end of the movement, sprinkling had come to be preferred.[44] Worth noting in this context is that Reverend Roberts had refused to baptize Hong during Hong's visit to the Canton chapel, as the missionary had been led to believe that Hong was insincere

Worship and Witness in the Taiping Heavenly Kingdom   129

A mother teaches her child the Lord's Prayer.
(*Lindley,* Ti-Ping Tien-Kwoh.)

in his faith. The foreign missionary's denial of baptism did not stop Hong or the rest of the Society of God Worshippers from administering this rite themselves to all their converts. In their preaching tours, these early leaders baptized all who believed in their message.

Rev. Theodore Hamberg describes the Taiping rite as a part of the Society of God Worshippers' congregational worship service. After converts had expressed their faith in God and their intent to turn from idolatry,

> two burning lamps and three cups of tea were placed upon a table, probably to suit the sensual apprehension of the Chinese. A written confession of sins, containing the names of different candidates for baptism, was

repeated by them, and afterwards burnt, whereby the presenting of the same to God was to be expressed. The question was then asked, if they promised, "Not to worship the evil things, but to keep the heavenly commandments." After this confession, they knelt down, and from a large basin of clear water, a cupful was poured over the head of every one [*sic*] with the words, "Purification from all former sins, putting off the old, and regeneration."[45]

After rising, the converts drank the tea and washed their chests with water, further showing their cleansing from sin. Each convert would then receive the various forms of prayer used in the Society of God Worshippers' rituals, which the new converts then took, memorized, and began to practice.

The sacrament of communion is nowhere mentioned in Taiping documents, and its omission is not explained. When Rev. Joseph Edkins specifically asked Hong Rengan, the Shield King, about the observance of this ritual and the manner in which it was observed, the Taiping king answered that the sacrament was not observed. Reverend Edkins commented: "It is not known among them. Wine is not used in any of their religious observances, and the private use of it is strictly forbidden by law."[46] It probably was not reluctance to partake of wine that prevented them from celebrating the sacrament. The early leaders of the God worshippers, including Hong Xiuquan and Feng Yunshan, who were new converts themselves, may not have known about communion as they had not been allowed to participate in the rite. And the missionaries may not have celebrated communion because no church had yet been formed; in the early stages of mission enterprise, only preaching chapels had been established.

The opinion has often been expressed that the constancy of devotion and consistency of practice declined among the Taiping rank and file especially in the last stages of the rebellion. In many ways, this matter is similar to the issue of geographic diversity that I discussed at the beginning of this chapter. Several observers of the movement at the time noted and many scholars today have assumed that in the early stages of the movement, all Taiping followers were zealous in their faith and conscientious in their practice, but that in the later stages, with the arrival of newer recruits, practice fell off to the point of abandonment. Such a decline is not surprising. In the early stages of the movement, when the Taiping were winning all their battles, people would have been more passionate to fight for what looked like the winning side, and so were eager to participate in the full range of Taiping religious activity. The large number of men and women recruited in Hubei and Hunan testify to the motivating force of this chain of victories. During the later stages of the movement, when victories were not as frequent and future triumph not so certain, even the Guangxi "old brothers" were probably not as zealous in their devotion.

In the Rev. Joseph Edkins's interview with the Shield King, Hong Rengan, the Taiping chief seemed to support this view, declaring that the religion had "deteriorated considerably."[47] It should be kept in mind that the Shield King was comparing the devotion of the demoralized, final stages of the movement with the fervent early years of the Society of God Worshippers.

This decline in religious devotion was not a precipitous fall but a gradual slip. It reflected the demoralization of defeat more than the complacency of unbelief. An account from Zhejiang from the years 1860–62, the years of decline and supposed waning of Taiping zeal, is illustrative. In this account, a Qing sympathizer who had been kept captive by Taiping soldiers reports that they worshipped on only two Sabbaths a month. Nonetheless, they still engaged in their rituals, including singing (chanting) the doxology, writing down the proceedings of their worship, and, by burning the paper, submitting this worship as a memorial to the Heavenly Father.

The doxology they sang added a few lines to the traditional Taiping doxology (this was a common occurrence). The lines in question appear in other records of Taiping worship but are not universal. Following the doctrinal core that praises the Father, Son, and Holy Spirit, the Three-in-One, this group sang:

> How can the true way have anything in common with the way of the world; only it can save the people, it will grant them the pleasure of blessing without limit. Those who are wise will leap and jump [for joy], since they will know what constitutes blessing. Those who are foolish will awaken and apprehend, since the road to the Heavenly Paradise will be open.
>
> Oh! The vast and profound mercy of the Heavenly Father! Its breadth

is great and without boundary. He did not spare even the Crown Prince [Taizi], but rather sent him down to us, contributing his life to redeem us from the consequences of our crimes [or, sins]. When people understand this, let them repent. May the Son of Heaven live forever![48]

What is relevant here is not what later followers understood of this doctrine or how they understood it, but that the Taiping continued to practice the core of their religion faithfully through even the final stages of the movement. This report suggests that later followers of the Taiping, the so-called younger brothers, still knew their religion, although they were perhaps not as zealous as their older Guangxi brethren. They knew the Ten Commandments and they knew the rudimentary outline of Christian doctrine: beliefs about the Heavenly Father, Son, and Holy Spirit, and the mission of Jesus as the Crown Prince.

This was not an isolated case. Even in Suzhou, the city governed by Li Xiucheng, the Loyal King whose commitment to the religion was characterized as a few degrees short of lukewarm, the soldiers still memorized the Ten Commandments, chanted the doxology, and worshipped on the Sabbath day.[49] Augustus Lindley reports that he participated in one such worship service in Suzhou.[50] Rev. Griffith John remarked after his visit to Suzhou, "Comparing the present religious state of the revolutionists with what they were at Nanking and Chen-kiang eight years ago, there seems to be little difference."[51] His comparison is meant to be understood positively. Although such a statement is probably to be expected from one like John, who sympathized with the movement, his colleague Rev. Joseph Edkins, who was convinced that the Taiping barely rose above the level of the crudest idolaters and syncretists, even lodged a positive report. When he visited a town twelve miles from Nanjing he found the chief of that city to be devout, praying the daily prayers and supervising his son in the learning of the *Three Character Classic* (Sanzijing) and the Ten Commandments.[52]

These Taiping followers in Suzhou were joined by the hardened Hubei war veterans and the young Anhui firewood boys in the practice of their faith. All were required to learn the Ten Commandments within three weeks (and to comply with their prohibitions) as well as to sing the doxology at the morning and evening meal, pray the common prayers, and attend the worship service on the Sabbath. There is little evidence that suggests this activity was an onerous burden or an irksome task, and much to suggest that it was an edifying and encouraging expression of their faith.

THE TAIPING MISSION

The Taiping were not just Sabbath sectarians; their religious practice was not confined to worship service or ritual activities. The Taiping mission was also an integral aspect of their religious practice, and they were serious about it. Their aim was to extend the boundaries of the Heavenly Kingdom to encompass all of the lands of the empire.

In support of their mission, the Taiping engaged in three different activities: attacking the Manchus and destroying the old imperial and idolatrous order; setting up a model of the new Taiping order; and propagating their views to all those uncommitted to either side.

The Ten Commandments were the theological and ideological basis of the Taiping mission. The first three commandments (those which speak against the worship of other gods, idolatry, and blaspheming the name of God) dictated the destruction of the old imperial order and the shattering of that order as represented in its images. Western observers frequently commented on the decalogue's paramount position in Taiping ideology. In the very first foreign contact with the Taiping following the establishing of the Heavenly Capital, E. G. Fishbourne, the captain of the *Hermes*, and the English consul Thomas T. Meadows recounted a conversation they had with the Northern King, Wei Changhui (whom Meadows misidentifies as the "Northern Prince"):

> To all this the Northern Prince listened, but made little or no rejoinder; the conversation, in so far as directed by him, consisting mainly of inquiries as to our religious belief, and expositions of their own. He states, that, as children and worshippers of one God, we were all brethren; and after receiving my assurance that such had long been our view also, inquired if I knew the Heavenly Rules (Tien teaou) [*sic*]. I replied, that I was most likely acquainted with them, though unable to recognize them under that name; and after a

moment's thought, asked if they were ten in number? He answered eagerly in the affirmative. I then began repeating the Ten Commandments, but had not proceeded far before he had laid his hand on my shoulder in a friendly way, and exclaimed, 'The same as ourselves! The same as ourselves!'[53]

Taiping devotion to the Mosaic code was the fundamental core of their faith. Much is made of Hong Xiuquan's vision in shaping Taiping religion, and even more is made of Liang Afa's tract for its own contribution, but neither of these men's works were placed in every Taiping household, as was a copy of the Ten Commandments.

Both Qing and Western observers noted that conforming to the rule of the Ten Commandments served as the essential standard of Taiping religious practice, and that rule was strictly enforced, especially for army recruits. Zhang Dejian discussed the severity of Taiping discipline, particularly in relation to the Ten Commandments. The commandments were to be memorized by all army recruits within three weeks—the penalty for failing to do so was decapitation.[54] Those who were literate were to help those who were not by reading the commands aloud until they learned them by heart. The penalty for transgressing the commands was the same as that for not knowing them.

The first three commandments concerned the proper worship of the one, true God. He, his image, and his name should be honored, while other gods should be dishonored. These commandments propelled an iconoclastic crusade, which served to express the recruits' loyalty to Shangdi just as their worship did. The *Taiping Imperial Declaration* states that "The Great God commanded Moses, saying, 'I am the Supreme Lord, the Great God; you men of the world must on no account set up images resembling anything in heaven above or on earth below, and bow down and worship them.' Now you people of the world who set up images are in absolute defiance of the Great God's [Huang Shangdi's] expressed will."[55] These images, therefore, had to be destroyed.

Iconoclasm was a distinguishing feature of the kind of Protestantism Hong had encountered in *Good Words to Admonish the Age* and at the Baptist chapel at Canton. The Calvinist wing of the Reformation was characterized from its beginnings in the sixteenth century by such iconoclastic activ-

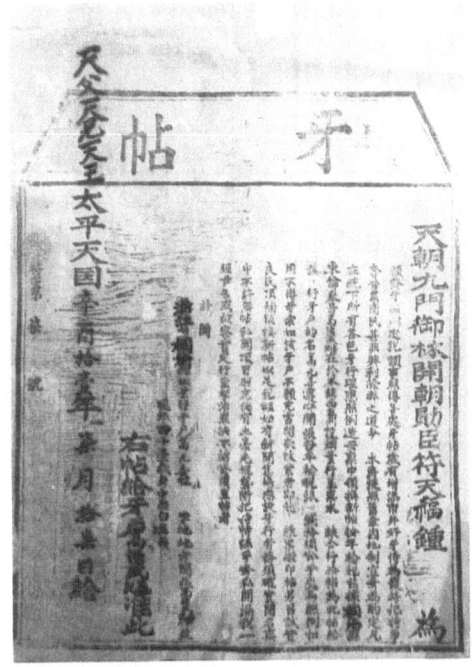

Cemetery title deed issued by the Taiping Loyal King, Li Xiucheng, to the Huang family, Jiangsu province, 1862. Note the customary Taiping declaration along the left side of the document: "The Heavenly Father, the Heavenly Elder Brother and the Heavenly King." Courtesy of the Jiangsu People's Publishing House.

ity.[56] As Carlos Eire has shown in his study of the role of iconoclasm in the Reformation, Ulrich Zwingli and other Swiss reformers read the Ten Commandments in a fashion that compelled the followers of Reformed Protestantism to take action against physical representations of the sacred.[57] During the Reformation, in city after city, the sound of shattered stained glass announced the arrival of Calvinist Reformers.

Eire documents how iconoclasm was a prelude to revolution in Switzerland and to the Wars of Religion in France. He describes iconoclasm as a "revolutionary act," a directed act of violence shattering the accepted social myth.[58] Eire recounts how in Basel the power of Rome and the established oligarchy were "swept away with the images" and how in Bern in 1528 "the people marched on the Cathedral to wage war on the idols. From the Cathedral alone, forty-six wagons of rubble were carted away to be burnt."[59] Bernese soldiers were then dispatched to other Swiss cities. When they entered Geneva in 1530, they beat the priests and stripped them of their habits, and then fed a consecrated host to a goat.

One soldier plucked the eyes out of a statue of St. Anthony with his sword in full view of the friars.[60]

Given the parallels with Taiping iconoclasm, the development in early Calvinism toward a theory of resistance that viewed tyrannicide as a form of iconoclasm is especially significant. As Eire notes, "Although none of the major continental Reformers ever advocated tyrannicide or revolution as a way of effecting religious change, their followers would not always be restrained from applying the same rule to governments that they applied to the 'idols.' As a form of aggressive disobedience to established authority, iconoclasm is closely related to the more radical forms of political revolution."[61] The Taiping made this same connection between smashing idols and rebelling against idolatrous governments in their own crusade for religious change.

Such iconoclastic fervor marked the Taiping movement from its beginning in southern China. The destructive aspects of the Taiping mission began with smashing idols. Hong's attack on the idol at a temple in Xiangzhou, in which he dug out the eyes of the idol and broke off its arms, mirrors the Calvinist soldier's desecration of the statue of St. Anthony. The targets of this iconoclasm were not limited to temple statues, as Hong also smashed his village school's Confucian tablets. This crusade, which began with iconoclasm, culminated in the toppling of Confucius and the slaying of Manchus, for each of these cultural artifacts defined and supported the blasphemous claims of the imperial office. The Taiping rebels left a trail of shattered idols wherever they ventured.

Western observers often described these iconoclastic spectacles as one of their first impressions when visiting Taiping-occupied lands. Capt. E. G. Fishbourne was one of the first witnesses to describe this aspect of the rebellion. He found that the rebels had spared the Buddhist priests (though the Taiping did require them to grow their hair), but that no mercy was shown to their religious representations. "The idols, it is true, were all destroyed; some of these must have been magnificent, made of clay, and forty or even sixty feet high. Those of wood or stone were defaced, and many thrown into the water."[62] Dr. Walter Medhurst, in an interview with a man who had served as a Taiping soldier, was told that "everything belonging to Buddha and Taou [sic] . . . were indiscriminately destroyed. . . . As for the priests, opium-smokers, and whoremongers, they dared not show their faces."[63] From Fuzhou, too, came a report describing the demolition of temples, and an equally sanguinary fate for the priests.[64] Alexander Wylie, who surveyed Taiping China from Nanjing to Anjing, filed a report in 1859 in which he comments on this signature mark of the Taiping movement:

> The temples have been especially marked out for destruction, and I find that it is an invariable practice with them, for there is not a single temple for idol worship to be seen anywhere within their reach. In the temple of the god of war, nothing remains but a semi-calcined marble tablet, and a pivot of clay seated on a pedestal, which formed the nucleus of the grim idol—apparently reproaching his besotted worshippers for their folly.[65]

A more vivid description yet came from Rev. Griffith John's journey to Suzhou, where even in 1860 he was able to record that "The iconoclastic tendencies of the Taipings are still in full vigor. Nowhere, apparently, do they leave the idols untouched. . . . It is common to see the nose, chin, and hands cut off. The floors of these buildings are bestrewn with relics of helpless gods. . . . Some are cast into the canals, and are found floating down the stream mingled with the debris of rifled houses and the remains of the dead."[66] In the early stages of the rebellion, missionaries greeted this iconoclasm as a positive omen, as a preparation for a new era in China, but in the later stages, many of these same missionaries encountered such scenes with a sense of foreboding, anxious about the apocalypse they in part had unleashed.

Chinese observers noted this signature mark of the movement in less approving terms. In Nanjing, near Moqiu Lake, stood the statue of one King Zhongshan. The Taipings did not know to which god it was dedicated, and the issue was irrelevant to them anyway; they cut off its head and destroyed the statue, after which they set fire to the building in which it was housed.[67] One loyalist observer explained this penchant for pulverizing: "The bandit's religion involves looking up toward the empty skies to worship, they are upset by idols [*shenxiang*, statues of gods]. Seeing one, they immediately smash and destroy it; they show no tolerance for any kind of idol."[68] The effect on Chinese worshippers, who witnessed attacks on their sacred objects, must have been traumatic. That the idols proved to be no match for the Taiping forces, thereby graphically demonstrating the powerlessness of these gods against the Taiping deity, must have been especially disconcerting.

Another object of Taiping wrath was Confucius and the classics. Hong Xiuquan had shown this iconoclastic posture towards Confucianism early, when in the vision of his ascent to Heaven he beat Confucius with a whip in spite of the sage's cries for mercy. The Taiping acted out this rage by defacing statues of Confucius and leveling his temples. Even more sacrilegious in the eyes of Qing officials was the Taiping effort to replace the Confucian canon with the Christian Canon in the Taiping official exams. Though the Eastern King, Yang Xiuqing, sought to moderate the Taiping stance toward Confucius, Hong would not relent.

The punishment for reading or teaching the classics—the "demon books," as they were described in the Taiping regulations—was decapitation.[69] One poet lamented that the Taiping did not read books, that books had no pleasure for them, that they did not know Confucius or recognize Mencius, that they thought it was good to burn these books and better to throw them in the water. All those who read books or collected them, along with those who bought and sold them, were executed.[70] These complaints may be hyperbolic for literary, or more probably propagandistic, effect; but the Taiping disposition toward the Chinese classics was well known.

Even more than Confucius, the Manchus aroused the fury of the Taiping. They were the demons who had plundered and pillaged Chinese civilization,[71] and the Chinese Taiping demonstrated their loyalty to the Heavenly Kingdom by letting their hair grow, since the partially shaved head signified Chinese submission to the Manchus.[72] Everything associated with the Manchus and the Qing court was identified by the adjective demonic, as is vividly described for us by one loyalist: "The bandits regard officials as demons, when they see dynastic clothes and headgear, . . . these are also regarded as demonic paraphernalia. They call scholars, 'demon scholars,' soldiers, 'demon soldiers,' messengers, 'demon messengers.' There is nothing they do not demonize; they even call the people's militia 'demon maggots.'"[73]

The Manchus were the enemies of Shangdi because the Manchu Qing

Business license for a tobacco shop issued by Taiping general Zhong Liangxiang, 1861. Note the customary Taiping declaration along the left side of the document: "The Heavenly Father, the Heavenly Elder Brother and the Heavenly King." Courtesy of the Jiangsu People's Publishing House.

emperor had profaned Shangdi by taking his name in vain. In effect, the emperor had set himself up as an idol, and so he, like every idol before him, was targeted for destruction. The Taiping thus reached a conclusion similar to that of the Calvinists in Reformation Europe: tyrannicide is but one form of iconoclasm. This connection is explicitly noted by a missionary who reported in an account of the occupation of the treaty port of Ningbo that the Taiping war cry heard throughout the city was "Down with the Tatars. . . . Down with the Idols."[74]

In his original commission to Hong, the Heavenly Father had ordered him to exterminate these demons. The Taiping carried out that commission faithfully. After breaching the wall of the cities they conquered, their first objective was to make for the Manchu section of the city. In Hunan, a loyalist observer wrote of the "pitiful Manchus," men and women, young and old, who were devoured by the hungry swords of the Taiping. When they reached Nanjing, the Taiping warned the common people to stay in their homes as they headed for the Manchu quarter. The holy soldiers killed all the Manchu men, and then drove several thousand Manchu women to the outside of Chaoyang Gate, surrounded them, and burnt them to death.[75] When Hefei, in Anhui province, fell, one observer heard shouts of "Kill the demons!" filling the streets and alleys of the Manchu city.[76] We know that these reports were not exaggerated, and if the clipping of a queue could arouse fear in the Manchus, it is not difficult to imagine what kind of response these reports elicited at the Qing court.[77]

The Taiping destroyed the idolatrous old order to clear the way for building a faithful new order. Their iconoclasm served a larger purpose. In the second component of their mission, the Taiping began to build their Christian culture, modeling the future for all to see. The commandments played a role in this enterprise as well. The seventh commandment, for example, which prohibits adultery, and in the Taiping version also denounces licentiousness, prompted restrictions forbidding any kind of social contact between men and women. Sexual relations were especially forbidden, and this rule extended even to married couples. According to one observer, the separation of the sexes was carried to such an extreme that fathers could not even communicate with their daughters, or mothers with their sons.[78] This custom of separating the sexes is reported by a number of observers, although the Taiping strictly enforced this regulation only in the early years.

Along with gender segregation, Confucian observers also attacked another Taiping social custom, the habit of addressing each other as brother and sister, which conflicted with Confucian ideas about the hierarchical structure of the family. As Zhang Dejian comments,

> As for the great ethical code of father and son, husband and wife, the bandits rebel against Heaven, and they turn their backs on reason; they do not acknowledge the order of older and younger, of noble and mean; they only know brother. And concerning these so-called brothers, not only are you yourself a [an elder] brother, but all are [elder] brothers; not only are you yourself a [younger] brother, but all are [younger] brothers. . . . Compelling wives to be addressed as "sister" so that you have old "sisters" and new "sisters" as terms of address [is another of their objectionable customs].[79]

The bandits rebel against Heaven, Zhang argues, in not following the distinctions that Heaven had determined, specifically the natural order between older and younger.

The commandments forbidding stealing and coveting, the eighth and tenth, were enforced with as much severity, as they reflected the Taiping understanding of Shangdi as the Creator of the Heavens and the Earth; He created the earth, the land belonged to Him, and He willed that it be apportioned fairly among all his children. Both Chinese and Western observers alike noted the Taiping commitment to economic equality and social justice, values enshrined in the widely circulated document *Land System of the Heavenly Dynasty*, which proclaims,

> The whole empire is the universal family of our Heavenly Father, the Supreme Lord and Great God. When all the people in the empire will not take anything as their own but submit all things to the Supreme Lord, then the Lord will make use of them, and in the universal family of the empire, every place will be equal and every individual well-fed and clothed. This is the intent of our Heavenly Father, the Supreme Lord and Great God, in specially commanding the true Sovereign of Taiping to save the world.[80]

Although many observers and scholars have questioned the sincerity of the Taiping in publicizing this document and have doubted whether the Taiping intended to institute this system, it now appears that Taiping intentions were more naïve than insincere.

That the Taiping shared a community of goods, best exemplified in the institution of the sacred treasury (*shengku*), has never been challenged. This institutional expression of the Taiping belief in economic equality is abundantly attested to and can be copiously documented. In Wuchang, one of the first actions of the Taiping army after entering the city was to set up the treasury.[81] Nanjing's sacred treasury was still operating and "carried out to its fullest extent" when Rev. Griffith John visited in the 1860s.[82] Even as far afield as Fujian, whatever food or clothing was obtained was shared with all.[83] Troop behavior was regulated by a requirement that all loot left by "demons," including gold, jade, and clothing, be contributed to the treasury,[84] and all meals were shared. The Taiping thus ensured that all the wealth of Shangdi would be distributed equally among all his sons and daughters.

Kathryn Bernhardt's study of Jiangnan-area rent rebellions discloses, through the patterns of these rebellions, the impact of Taiping socioeconomic doctrine and policy. As Bernhardt emphasizes, even though the Taiping were not able to implement their land system, they did implement other equitable policies that permanently changed the landscape of landlord-peasant relations in the area, some as rudimentary as compelling gentry households to pay their fair share of taxes. In contrast with the traditional argument about the long-term impact of the Taiping Rebellion, Bernardt's study has shown that it was Jiangnan peasants, not the elite, who derived the most benefit from the upheaval.[85]

The Taiping mission did not end with their efforts to destroy the Qing empire and build their own Heavenly Kingdom. The third dimension of their mission, directed at those who had not yet thrown their lot with either side, involved the propagation of their complaints about the old order and their promises for the new. The Taiping invested a great deal of effort in winning the hearts and minds of the people by getting their message out and persuading the people of the righteousness of their cause.

Rudolf Wagner describes how the Taiping engaged in proselytizing efforts similar to those of various sectarians who preceded them. He emphasizes, however, that the Taiping efforts were far more intensive and extensive, and compares them to the Qing village lectures that were delivered by local gentry twice monthly throughout the empire. After considering this array of indoctrination practices, Wagner observes, "Like the other religious moral educators, the Taipings operated through the public sphere. Like them, the Taipings distributed books, held public lectures, and introduced ceremonies to publicly reinforce their message."[86]

The Taiping were able to extend their influence through the distribution of literature even into areas they did not occupy. Ironically, the Qing were thus compelled to engage in the same kind of proselytizing and often wound up spreading the Taiping message in their own attempts to counteract it. The declarations posted up on anonymous walls were especially conspicuous in cities under siege by the Taiping, such as Nanjing, where a Qing observer described the scene for his readers: "The rebel bandits set up their Heavenly Father religion [the only time this phrase is used] coercing foolish people [to join]; the center of the city was plastered with false declarations. Regardless of what matter, these all begin with 'The Heavenly Father has greatly poured out his heavenly grace and mandated that our Heavenly King serve as the truly-mandated Lord, and to establish the Heavenly Capital' and such, these several phrases."[87]

Zhang Dejian tells us that in the very beginning of the rebellion, such literature was not so plentiful, and the wording did not so openly challenge the dynasty. But all that quickly changed when the Taiping captured Yongan in 1851, and along with the city came all its resident literati, and so the Society of God Worshippers could call on these talents for their help in the publication of a greater volume of this literature. Zhang's account features many of these "false declarations," which he states are representative of the different types of literature posted in areas of Taiping activity. The one that leads off this representative sampling is by far the most grave:

> The Heavenly King [hereby] proclaims "All you Qing fellow-Chinese, you whose position is so clear; order all your soldiers and officials to obey the mandate and adhere to the Commandments. In all the great universe, the Supreme God [Huangdi; usually the title used for the emperor but used here for God] is alone one. He is the Heavenly Father, the High Lord, the Supreme Sovereign on High [Huang Shangdi]. Apart from the Heavenly Father, the High Lord, the Supreme Sovereign on High, if there is a man who calls himself the Supreme God [Huangdi], with respect to the law of Heaven this transgression involves snow in the midst of the clouds [i.e., execution]. In the universe, the Great Elder Brother is alone one. He is the Heavenly Elder Brother, Yesu [Jesus]. Apart from the Heavenly Elder Brother, if there is a man who calls himself the Great Elder Brother, with respect to the law of Heaven this transgression involves snow in the midst of the clouds. Continuing from this moment, I am clearly proclaiming this to the whole universe. After this, anyone who transgresses [these commands] should not blame us [for what befalls him]. Respect this."[88]

This representative declaration contains a very serious accusation: that the emperor, in referring to himself as Huangdi, had transgressed the law of Heaven and so was judged to be worthy of execution. Although somber and sobering, this indictment sums up the charge the Taiping had against the emperor—the charge of blasphemy, and this was the reason behind the Taiping attempt to overturn the whole imperial institution.

All but a few of the different Taiping declarations Zhang included began with the line "The True [Bearer] of the Mandate of Heaven, the Heavenly

Kingdom of Great Peace," followed by the name of the particular king in whose name the declaration was issued, along with his various titles. Then came the line, "The Heavenly Father and the Heavenly Elder Brother have greatly displayed their Heavenly mercy, specially sending my True Lord, the Heavenly King to descend into the world to rule with sovereignty over all the world."[89] The heading of some declarations concluded with the phrase "to slaughter and exterminate the demons," replacing "to rule with sovereignty over all the world."[90] This heading was followed by the declaration itself.

Thus, from only the formulaic heading of such declarations, the populace reading them (or having them read, in the case of those who were illiterate) would know some basics about the religion of the Taiping Kingdom, even if they never had the opportunity (or, as these observers viewed it, misfortune) to live under rebel rule. They would know that this movement challenged the claim of the imperial regime to be the bearer of the mandate of Heaven; that the challengers called themselves kings and not emperors (and the curious peasant would wonder why that would be); that there were Chinese who disputed the legitimacy of the imperial title and the entire imperial system; that as part of the challenge, the Taiping were engaged in a particularly provocative form of iconoclasm and a demonization of the ruling race; and finally that the challengers backed their enterprise with religious appeals to the mandate of Heaven. In sum, the populace would learn about some of the more important religious aspects of the rebellion, including many of the more distinctive Taiping religious doctrines, along with the full political import of these Taiping beliefs.

Such declarations, on yellow paper with dragon borders (the kind of paper used by the emperor), appeared first in Yongan. They were "posted on every street corner" in Changsha, even though the Taiping failed in their attempt to take the city.[91] Secret society allies often posted such declarations in cities where they resided. When the Taiping laid siege to Nanjing, they used even more creative means for disseminating their message: the God worshippers shot their literature into the city by bow and arrow, both declarations and documents.[92]

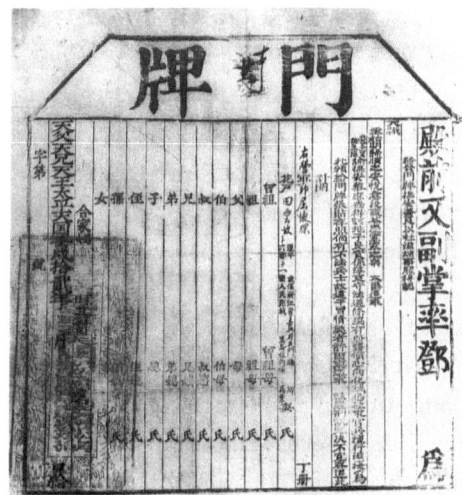

Household register issued by Taiping general Deng Guangmin, 1862. Note the customary Taiping declaration along the left side of the document: "The Heavenly Father, the Heavenly Elder Brother and the Heavenly King." Courtesy of the Jiangsu People's Publishing House.

In Suzhou, the yellow paper declarations were displayed when criminals were paraded through the city and were festooned over the cangues placed around the necks of transgressors. A typical Suzhou banner read, "The Loyal King has a command; let all the brothers hearken: such and such a person did such and such a thing; he transgressed the Heavenly Commandments; we will punish his crime."[93] Also issued around Suzhou was a denunciation of the Qing "demon court" that showed contempt for the sacred things of the former Ming dynasty (1368–1644), a message with secret society overtones.[94]

After the Taiping breached the walls of Nanjing, one of their first actions was to plaster the walls with all kinds of declarations and announcements. Some concerned a decree of one of the kings; others concerned matters of belief or conduct, such as: "When people do not know how to revere Heaven, the Heavenly Father is greatly enraged; the first time, he sent down flood waters."[95] Another, on red paper, read, "The Heavenly King has been invested with the mandate of the Heavenly Father and the Heavenly Elder Brother, in order to save the people of the world; everyone must know the Heavenly Father and submit to the Heavenly King." On top of the doorposts leading into Taiping living quarters was written this exhortation: "Let everyone worship Shangdi, then each person will ascend to the Heavenly Paradise; come quickly, come quickly, worship Shangdi."[96]

The effort the Taiping expended to widely distribute this literature and to secure an audience for their message testifies to their confidence in their message and their mission. They seem to have been convinced that the more the people knew about Taiping doctrine and purpose, the more willing they would be to give allegiance to the movement. Was this confidence in the common people misplaced?

In addition to these official declarations and pronouncements, there was the mundane literature of everyday life, all of which further testified to the mission of the Heavenly Kingdom. An example of this is the memorial to the calendars the Taiping regime issued, proclaiming the religious legitimacy of the Heavenly Kingdom. Each prologue contained a statement such as "Now that our Heavenly Father, the High Lord and Supreme God [Shangzhu Huang Shangdi], has out of his great goodness sent down our sovereign into the world to become the sovereign of the Taiping, we consider that these are truly the days of great peace."[97] Bureaucratic documents that were a part of the routine workings of government were usually imprinted with "The Heavenly Father, the Heavenly Elder Brother and the Heavenly King" emblazoned across the top. These include such pedestrian documents as a business license for operating a salted meat shop, a cemetery title deed, a firewood receipt, and a land tax return.[98] Finally, even the currency alluded to the Taiping mission: each coin minted in the kingdom was stamped with the words "Sacred [or, Imperial] Treasury [*sheng ku*]."[99]

Beyond these declarations, proclamations, bureaucratic documents, and calendar notices, which were largely political in nature, was the specifically religious literature that poured out of the Taiping printing presses. In these the evangelical purpose of the sectarians was all the more evident.

A common feature of many Qing loyalist observer accounts is the list of Taiping publications they include, which in itself testifies to the wide and effective distribution of these materials. Zhang Dejian provides a list of nineteen titles that played an important role in the movement, including the Old Testament, the New Testament, the Ten Commandments, the *Three Character Classic,* and the *Land System of the Heavenly Dynasty.*[100] Although some scholars have emphasized other documents and other sources for the Taiping, it is instructive how these observers continue to point out literature that is most distinctively Christian in nature. And that is how it should be, for only this kind of literature received the Taiping imprimatur and appears on the Taiping lists of authorized texts. The Old and New Testaments, for example, appear both on the earliest and the latest lists of authorized works, whereas the documents discovered by Wang Qingcheng do not, nor does even *Good Words to Admonish the Age*.[101]

A loyalist named Wang Kun lamented the fact that the Taiping had broadcast (*chuanbo*) their "demon books" to the four corners of the empire. He used word play to refer to the new and old "cursed" books, replacing the character *zhao* in Xinyizhao (the New Testament) and Jiuyizhao (the Old Testament) with the character *zhou*, meaning "cursed."[102] This broadcast distribution of books was one of the first steps the Taiping took in establishing the new order in the cities they subjugated. One Qing observer stated that after the rebels and bandits entered Nanjing, they "distributed and scattered their false books and ordered that we chant and read them. There were titles such as the *Old Testament*, the false *Taiping Military Organization*, the false *Taiping Camp Regulations*, the *Ode to Youth*, . . . and the *Three Character Classic*."[103] Two other Nanjing observers provide similar lists, mentioning titles including the Old and New Testaments, the *Three Character Classic*, and the Ten Commandments.[104] These books were also used to educate the schoolchildren of the Heavenly Kingdom.

It is hard to know just how long this distribution of literature continued. Books were probably not as generously spread abroad in the later stage of the movement as in the early years, but broadsheets and declarations were posted everywhere the Taiping advanced through the final years of the Kingdom.

Alongside questions of the duration of their mission, there are questions of place. Just how far did their evangelistic crusade reach? To be sure, the physical and ideological impact of the Taiping was strongest in cities along the Yangzi River that the Taiping occupied for two years or more, such as Wuchang (capital of Taiping Hubei province; governed from June 1854 to December 1856), Anqing (capital of Taiping Anhui province; governed from June 1853 to September 1861), Jiujiang (capital of Taiping Jiangxi province; governed from September 1853 to May 1858), and later Hangzhou (capital of Taiping Zhejiang province; governed from December 1861 to March 1864) and Suzhou (capital of Taiping Su-fu province; governed from June 1860 to December 1863).[105] Each of these cities was large and influential, and we can assume that in them the more sympathetic residents would have been totally indoctrinated through sermons, prayers, and hymns, along with literature such as the *Three Character Classic*, and that their children would have learned much of the doctrinal corpus at Taiping schools.[106] Even residents hostile to the new order but unable to flee—and who would have resisted indoctrination—would have been familiar with all aspects of the Taiping faith, as is proved true from each of these observers' accounts.

This list of cities does not include those of lesser importance in Taiping-controlled areas, or those the Taiping held for a brief time only to be driven out, or from which they chose to pull back. Some of these may have been under Taiping control only for several months, which would still have given the residents enough time to become familiar with the Taiping creed. The number of such cities is not small. Yongan, in Guangxi, was occupied for seven months; Yangzhou traded hands a number of times; Jiaying, Guangdong, was captured twice by the Taiping (in 1859 and 1865); Linqing, Shandong, fell to the Taiping in 1854. We have not even considered the cities that were captured during the Northern Campaign or were overrun by Shi Dakai, the "Wing King" during his independent campaigns in Fujian and in the west.[107] We have not included cities occupied and governed by groups allied with the Taiping, such as the Chinese city of Shanghai, which was ruled by the Small Sword Society, a traditional secret society, and the cities and towns of the Huai River Valley, which were taken over by the Nian rebels, one of the few popular groups that did have ties to the Taiping (their rebellion lasted from 1851 to 1868). Augustus Lindley offers an anecdote about the inventiveness of the Taiping proselytizing campaigns: in one encounter, the Taiping even floated copies of the Old and New Testaments downstream in the hope that Imperialist sailors would read them and convert.[108]

This kind of propaganda campaign was active not only in the areas the Taiping and their allies controlled. The Qing disseminated information about Taiping doctrine to the Chinese public in the areas they themselves controlled. In their efforts to win the propaganda war, the Qing had to address Taiping doctrines and formulate responses. Their observer accounts are records of just this very process. Many accounts were written in the 1850s but were published only after the Taiping capital fell in 1864 and the rebellion was suppressed, thus finding new life in the period of reconstruction, when the gentry took the lead not only in rebuilding the dikes and restoring the administration of Taiping China to the Qing, but also in reconstructing the ideological world of the common people.

How challenging a task did the gentry face in this regard? What was the impact of all this Taiping iconoclasm—the smashing of the idols, the slaying and demonization of Manchus, the assault on the imperial office as a blasphemous transgression of Shangdi's holy name—on popular thinking? Rev. Joseph Edkins succinctly summarizes the religious impact of Taiping iconoclasm while visiting Suzhou after the fall of the Heavenly Kingdom: "The rebels have shown their scorn of the idols, by chopping off their noses, and placing them in ridiculous attitudes. A blow has been inflicted on Chinese idolatry, by the actors in this movement, such as it has never received."[109] The Taiping controlled vast stretches of both the middle and the lower Yangzi Valley for years, whole provinces in some of China's most populous and wealthiest regions, and hundreds of thousands were enlisted to fight for their cause. Millions more witnessed the leveled temples and crowded around the declarations denouncing the emperor. Did these events yield changes in the popular perception of imperial legitimacy?

Qing loyalist armies broke through the walls of the Heavenly Capital in 1864, and all the Heavenly soldiers fell by the sword. Did the people regard the defeat of the Taiping as just deserts for their attack on the old order and the hardened-clay gods, or did they see the Taiping as martyrs who were sacrificed in a just cause? The gentry's interpretation of the Taiping defeat has been meticulously chronicled in observer accounts. But where is the interpretation of the common people? Where are their accounts?

Unfortunately, such accounts are not available. Beyond these gentry accounts of the impact of the Taiping, there is only one other kind of record that documents the legacy of the Taiping, and these records belong to the Christian missionary enterprise in the period following the rebellion.

5
The Taiping Legacy and Missionary Christianity

After the fall of the Taiping Heavenly Kingdom in 1864, the victorious Qing imperial government moved quickly to efface all memory of the Taiping and their challenge to empire. Only one aspect of the Taiping legacy survived, and that was its connections to missionary Christianity. Yet it would not be the Protestants who would suffer most from this association, but the Catholics, the Heavenly Lord sect, since they were the only form of missionary Christianity present in the provinces at this time. During the era of proscription, the Heavenly Lord sect was regarded more as a heterodox than alien creed. The authorities identified the sect with native Chinese heterodoxies. This perception changed with the Opium War and consequent treaties. Beginning with the Tianjin Treaty (1858), which legalized the practice of the Heavenly Lord sect outside the treaty ports, Chinese officials moved the Heavenly Lord sect from the official category of illegal and heterodox, identified with native sects, to that of legal and heterodox, identified with foreign ones.

The circumstances of the Taiping Rebellion called into question the wisdom of establishing this new legal status for the Heavenly Lord sect. Indeed, the rebellion radically changed the official assessment of the sect as peaceful, although heterodox. Catholic sectarians were now regarded as more threatening to the status quo than Buddhist sectarians. During the rebellion, Chinese officials and gentry began to view the Heavenly Lord sect (and in time, Chinese Protestants as well) as a challenge not only to the political status quo, but also as a threat to the entire Confucian and imperial order. In one gentry-sponsored tract (examined at length later in this chapter), Chinese officials and gentry accused the Heavenly Lord sect of embodying every imaginable evil of sectarian heterodoxy, from moral turpitude to political rebelliousness.

This change in the official attitude toward the Heavenly Lord sect was wholly a result of the sect's identification with the Taiping rebels. Moreover, the hostile reaction of gentry and officials to the Heavenly Lord sect during and following the rebellion underscores their fear of the Taiping restorationist appeal and hatred of its iconoclastic message. While Hong Xiuquan's call to return to the classical religion echoes Matteo Ricci's earlier call, Ricci had never attacked the imperial institution as blasphemous, and he had never advocated a return to the political institutions of the classical period.

Ordinary reference to the Taiping rebels in government documents was made by the terms Yuefei (Guangdong/Guangxi bandits) or *changfa fei* (long-haired bandits). When the documents did identify the rebels beyond this, and especially when they sought to specify the source of the Taiping religious doctrines, officials and gentry observers alike associated them with the Heavenly Lord sect. Reports from Wuchang, Nanjing, Yangzhou, and Suzhou all describe the Taiping religion as being of the sect.[1] For example, this description of the Taiping religion comes from an account written during the occupation of Suzhou:

> Amidst the rebels [*zei*] is practiced the religion of the Heavenly Lord. It is the same as that practiced by the Western barbarians. Every seventh day they worship, at which time they chant a twenty-eight line hymn whose first line reads, "Praise be to the High Heaven." The third line reads, "Praise be to the Heavenly Father." The fifth line reads, "Praise be to the Heavenly Elder Brother [Tianxiong]." This Tianxiong is the barbarians' so-called Jesus.[2]

The pointed description of the Heavenly Lord sect as originating with the Western barbarians and resulting in the Taiping sect was everywhere assumed in official accounts.

The identification between the two groups was a matter of course, given the similarity of the Heavenly Lord and Taiping teachings. For example, in his chapter on the religion of the Taiping, Zhang Dejian, chief of intelligence for the loyalist general Zeng Guofan, devotes almost as much attention to the Heavenly Lord sect as to the Taiping, even providing a brief history of the coming of the Heavenly Lord sect to China with the Western missionary Li Madou (Matteo Ricci).

A gentry account of the fall of Wuchang describes how, soon after the Taiping scaled the walls, they began propagating such teachings as the Heavenly Father's creation of the earth, hills, and rivers in seven days and seven nights. The observer concludes that "it is all trusting in gods and ghosts, trying to stir up and frighten, together with White Lotus and Heavenly Lord sectarian bandits, only these bandits [i.e., the Taiping] are even more perverse."[3] A few observer accounts point to the custom of dividing up time into seven-day weeks, with the seventh day set aside for a day of worship.[4] Others remark on the shared propensity of Taipings and Catholics to smash idols and raze temples.[5]

This identification quite naturally led to a perception among officials and observers alike that the Taiping sectarian rebels were a branch of the Heavenly Lord sect: the Heavenly Lord sect had somehow given rise to the Taiping. For example, in 1853, the acting governor-general of Liangguang, Ye Mingchen, reported that he had seized a common bandit by the name of Ling Shiba, who "had in the twenty-ninth year of Daoguang [1850] at Jintian in Guangxi Province linked up with Hong Xiuquan [the wrong character is used here for *quan*] and the rest. Because the name of the Heavenly Lord sect had already been around too long, they changed the name to the Shangdi society, and together they swore allegiance [*jiebai*, a secret-society term] to that same criminal."[6] This view that the Society of God Worshippers had evolved out of the Heavenly Lord sect and had simply changed its name was repeated almost verbatim in several Qing observer accounts.

In the chapter of his reconnaissance report for Zeng Guofan devoted to the "bandit religion," Zhang Dejian recounts how White Lotus and Eight Trigrams sectarians had used religion to stir up the common people in past rebellions. Zhang notes that Guangdong and Guangxi had many followers of the Heavenly Lord sect (these two provinces actually represented a very small contingent) who, under persecution from the authorities, concealed their name by changing the term *jiao* (teaching) to *hui* (society—i.e., signifying a secret society), so that there were now such names as Shangdi Hui (Society of God), Tiandi Hui (Increasing Brothers Society), and Xiaodao Hui (Small Sword Society). Zhang traces the genealogy of the Taiping:

> Hong and the other rebels, when they first swore brotherhood, called themselves the Shangdi Hui. Then they changed the name to the Tiandi Hui [Heavenly Emperor Society], and also went under the name of the Tiandi Hui [Increasing Brothers Society]. This is why all those who enter these societies, irregardless of whether they are old or young, afterwards all consider each other brother. Even though there have been these multiple changes in the name, in substance it is all still the Heavenly Lord sect [Tianzhu jiao].[7]

This is a fairly broad sweep. The Heavenly Lord sect is depicted as the origin of not only the Taiping but of all the secret societies as well.

A similar account was recorded by a Qing loyalist in the early years of the rebellion:

> A villainous man from Guangdong by the name of Zhu Jiutao set up the Shangdi Hui. The rebel Hong, along with Feng Yunshan, began to take him as their teacher, and then afterwards, because they could not recruit a big enough following, they established a Heaven and Earth Society also going by the name of the Triad Society. After this, because in recent years the Heavenly Lord sect has become quite flourishing, they wanted to ride it, and so they hopped on.[8]

In this telling of the history, the Society of God Worshippers did not arise from the Heavenly Lord sect, but linked up with them early on in their development.

This identification of the Taiping rebels with Heavenly Lord sectarians alarmed Catholic missionaries. The allegation of a Catholic conspiracy with the Taiping imperiled the entire mission and the mass of believers. In the earliest stages of the rebellion, Catholic missionaries reported to superiors that Chinese officials were linking the Taiping and the Heavenly Lord sect.

One such report submitted by an Italian Franciscan missionary concerned the state of the Catholic church in Hunan and Hubei at the time of the Taiping campaign there:

> The extraordinary conduct on the part of the rebels renders it impossible to say to what religion they belong, or what form of worship they are thinking of establishing in China.... Now, as the destruction of the temples and the idols is an act opposed to the principles of all the pagan sects, not excepting that of Confucius, the government of the celestial empire is beginning to believe that the leaders and instigators of the rebellion are Christians, and supports this suspicion on the fact that, of all the religions in China, the Gospel is the only one professing the hatred of idols and the worship of them. My couriers assure me that lately, in consequence of this suspicion, the imperial government has made a prisoner of an old man of upwards of sixty years of age, who is well known to me, and whom all the Christians hold in great veneration, as being the principal catechist in the province of Hou-nan. On his premises were found a few treatises against idolatry, and this circumstance has aggravated his fault in the eyes of the authorities, who have declared the doctrine of these books conformable to that of the insurgents.[9]

The missionary reasoned that the rebels could not be followers of the Heavenly Lord sect because the words "Xam-ti houoei" (Religion of the Supreme Emperor) were inscribed on the banners leading them into battle. "Who is not aware," wrote the missionary, "that Benedict XIV forbade the Missioners to make use of these two words [the early Catholic romanization of Shangdi Hui was Xam-ti houoei] to represent the name of God, because these words, expressing only the great and supreme emperor, were inadequate to express the name of the omnipotent God." He nevertheless lamented the fact that the imperial authorities were not in the habit of making such fine distinctions among heterodox sects. The same missionary admitted, in a later report, that missionary protestations of innocence were certainly muted when it was discovered that the Taiping had destroyed all the temples in the city but spared the Catholic church.[10]

There may have been more substance to these allegations of conspiracy than Catholic missionaries dared to admit. One Western report suggests that Heavenly Lord sectarians were indeed going over to the Taiping. Captain E. G. Fishbourne found in his contacts with Taiping followers that "one or two told us they were worshippers of T'ien-chu [Tianzhu], by which I understand them to say that they were different from others in the movement, and they appeared not to wish it to be generally known that they said so; it might be that they meant to say merely that they had been such, until they had joined the movement."[11] This is the only reference in Western reports to such contacts.

Missionary correspondence more often revealed that the Taiping often did not know what to do with Catholic believers. Were Catholics followers of Shangdi, or were they worshippers of images? Some Western reports described how the Taiping persecuted Heavenly Lord sectarians, and others described how the Taiping protected them. For example, the Catholic bishop of Nanjing recounted how, when the Taipings captured his city, the Catholics were ordered to pray to Tianfu (Heavenly Father). According to the bishop's account, the Catholics answered that they were Heavenly Lord sectarians and did not know any other religion, and could not pray to the Heavenly Father. They were commanded again to recite a prayer to the Heavenly Father but remained steadfast in their refusal. Some of the men later relented since they considered that the prayer "contained nothing contrary to our Holy Religion." These same men, however, later expressed contrition for their lack of faith.

This account is puzzling in that the Heavenly Lord sect had many prayers addressed to the Heavenly Father. The bishop was no doubt antagonistic toward the Taiping for shutting down his church and killing some of his followers (deaths that appear to have been a circumstance of the fighting and not a result of their religion); perhaps this antagonism distorted his description of the events that transpired.

Other reports offer dramatically different characterizations of the treatment of Catholics at the hands of the Taiping. A Catholic missionary who visited Taiping territory aboard the *Cassini* found the Taiping much more accommodating to the needs of the Heavenly Lord sectarians than Qing armies had been. The Taiping promised one missionary that they would treat Catholics as brethren "because they worshipped the Heavenly Father." The missionary concluded that "Our Christians have not been maltreated in so far as they are Christians, and if a cross and images have been destroyed at the hands of some subordinates, the chiefs have received such things from ours—with much respect."[12] A missionary report submitted from Jiangxi confirmed that when the Taiping learned that the Heavenly Lord sectarians called on the name of Jesus and combated idolatry, the Taiping respected them and were even described as being "favourably disposed towards us."[13]

An apologetic tract published during the rebellion addresses the official suspicions of an alliance between Heavenly Lord sectarians and the Taiping. It is no accident that this work, *A Treasured Raft which Rescues the Drowning* (Yuanni baofa),[14] was published in Hubei in the tenth year of the Xianfeng reign (1860), at the height of the rebellion. The general impression among gentry and officials that there was an active alliance between the Heavenly Lord sect and the Taiping was nowhere stronger than in Hubei and neighboring Hunan.

These two provinces served as recruiting grounds for both the Taiping and the Qing loyalist Hunan army during the Taiping Rebellion. Hunan also functioned as the ideological nerve center of the cultural war, first against the Taiping and then against the Heavenly Lord sect. Zeng Guofan's Hunan headquarters poured out some of the most vituperative literature employed in this battle.

Hubei and Hunan had always been a stronghold of the Heavenly Lord sect. As early as 1844 the two provinces formed one of four vicariate apostolics, and included some 18,000 believers in 100 congregations.[15] In spite of the depredation of the rebellion, the numbers held constant, with the ranks of those who had fallen during the war being filled by new converts. In 1856 the provinces were split into two different vicariates. By 1866, Hubei, which earlier had by far the greater number of believers, still had 16,000, and in that year alone gained 321 more through adult baptisms (i.e., converts to the faith).[16]

A Treasured Raft which Rescues the Drowning was intended to be both an encouragement to the faithful and an apologetic treatise aimed at rescuing "those who are drowning in Buddhist and Daoist" heterodoxies. Although 1860 was not an auspicious time to publish this tract, it was necessary to do so, for the Heavenly Lord sectarians had become subjects of rumors and objects of contempt. They were accused of heterodoxy of the most egregious kind, that leading to rebellion.

The arrival of the Guangxi rebels made the publication of this tract even more urgent. The authors pointed out to their devout readers why their good and orthodox religion was being maligned. It was jealousy, the native preachers explained, that incites people to create falsehoods and spread rumors. "So it is that when the Guangxi rebels rose up that people speculated, saying that they were part of the Heavenly Lord sect; when Hunan's Gedi Hui [Elder and Younger Brother Society] gathered together, people gave voice to their suspicions, saying that they also were part of the Heavenly Lord Sect."[17] The authors sought to reassure the followers of the Heavenly Lord sect that they neither aided heterodoxy nor abetted rebellion.

THE FACTS OF HETERODOXY

The case for collusion between Taiping rebels and Catholics was made much more powerfully by a Qing loyalist tract, the notorious and salacious *A Record of Facts to Ward Off Heterodoxy* (Bixie jishi), which was also published by a Hunan press during the final years of the Taiping Rebellion. This publication enjoyed a long career, starring in several different anti-Catholic and, later, anti-missionary productions. Paul Cohen, in his influential *China and Christianity: The Missionary Movement and the Growth of Chinese Anti-Foreignism, 1860–1870*, spotlights the role the text played in "the anti-foreignism" of the 1860s, which he associates with the growth of the missionary movement. This tract played an even more critical role in the Taiping Rebellion.

A Record of Facts to Ward Off Heterodoxy first appeared in events that preceded the "anti-foreignism" of the 1860s. The author targeted the Heavenly Lord sect in part because of its alleged connection to the Taiping rebels. The author associated the doctrine and practices of the Heavenly Lord sect with the Taiping movement, and he found them to be equally damaging to the imperial order.

The version of the text I consulted is that which Cohen used. Although published in the tenth year of the Tongzhi reign (1871), the title page notes that the edition is a reprint; both prefaces, from 1861 and 1862, were composed while the rebellion was still raging.[18] The earlier preface identifies the author only as "the person whose heart is the most wounded under Heaven." Cohen concluded that the ultimate responsibility for the tract lay with Zeng Guofan, the Hunan army general. In an appendix, Cohen notes how a Chinese Catholic scholar claimed that this work was composed by Zeng's headquarters for use in their ideological campaign against the Taiping. This claim can be easily substantiated by an analysis of the work's content.

The one "whose heart is most wounded" begins his propaganda piece with a quote, several pages in length, from the section of *The Sacred Edict* (a collection of Confucian maxims first compiled by Emperor Kangxi in the early Qing dynasty) concerning heterodoxy. The table of contents features the chapters: "A Collection of Sayings Concerning the Heavenly Lord Sect," "An Outline of the Heavenly Lord Sect's Entrance into China," "A Discussion about Warding Off Heterodoxy," "Miscellaneous Quotes," "Criticizing and Disputing Heterodox Teachings," and "Testimonials." An appendix includes a "Warding Off Heterodoxy" song, a manual on setting up local militias, and a discussion of the Elder Brother Society (a secret society that arose at the time of the Taiping Rebellion). This anthology is similar to sectarian prosecution manuals such as *A Detailed Refutation of Heterodoxy* (Poxie xiangbian), which was published immediately prior to the Taiping uprising (and was then reprinted in 1883) and which was used against Buddhist sectarians. Such texts served as guidebooks for use in local ideological emergencies.

In the introductory chapter to *A Record of Facts to Ward Off Heterodoxy*, the author discusses the origins of the Heavenly Lord sect and its founder, Jesus. Some comments are necessary here, especially in light of the relationship between the Taiping and the Heavenly Lord sect, for the very first paragraph describes how those who practice this religion slanderously declare that "Jesus is Shangdi incarnate" *(Yesu ben Shangdi huashen)* and further identify Jesus as Tianxiong (Heavenly Elder Brother).[19] These "true facts" are a little distorted, since Catholics did not speak of Shangdi after the Rites Controversy and never had called Jesus the Heavenly Elder Brother. The Taiping, on the other hand, did employ these terms.

The author never discusses the Heavenly Lord sect's association with the Taiping. He merely asserts it. He does point out in a couple of places that the Heavenly Lord religion was that to which the Taiping gave their allegiance. For example, in chapter 1, after having examined the perverseness of the sect in both its moral and political dimensions, the author says of the Heavenly Lord's association with the Taiping: "This being so, our country early on prohibited and severely restricted the [Heavenly Lord] sect. Those who propagated and practiced it then did not dare to gather together or reveal their vile form, down to the latter years of Daoguang. Thereupon, the bandits Yang Xiuqing and Hong Xiuquan [the Taiping Eastern King and the Heavenly King] and the others, in the name of this very religion gathered a following and began to stir up chaos."[20]

After this the salacious character of the tract quickly manifests itself, and this is what caused the missionaries to hesitate somewhat before publishing their translation of the related tract *Death Blow to Corrupt Doctrines*. The missionaries were "aware that serious objections may be urged against publishing in English a book so full of obscenity" but did not want to seem too squeamish to expose human depravity. So they forged ahead, concluding that post-Taiping attacks on missionaries warranted its perusal by the foreign community.

The missionary translators were prudent to issue this warning about the obscene contents of the tract, for the allegations in the tract they translated and in *A Record of Facts to Ward Off Heterodoxy* did tend toward the lurid. One oft-quoted accusation claimed that Catholic missionaries scooped the eyeballs out of the dead in order to brew magical potions and prepare evil concoctions. Another stated that the Heavenly Lord sectarians smeared menstrual discharge on their faces in preparation for worship. A third charged that a man who had "unintentionally" peeked through a neighbor's wall had witnessed a father and son, who were well-known adherents of the Heavenly Lord sect, engaging in all kinds of illicit relations with each other.[21] Much of the first part of the tract is devoted to this kind of slander.

But not all of the work is of this temper. One chapter lifted out of a work by the seventeenth-century critic of Jesuit Christianity, Yang Guangxian, and one written by the one "whose heart is most wounded" titled "Criticisms and Disputations of Heterodox Doctrines" are actually reasoned examinations of the Heavenly Lord Doctrine. The "Criticisms" chapter is directed at the Heavenly Lord sect but must be based on a Protestant pamphlet, since the author refers to Shangdi throughout and when discussing the sacraments lists only baptism and communion.

The anonymous author treats the material in a serious manner, although he employs a substantial dose of sarcasm when he wants to deliver his point with particular force. He begins with the doctrines of heaven and hell, which were favorite targets of the Buddhist anti-sectarian manual *A Detailed Refutation of Heterodoxy*. He discusses God (Shangdi), wondering why, when God himself has commanded that men not add to the name of Shangdi, he is called by so many names—Yehehua, Heavenly Father, Shangdi, Heavenly Lord. And, although Jesus committed no sin, keeping Shangdi's commands completely, why was he punished by the Kingdom of Israel for transgressing its laws?

Then there was the matter of God's Kingdom ("Shangdi's Kingdom," not Heavenly Kingdom, the name the Taiping favored). If there were two kingdoms, as the Heavenly Lord doctrine states, the kingdom of God and that of the devil, and those who revere Shangdi belong to the former and are therefore called the "people of God," did all the ancient and worthy sages of the Chinese empire, along with all rulers and ministers of the Great Qing, who did not know about or follow Jesus, then belong to the devil? Moreover, did this mean that the Yue bandits (i.e., the Taiping), who adhered to this religion and were instigating such tumult, were the people of God as well?[22] The prosecutor, satisfied with exposing the true nature of the sect, then rests his case.

In order to avoid such heterodox teachings and to properly indoctrinate the illiterate in orthodox teachings, the "person whose heart is the most wounded under Heaven" includes the "Warding Off Heterodoxy Song," a long tune of 294 lines, with seven characters to a line, which encapsulates the main points of the preceding chapters. While directed at the Heavenly Lord sect, it contains vocabulary more properly suited to the Taiping. There is a reference to God the Creator as "the Heavenly King" and to the Heavenly Lord as both Shengzi (the Holy Son) and Tianxiong (Heavenly Elder Brother, a title used exclusively by the Taiping)[23] in addition to multiple references to Shangdi.

In this song, as in the body of his tract, the author makes the connection between the Heavenly Lord sect and the Taiping explicit:

> In the final years of Daoguang, the disaster gradually started to sprout, Hong Xiuquan and Yang Xiuqing holding high this heterodox religion in like manner chaos brought about. Spreading out from the southeast it became the great calamity, these ten-odd years we have not been able to enjoy peace and security. The perverse barbarians [referring to Europeans] ascertained China's situation, they knew about the heterodox religion and the sectarian bandits' devotion, in the chengwu year, they entered Guangdong and began a commotion.[24]

One of the more intriguing parts of this song describes the terms which the sectarian bandits—whether these are Taiping bandits or Heavenly Lord bandits is not clear—use to refer to death resulting from persecution: "Death has three levels of holy status," determined by the kind of death one suffers. It is evident that all of these are punishments imposed by the state, with the one achieving the highest stage of holiness being death by dismemberment. Immediately following this description is a reference to an image the sectarians used to describe the death they suffer: "If one then transgresses the laws of the empire, and so has his life taken from him, this is called putting on a red robe, and ascending to Heaven."[25]

This image of putting on the red robe of martyrdom is critical for understanding sectarian life prior to, during, and after the rebellion. For this phrase is a word-for-word parallel to that found in *A Detailed Refutation of Heterodoxy*. That text was also a sectarian suppression manual, but it was directed at Buddhists and written by another government official who denounced the Buddhists for their refusal to recognize that the sword of the state would prevail in the struggle against the sectarians. In both that manual and this one the sectarians are depicted as responding to government threats by claiming that Heaven was taking their side and would drape them in the red robe. Thus, in martyrdom the doctrinal differences of the various sects—Taiping, White Lotus, and Heavenly Lord—disappear. What does this correspondence tell us about the Taiping legacy? First, sectarian heterodoxy was targeted both during and after the rebellion. But even more significantly, different sectarians had adopted a similar vocabulary for describing their suffering at the hands of the state. They—not the state, the officials, or the gentry—were on the side of justice and would be vindicated by Heaven.

The government was making threats, and they were not idle ones. The appendix following this song confirms the intention of the authorities to follow up on their threats. This appendix, *Methods of Militia Defense* (Tuanfangfa), is a ten-page instruction guide covering twenty different regulations of successful militia organization. Not published for everyday, generic village defense, this guide specifically targeted the defensive needs arising out of the Taiping Rebellion.

Paramount in this cultural war was constructing an effective ideological defense. Nine of the twenty regulations explicitly deal with ideological matters, and many of these specifically concern how to ferret out hidden Heavenly Lord sectarians. The primary target of this ideological campaign was the crypto-Catholicism of the Taiping rebels. Eliminating Heavenly Lord sectarians and other heterodox sectarians apparently was the first battle in the long war against the host of heterodox forces.

Though most of these regulations are phrased negatively, the fourth, which deals with religion, is positive in intent:

> Regardless of whether one belongs to an official, gentry, scholar or common person's household, in the middle of the hall [in the household] one must set up a shrine. One must offer worship to a tablet on which is inscribed these five characters: Heaven, earth, ruler, family, teacher. One must also offer worship to one's ancestors and the ancestral tablet. In each season of the year, the head of every militia unit must call together a meeting of the militia group. At this time, he should inspect every household to see whether such a shrine has been set up.[26]

Only in this way, the manual instructs, can the strong temptation of heterodox religion be resisted.

The positive work of indoctrination in good religious habits was not, though, considered sufficient. The remaining regulations, which call for expunging bad religious habits, are led off by a peculiar one, quoted here in full:

At the threshold [*yu*, "house threshold," and by extension, "city gate"] to every city, there should be etched in stone the figure of Jesus nailed to the cross. It should be carved according to this form: he should have no beard, his body should be naked, his hair disheveled, his two hands stretched out, with the left foot placed on top of the right. His head should lean to the right. At every port and every important pass there likewise should be etched this figure. On the ground of every street, of every market, of every village, and even on the threshold of every home, there should be this likeness. If anyone is unwilling to have this likeness etched, then he shall be considered a follower of heterodox religion. The militia unit head should hire a stone carver and order every family to comply.[27]

Some background is needed to understand the import of this regulation. During the period of Catholic proscription, officials compelled followers of the Heavenly Lord sect to step on and trample crucifixes in order to signify that they had recanted their belief in the heterodox sect. In the context of the Taiping Rebellion, this practice was now extended to households and even whole cities. The depiction of Jesus is a degrading image, with disheveled hair and without even the dignity of a loincloth—represented in a manner that therefore would magnify the shame of being executed as a criminal.

And what happened to those heterodox individuals who were not identified by this method? It became the responsibility of their families to expose their crime. At this point, there is no talk of recanting, there is only talk of imposing the death penalty, and imposing it immediately. The eleventh regulation demands, "Every family lineage must establish a lineage militia. If there are any in the lineage who follow a heterodox religion, and that person is discovered, then he must be bound up and transported to the lineage shrine where he is to be put to death. This should be quick and easy." ("Quick and easy" probably means not having to wait for the autumn assizes or not having to bring the accused to the magistrate's yamen.) That the guide called for the heterodox to be executed in the lineage shrine is telling. This was as much a religious war as it was a military battle.

The regulations make explicit that this guide equates heterodox religion with the Heavenly Lord sect. The head of each militia was required to read to his men from the Qing law code concerning the sect annually, and any Heavenly Lord sectarians were to be punished according to the code; there would be no excuse for misunderstanding.[28]

It is not known how many Heavenly Lord sectarians lost their lives in the Taiping Rebellion. To the official mind, as is evident in this manual, there was little difference between a Catholic believer, a Taiping adherent, and even a White Lotus follower. Most missionaries reported such losses only in the most general of terms, and then the deaths were attributed mainly to the cataclysm of the times.

And what of other sectarians? Although we do not know how many White Lotus and other Buddhist sectarians fell under the sword of the state, caught up in the net Qing officials set for the heterodox, we can assume that along with the hundreds of thousands of Taiping sectarians who perished in the conflict, and perhaps the thousands of Heavenly Lord sectarians, there were a significant number of Buddhist sectarians as well.

THE LEGACY OF THE TAIPING RELIGION IN WESTERN AND CHINESE MEMORY

After the signing of the 1858 Tianjin Treaty and the fall of the Taiping Heavenly Kingdom, the Heavenly Lord sect emerged from the shadows into the full light of legality, if not orthodoxy. While the memory of the Heavenly Lord sect's connections to the Taiping rebels may have continued to influence how Chinese officials viewed the Catholic and Protestant mission enterprise (*A Record of Facts to Ward Off Heterodoxy* was published with two different prefaces, the last being 1871), Western missionaries quickly acted to exorcise that memory, airbrushing their connections to the Taiping right out of the mural of Chinese Christianity. As incongruous as it may seem, and in contrast to how the Taiping legacy was regarded by Chinese officials, gentry, and common people, it appears from all the evidence that the Western missionaries summarily dismissed and wholly ignored the Taiping message about the blasphemy of empire. The missionaries learned little from the Taiping Rebellion and even less from the Taiping efforts towards the indigenization of Christianity. Indeed, the Christian faith became identified with imperialism and the West in a way it had never been prior to the rebellion.

Catholic converts had been most affected by the rebellion, yet Catholic missionaries seem to have been most oblivious to the changes the Taiping had sought to sow in Chinese society. For example, a Catholic version of the Ten Commandments, *A Discussion of The Holy Record of the Ten Prohibitions of the Heavenly Lord* (Tianzhu sheng jiao shijie quanlun shengji), appeared soon after the defeat of the Taiping.[29] While it is a reprint of a work first published in 1650, there is no sense of changed circumstances in the pages of this reprint, even though the missionaries themselves had recognized that the core of the Taiping faith was the decalogue and that the Taiping were referred to as the "Ten Commandments people." This was a missed opportunity. The Catholic missionaries might have published a preface to this work that discussed the Taiping and the Ten Commandments, but not even one line of commentary refers to the rebel religion. Evidently the missionaries did not feel this kind of explanation was necessary.

Instead, this piece of doctrinal literature is a traditional presentation of the commandments. For example, in the discussion of the first two commandments, which deal with idolatry and blasphemy, no reference is made to the Taiping smashing idols or to their accusation of blasphemy. Instead, the first commandment only declares, "Worship one Heavenly Lord [Tianzhu] above all the ten thousand things," which would have provided a natural context for such a discussion. Most of the pages of this publication concentrate on defending Catholic practices such as the use of Catholic "statues" in worship, while condemning the use of "idols" in Buddhist worship. In the discussion of statues and idols, an opportunity existed to speak to issues of idolatry and iconoclasm, since Catholic statues had been shattered along with Buddhist idols, but this opportunity also was passed by.

Nor does the discussion of the second commandment address the issue of blasphemy, which was the main thrust of the Taiping assault on the imperial office. Indeed, this discussion seems, when not just provincial, insulting in its superficiality. It is entirely focused on what Europeans took to be the import of the commandment, which from the catechism seems to be limited to rashly using God's name in making an oath. No consideration of the Taiping charge that the emperor had usurped the place of Shangdi is present in this doctrinal statement, nor is there a discussion of the different names of God. The names of Shangdi, or even Heavenly Father, do not appear on these pages. Rather than publishing a revision of the decalogue that could have spoken to the changes the Taiping made, or even discussed in a preface a Catholic response to the Taiping religious challenge, the missionaries published a reprint of a text with no acknowledgement of a different historical situation and a transformed historical context.

The Protestant record is not much brighter. Hong had first learned Christianity through Protestant missionaries, and throughout the period of the Heavenly Kingdom, he maintained regular contact with them. Surely, the Taiping Rebellion would have had a transformational impact on Protestant literature. This was not the case. Protestant catechisms, too, continued to follow a traditional format, usually presenting the Ten Commandments, the Lord's Prayer, and the Apostles' Creed, along with a short discussion of the church and sacraments, all in a question-and-answer format. One would expect that the missionaries would have noted ideas introduced in the rebellion in the discussion of these key documents of the church, but the lack of any reference to Taiping ideas and terminology in these discussions testifies to the virtual denial of the Taiping impact.

The third commandment, that prohibiting use of the Lord's name in vain, appears in various forms in the different catechisms. In a version attributed to Liang Afa, which bears the characteristic influence of Robert Morrison, the commandment reads, "People are not permitted to carelessly call on or blasphemously speak the name of the God of Heaven, Shangdi."[30] Morrison's colleague, Rev. William Milne, translated the third commandment, "You shall not in any instance vainly or recklessly call upon the Divine Lord [Shenzhu], your god's name."[31]

No changes in the presentation of these documents or in the accompanying discussion of points of doctrine appeared in the wake of the rebellion. A catechism published by Milne's son during the vigorous years of the Taiping movement featured this rendition of the commandment: "The name of your Shangdi Yehehua [transliteration of "Jehovah"], you shall not vainly call out; he who vainly calls out the name will commit a sin which cannot be forgiven."[32] Here, along with a bad translation, the Chinese convert received bad theology (that there is a sin that cannot be forgiven). A catechism published in Beijing in 1873, reflecting the long and continuous Catholic tradition in and around the capital, which was swimming against the tide of Protestant tradition elsewhere, prohibits vainly calling on "Your Heavenly Lord [i.e., Tianzhu] Yehehua's name."[33] These texts still do not translate the name of God consistently, yet there is also no indication that the missionaries referred to the Taiping experience in sorting out this inconsistency. The question of exactly whose name the third commandment prohibits the convert from blaspheming—the Divine Lord's, Shangdi Yehehua's, or the Heavenly Lord Yehehua's—is left unanalyzed.

Catechisms published after the rebellion show no evidence of a reexamination of the name of Shangdi in the light of the Taiping claim that the title of emperor was a form of blasphemy. Indeed, often these catechisms were simply mere reprints of catechisms published before the rebellion. Milne's *Young Scholar's Catechism* (Chuxue wenda), for example, was first printed in 1817 in the Jiaqing reign, but it was reprinted in much the same form in 1848, 1850, and 1892. This reprint was published with no revisions of the explanation of major terms and doctrines. Besides being an affront to the memory of the Taiping, that the reprint does not include a preface referring to the rebellion and its claims demonstrates a lack of respect for Chinese culture and society and for the changes that had occurred in the post-Taiping era.

Even though Protestant missionary work was often located in the very heartland of what was Taiping China, the birth, life, or death of the rebellion seems to have exercised no influence on the missionaries' choice of terminology or their explanation of doctrine. Shangdi was the name preferred by a slight margin of the authors of Protestant catechisms, but there was no real consensus. Nor did Catholic or Protestant missionaries address the issue of the Chinese term for "Christ," which transliterated as Jidu still retained its foreign feel. Learning from the Taiping experience, the missionaries might have experimented with a more meaningful term—a translation such as those chosen by the Taiping, either Tianzi (Son of Heaven) or Taizi (Crown Prince). But recognizing the political dimension of Christ's mission was a risk from which the apostles of the nineteenth century, unlike those apostles in the early church, shrank.

Nor did the missionaries appreciate Taiping efforts to integrate the Christian message with Chinese history and culture. Hong Xiuquan had placed China at the center of the world in a new, Christian adaptation of the traditional Sinocentric world order. This view was readily apparent in the Taiping version of the *Three Character Classic* (Sanzijing), which differed from both the traditional version and popular missionary versions in its reinterpretation of Chinese history in light of this new understanding of China's place in the world.[34]

The traditional Confucian version of this classic, which was fixed during the thirteenth century, served as a primer for Chinese children embarking on the arduous task of learning to read and write (it contains about five hundred different characters) and also served to introduce young minds to Confucian learning. The primer begins with a statement of faith in humanity, declaring that human nature is originally good. Most of the rest of the curriculum presents simple axioms promoting Confucian morality, with the three relationships of ruler and minister, father and son, and husband and wife being the capstone. The text also surveys books in the Confucian canon and finally turns its attention to history, beginning with the earliest dynasties and ending with the Song dynasty (960–1279), which was where history ended for the traditional *Three Character Classic*.

Several points of contrast with the Taiping version of the *Three Character Classic* deserve comment. The Taiping version begins in a very different place, with the Supreme God and His creation. It then introduces the nation of Israel and continues with this history for about one-third of the entire text, almost exclusively focusing on the story of Egypt's judgment and Israel's deliverance. A recounting of China's early history follows, which carefully emphasizes that the early Chinese people walked in Shangdi's ways. The kings had held their mandate to rule by virtue and justice, not by military force, and the kings thereby won the people's hearts. It was only with the Qin emperor, in the third century B.C.E., that the people were led astray. The Taiping version spells out how each dynasty after the Qin led China farther away from the Supreme God's ways. This historical narrative breaks off with the Song dynasty, but then resumes with Hong Xiuquan's ascension into heaven in 1837. The last part of the text concerns Hong's vision and the Taiping doctrines derived from it, ending with a litany of exhortations that emphasizes the importance of fearing Shangdi and keeping his commandments. In sum, the traditional version and the Taiping version define right doctrine and interpret Chinese history in radically different ways.

The Taiping version of the *Three Character Classic* contrasts even more sharply with the standard Protestant missionary version translated by Dr. Walter H. Medhurst, which was widely used in nineteenth-century evangelization. Although both versions begin with creation, after their opening lines they are completely different texts. The missionary version begins with the all-knowing and all-powerful nature of God. (Medhurst uncharacteristically refers to God as the "true Divine Lord" [*zhen* Shenzhu] and also as *shen*, but not as Shangdi. This nomenclature changed in a revision issued after Medhurst's death.) It then mentions the creation of humanity (Medhurst is careful to point out that human nature originally was good). The rest reads like a typical gospel tract that, although written in Chinese and in the format of the *Three Character Classic*, could have been published during any other century and at any other place. The topics covered are familiar: God and his nature; creation; the fall of man; Jesus' birth, death, and resurrection; and the means to salvation. Missionaries who issued a revision of this tract in 1870, following the fall of the Heavenly Capital, did not change these topics or add any new ones.

In this missionary version of the primer, there was not one mention of Chinese history or Chinese culture. Chinese students would learn that this true Divine Lord was concerned only with disembodied, ahistorical, culture-free souls. The Taiping version of the *Three Character Classic*, on the other hand, attempted to reclaim the Chinese past, placing that past in the more universal context of Shangdi's dealings with all humankind. Out of all the earth's peoples, the Sovereign on High (Shangdi) had singled out the Chinese for special favor, as he had appointed one of their number to serve as the Heavenly King. This sinification of Christianity by the Taiping did not affect how the missionaries presented their message.[35]

While Catholic and Protestant foreign missionaries may have felt that they could ignore the Taiping Rebellion, Chinese gentry and the common people did not forget the event or its connections to the Heavenly Lord and the Jidu (Protestant) sects.[36] The memory of the Taiping religion's association with the Heavenly Lord religion loomed large in the decades following the fall of Nanjing, the Heavenly Capital.

A CONTINUING LEGACY

The most important Taiping legacy was a continuation of the attack on and delegitimization of the old imperial order. The widespread conflation of the Taiping, White Lotus, and Heavenly Lord sects in the accounts of Qing loyalist observers and in publications such as *A Record of Facts to Ward Off Heterodoxy*, along with the tendency of White Lotus followers to convert to Christianity, shows that the Taiping legacy for the Heavenly Lord, Protestant, and even native Buddhist sects was a tradition of iconoclasm directed at the imperial office and the ascription of Heaven's approval to those persecuted by the government.

Even though missionaries worked to erase the connections between themselves and the Taiping, they could not nullify the doctrinal teachings common to Taiping and missionary Christianity. So it is that the essentials of the Taiping message continued to be proclaimed in the marketplaces and streets of formerly Taiping-administered cities, towns, and villages. Through the work of Catholic and Protestant missionaries and their Chinese evangelists, elements of the Taiping message continued to be preached throughout China, even while the evangelists seemingly ignored the Taiping legacy. How might former Taiping recruits and subjects have responded to hearing the missionary preaching of the Ten Commandments—the code that every recruit was required to memorize—and to hearing once again the commandments' condemnation of idolatry and its warnings against taking the name of Shangdi in vain? How might they have responded to hearing the sounds of doxologies wafting through the city? Would the stanzas that referred to the Heavenly King and to Jesus the Crown Prince have come to mind? While the missionaries and evangelists might have been oblivious to this legacy, it hardly seems that any Chinese person—be he woodgatherer supporter or gentry opponent—who lived through the years of the Taiping Rebellion could have failed to be reminded of it.

The missionaries could remain oblivious to the changes that the rebellion wrought in Chinese society, but the Chinese people—official, gentry, and peasant—could not. In doctrine and practice, the Chinese memory of Taiping iconoclasm, nationalism, and desacralization remained vivid, just as the wounds suffered during the struggle to promote these teachings remained fresh. The Taiping faith, this dynamic Chinese Christian faith, transformed not just the Taiping faithful, but affected to some extent how all Chinese thought about religion, the imperial office and title, and the entire traditional imperial and Confucian order.

Notes

INTRODUCTION

1. This success came when the religious commitment was at its strongest. As Kuhn comments in his chapter on the Taiping in *The Cambridge History of China*, "One may well ask whether, desperate for popular support, the Taipings hid their religious message under more traditionally acceptable nationalist appeals. An examination of these 1852-53 documents leads to the opposite conclusion." Kuhn, "The Taiping Rebellion," 276.

2. Deciding on the terms for describing various religious traditions and their adherents is always a difficult matter. For example, "popular Buddhist sectarians" would be a fairly accurate term for such groups. But some scholars would object to such terminology.

In describing these teachings and traditions as popular religion, I imply that the elite subscribed to these teachings and traditions but normally did not participate in the religious organizations that grew out of them. Concerning the label "Buddhist," Overmyer, in his study *Precious Volumes*, argues that these popular sects were a tradition apart from established Buddhism and Daoism, a fourth teaching, as it were. These groups often drew ideas from a number of different sources, including Confucianism, but the ideas and concepts seemed most heavily indebted to the Buddhist tradition. In *The White Lotus Teachings in Chinese Religious History*, ter Haar objects to using the term "sectarian" to refer to associations of believers. He recommends describing these associations as "religious groups," since he believes that "sectarian" is a pejorative term (the term was definitely used pejoratively in traditional China). A term like "cultists," on the other hand, would obviously impose a negative label on these groups.

3. These documents appear in Franz Michael's collection of Taiping docu-

ments, *The Taiping Rebellion*, translated in English. The Chinese-language originals appear in the collection of documents by Xiang et al., *Taiping Tianguo*.

4. Wagner, *Reenacting the Heavenly Vision*, 29.

5. Michael, *The Taiping Rebellion*, 2:57.

6. Wang Qingcheng, *Tianfu Tianxiong shengzhi*. This title does not appear on any of the lists of royally sanctioned works, though it is similar in content to one that does, the *Tianfu xiafan zhaoshu*. See Michael, *The Taiping Rebellion*, 2:86-97.

7. Ter Haar, "China's Inner Demons," 54-88.

8. The lists of these authorized works are dominated by texts whose content is strongly Taiping Christian. The lists are usually attached as an addendum to various documents. *Taiping Tianguo yinshu* offers several examples of these. See the page attached to "Treatises on the Establishment of the Heavenly Capital at Jinling" (416), published in 1853-54, which notes that only the twenty-one documents appearing on the list are royally sanctioned. The addendum attached to "Calendar by Imperial Sanction, the Eleventh Year" (718) pronounces that only the twenty-nine works appearing on this later list are sanctioned.

9. In his Chinese-language study of Taiping institutions, Jen does more explicitly characterize Taiping Christianity as a Chinese Christianity, similar to Greek Orthodoxy serving as a Greek Christianity and Coptic Christianity as an Egyptian Christianity. Jen, *Taiping Tianguo dianzhi tongkao*, 3:735-39, 2022.

10. This occurs in the Jiuyao (Nine Demons) Temple and is cited in *Taiping Heavenly Chronicle*. See Michael, *The Taiping Rebellion*, 2:72. Shangdi had conferred the title on Hong during his vision, but Hong only publicly announced his claim after visiting Rev. I. J. Roberts's chapel in Canton. Whether he made this claim at an earlier time does not seem to be of interest to the Taiping recorder of the event.

11. The most influential of these works studied the actual impact of the missionary movement in China. On the basis of their findings, however, the authors of these works usually argued for Chinese hostility towards the Christian religion. See Cohen's early study, *China and Christianity* and Gernet's more recent *China and the Christian Impact*. Work by such scholars as Standaert, Bays, and Mungello, along with several others, have mitigated somewhat the negative blow delivered by these influential works, and my hope is that this study on the Taiping contributes further to the efforts of these scholars.

1 / THE EARLY CATHOLIC SEARCH FOR THE NAME OF GOD

1. Zürcher believes that the missionary failure to resolve this contradiction of drawing nearer to Confucianism in some areas and to Buddhism in others was ultimately a greater factor than the Rites Controversy—which heated up during the reign of the Emperor Kangxi (1662–1722)—in preventing Christianity from becoming anything more than a marginal phenomenon in Chinese culture. Zürcher, "A Complement to Confucianism," 92.

2. In this study, I generally use the terms Catholicism, Christianity, Heavenly Lord teaching, and Heavenly Lord sect more or less synonymously. While overlapping, the terms do have their distinct referents. The only Christianity in China until the early 1800s was Catholic Christianity, and the name by which Catholic Christianity was and still is designated in Chinese is the "Heavenly Lord teaching." At times, however, I use one term predominantly. For example, when discussing Christianity during the time of proscription, I refer to it as the Heavenly Lord sect, as did Chinese officials, rather than as the Heavenly Lord teaching or religion. The latter description bears a more positive connotation, which Chinese officials during this time would not have ascribed to Christianity.

3. The Rites Controversy pitted the Jesuits and the Chinese emperor against the pope and orders such as the Dominicans. The controversy arose over issues such as Christian participation in Confucian rites and the proper translation of the name of God. The Mandate of Maigrot (1693) ordered the sole use of Tianzhu while forbidding the terms Shangdi and Tian (Heaven). This decision was confirmed by the papal decree of 1704 and a formal papal bull in 1715. In 1724, the Chinese emperor banned the propagation and practice of Catholicism. See Standaert, *Handbook of Christianity in China*, 680–84, for a brief summary of the controversy.

4. Gernet, *China and the Christian Impact*, 32.

5. The studies that deal with this topic are numerous. Among the most recent and influential are Gernet, *China and the Christian Impact*; Young, *Confucianism and Christianity*; Mungello, *The Forgotten Christians of Hangzhou*; and Nicolas Standaert, *Yang Tingyun, Confucian and Christian in Late Ming China* (Leiden: E. J. Brill, 1988).

6. Mungello, *The Forgotten Christians of Hangzhou*, 122. See also Gernet, *China and the Christian Impact*, 66.

7. Almost all of the major studies except Gernet's focus very narrowly on the work of the Jesuits, and then mostly on their work at the court rather than in the provinces. Mungello, in his 1994 study, while still focusing on the Jesuits, does examine what was happening in the provinces. In his newest work, *The Spirit and the Flesh in Shandong*, Mungello examines the missionary efforts of Franciscans in the provinces.

8. The use of this term is the subject of Young's *Confucianism and Christianity*.

9. Ricci, *Tianzhu shiyi*. In his introduction, Ricci uses all four of these terms (57–61). I have employed the English translation provided by the editors of this text (including their romanization of terms, most notably, Shang-ti).

The title that Ricci selected might itself indicate a preference for using the translation Lord of Heaven. Yet Ricci was merely following the lead of the very first missionary to China, Michele Ruggieri (1543–1607), who opted for the term on the basis of advice from some of his converts. See Lundbæk, "Joseph de Prémare and the Name of God in China," 132.

10. Ricci, *Tianzhu shiyi*, 121, 123.

11. Ibid., 125. In his article on the figurist Joseph de Prémare, a Jesuit serving in China from 1669 to 1736, Lundbæk refers to comments de Prémare made concerning Ricci's views. De Prémare notes, "He [Ricci] said and wrote to the Chinese—all of them applauded him and did not contradict him—that the true God whom he had come from the Extreme West to preach about, was exactly the same as the Tian and the Shangdi they knew about from their own old books." This is exactly what Ricci states in *Tianzhu shiyi*, though he probably would not be too happy being associated with de Prémare's views. Lundbæk, "Joseph de Prémare and the Name of God in China," 137.

12. Zürcher, "A Complement to Confucianism," 76–77.

13. Standaert, *The Fascinating God*, 33–47.

14. Zürcher, "A Complement to Confucianism," 71–73.

15. Standaert, *Handbook of Christianity in China*, 581.

16. Ricci, *Tianzhu shiyi*, 99.

17. Ibid., 107.

18. Ibid.

19. Ibid., 209.

20. Ibid., 241.

21. Wright, *Buddhism in Chinese History*, 36.

22. Zürcher appears to disagree with Wright on this issue. Zürcher states that terms of specifically Daoist provenance constitute a very small percentage of the Chinese Buddhist vocabulary. See his *The Buddhist Conquest of China*, 33–34.

23. Ibid., 40. I have been able to find only scattered references to the enterprise of Buddhist translation. Besides Zürcher, Wright, *Studies in Chinese Buddhism*, has been the most helpful. Chen, *Buddhism in China*, discusses the topic briefly (365–72). Gregory, *Tsung-mi and the Sinification of Buddhism*, examines how different classification schemes allowed Buddhist leaders to highlight scriptures that would appeal to their Chinese audiences. He does not deal at any length, however, with the role of the translation effort itself in the process of sinification.

24. *Zhongwen da zidian* (The Great Dictionary of the Chinese Language) (Taipei: n.p., 1973) offers several classical proof texts for the term hell (*diyu*), but as used with the corollary of heaven (*tiantang*), it offers only Buddhist references (8:317).

25. Wright, *Buddhism in Chinese History*, 102.

26. Ricci, *Tianzhu shiyi*, 143.

27. Soothill and Hodous, *A Dictionary of Chinese Buddhist Terms*, 143, 145.

28. Lundbæk, "Joseph de Prémare and the Name of God in China," 132.

29. Actually, using a word like "secular" to describe this kind of language can create misunderstanding. The word may be too tied to modern Western distinctions between secular and sacred realms. This restricts all religious language and liturgy to the sacred realm and usually identifies such language and liturgy with the institution of the church. The Jesuits would have distinguished between a political and ecclesiastical realm, but would nonetheless have affirmed that those occupying a political office were still entrusted with religious obligations. This is, of course, closer to the Chinese situation, where all secular (and political) activity had religious dimensions.

In Chinese culture and society, there were no realms. Instead, there were levels in a hierarchy, and all those levels were religious. No distinct ecclesiastical realm was embodied in a separate institution. Each office of political authority had an inherent set of religious responsibilities. The imperial office, for example, was at once a political (secular) office and a religious office. The emperor was both king and priest. Alongside his so-called secular duties, he worshipped at the Temple of Heaven, prostrated himself at the Temple of Earth, venerated the imperial ancestors, and prayed to the spirits of the imperial mountains and rivers.

30. *Zhongwen da zidian* gives over forty possible definitions for *zui* and its cognates, all but one having this strictly legal sense. The one exception involves the Buddhist idea of moral retribution (26:223).

31. Wright points to the work of the monks Dao An and Kumārajīva, who translated the message of Buddhism with far greater precision than had been done before. *Buddhism in Chinese History*, 62–63.

32. Bai, *Tianzhu sheng jiao bai wenda*. No date or publisher is given in the text itself. The title page identifies the author only as a Western Jesuit missionary, or more precisely, a Western scholar who belongs to the Yesu Society. Bai Yingli is in fact the Chinese name for Father Philippe Couplet; see Dehergne, *Répertoire des Jésuites de Chine*, 66–67.

In *Notices Biographiques et Bibliographiques sur Les Jésuites de L'Ancienne Mission de Chine*, Pfister provides the date and place of publication for the catechism: Peking, 1675 (310). Pfister notes that the catechism was reprinted in 1859, a year which coincidentally marked the revival of the Taiping under Hong Rengan.

33. Dehergne, *Répertoire des Jésuites de Chine*, 66–67.

34. Bai, *Tianzhu sheng jiao bai wenda*, 2a.

35. Ibid., 7a.

36. Cary-Elwes, *China and the Cross*, 134–35. For biographical details on Father Buglio, see Dehergne, *Répertoire des Jésuites de Chine*, 39.

37. Standaert, "The Bible in Early Seventeenth-Century China," 36–37. Professor Standaert states that these translations were primarily intended to secure permission for the liturgy to be translated into Chinese. *Handbook of Christianity* states that after Pope Innocent XI's ruling in 1680, "these manuals were hardly used after their publication" (627). It is not clear from Standaert's discussions in "The Bible in Early Seventeenth-Century China" and *Handbook of Christianity* whether this ruling affected only the celebration of the mass or whether it also affected the administration of the sacraments.

These discussions do suggest that these Chinese translations of sacramental rituals were in use prior to the papal withdrawal of permission. Thus, even though it is not clear to what extent missionaries used Buglio's manual in their administration of the sacraments after the papal ruling, it does seem safe to assume that the missionaries would have used the same language Buglio employed in their explanation of the meaning of the sacraments. Therefore, we can still study Buglio's manual as a record of the kinds of language and concepts used in the administration of the sacraments.

38. Buglio, *Shengshi lidian*, 1b of section on baptism.
39. Ibid., 6b. This term will be important for the Taiping.
40. Ibid., 8b.
41. Ibid., 8b-9a.
42. Ibid., 56a.
43. Ibid., 69a.
44. Such differences are addressed in Jordan, *Gods, Ghosts, and Ancestors*.
45. The term *jing* can be translated with a Confucian sense, as I do here. Or it can just as easily be translated with a Buddhist sense, which would then best be rendered as "sutra." Since sutras are usually chanted as a form of praise, I have chosen to translate this term with the word "classic."
46. Buglio, *Shengshi lidian*, 95a-b.
47. Pope Clement XI had first ruled on the Rites Controversy in 1704. The 1715 decree was in the form of an "apostolic constitution," which was a more solemn judgment. Minamiki lists and discusses these various papal correspondences and decrees in *The Chinese Rites Controversy*, 25–76.
48. Mungello, *The Forgotten Christians of Hangzhou*, 171.
49. Ibid., 172. There is more than just anecdotal evidence for this statement. *Handbook of Christianity* has calculated that even at the peak of elite interest in Christianity at the end of the Ming dynasty, the number of Catholic degree-holders and officials among the overall Catholic population was only some 0.85 percent (387). But this number approximates the number of degree-holders among the general population, and so the Catholic population mirrored the social stratification of the general population.
50. This adds an important dimension to Zürcher's comments, referred to in note 1 of this chapter, concerning the contradiction of the missionary strategy. This contradiction may not have been something the Catholic missionaries could have avoided, given the divide between elite and popular religion.
51. I always find it curious, however, that modern Western scholars such as Gernet have no problem understanding what is happening between the mandarins, representing traditional China, and the missionaries, representing traditional Europe. How is Dr. Gernet, this modern Western scholar, able to understand these

traditional worlds that seem even more alien to the modern West than they seem to each other?

52. Gernet, *China and the Christian Impact*, 93.

53. Ibid., 90.

54. Ibid., 96.

55. For a discussion of the autocratic policies of Emperor Yongzheng in his institution of the Grand Council, see Bartlett, *Monarchs and Ministers*. For an account of Yongzheng's fiscal policies, see Zelin, *The Magistrate's Tael*. Professor Guy's work on intellectual developments and political policy in the late Qianlong era, *The Emperor's Four Treasuries*, also deals with the issue of autocracy and its relationship to ideological control and intellectual life.

56. DeGroot, *Sectarianism and Religious Persecution in China*, 274.

57. Standaert, *Handbook of Christianity in China*, 523, 564.

58. *Daqing lüli huitong xinzuan*. This legislation appears in the conspectus (1414–18). I have used the pagination of the reprint edition.

59. *Daqing lüli huitong xinzuan*. The sub-statute that criminalized the practice of the Heavenly Lord sect is reflected in all cases taken from the conspectus and the commentary. Many of the memorials from the *Chouban yiwu shimo* address the sub-statute, and one memorial from the volume submitted in 1846 summarizes the various legal stages in the history of the Heavenly Lord sect for the emperor: "the Heavenly Lord sect formerly during the Ming dynasty was propagated into China. Prior to the reign of Kangxi, it was not proscribed. From the time of Yongzheng, the propagation and the practice of the religion began to be forbidden. During the reign of Jiaqing, a law was enacted which criminalized sectarian practice, but also allowed for repentance. In summary, the time it was proscribed was little, the time it was not proscribed was much." *Chouban yiwu shimo*, Daoguang, chap. 75, 4a-4b.

The editions of the law code from the Tongzhi reign (r. 1862–74) and after rescinded this sub-statute, but still included the separate case dealing with Western missionaries in the conspectus. An early Guangxu edition, however, effaced all legislation dealing with the sect. See *Daqing lüli huiji beilan*. One of the first cases tried under this law appears in the commentary section of the law code of the Qing, especially as expressed in the editions of the *Daqing lüli huitong xinzuan*. The law which criminalized the practice of the Heavenly Lord sect aimed to compel followers of the sect to renounce their faith regardless of whether the sect had peaceful or rebellious intentions. In the following extract from the conspectus of *Daqing lüli huitong xinzuan* (1418–19), the Board of Punishments adopts the strictest interpretation of the decree:

> Ma Huiyou [the governor-general of Huguang] and others have submitted a memorial inquiring about whether persons who have practiced the Heavenly Lord sect from birth, and, though appearing after the term of immunity has expired, renounce the religion and come in person to [an official] to confess, can such persons still be pardoned of their crimes? This question refers to a case in Hubei Province, Jingshan County, where a man named Liu Yi and eight others recently reported to an official. They stated that their grandfathers and fathers had followed the Heavenly Lord sect. But now since there has been a series of investigations in their *baojia* districts, along with the publishing of the imperial decree on this matter, they have now come forward, pledging repentance. However this took place after the year of immunity had expired. These criminals, however, are farmers from a distant village, and so they could not have known of this law any earlier, and so the period of immunity had already passed once the decree became known. Moreover, they came to confess of their own accord, they truly fear the law, and their repentance seems more sincere than those who repented after being discovered by the magistrate. Might we then exempt them from punishment?

60. *Gongzhong dang*, 662–65, Daoguang 11/7/6.

61. The new edition of *Lettres Edifiantes et Curieuses* published in Toulouse from 1810 to 1811 included material through only the early 1780s.

62. Latourette, *A History of Christian Missions in China*, 183. Cary-Elwes gives an estimate of 300,000 for the year 1840; *China and the Cross*, 188.

63. Standaert, *Handbook of Christianity*, 383. The *Handbook* comments on the slippery nature of these figures. These numbers are difficult to calculate and even more difficult to compare. Some reports submit figures for accumulated number of baptisms, and others submit the number of living Christians. Often sources do not distinguish between child and adult baptisms, which would have a tremendous impact on the reliability of these figures, since missionaries and Chinese priests baptized abandoned babies who were often close to death (380–81).

64. Ibid., 385–86. Although Jiangnan lost ground, it still was home to a large number of believers.

65. Society for the Propagation of the Faith, *Annals of the Propagation of the Faith*, 1841, 308. For 1838–39, I used the editions published in Paris. After that, I used those published in London and Baltimore.

66. Ibid., 1841, 171–72. This was gleaned from a letter submitted by the vicar general of Huguang province. This ecclesiastical title corresponds to the office of Chinese governor-general of the region encompassing the two provinces of Hubei and Hunan.

67. The ecclesiastical administration of the empire had been established in 1696, with the empire divided into three bishoprics—Macao, Nanjing, and Beijing—and nine vicariates, organized along the lines of the provinces; these divisions continued to structure mission activity at this time.

The organization of part of the Chinese mission into bishoprics and part into vicariate apostolics was a measure adopted by the papacy to get around having granted the right of appointment to the king of Portugal. In this scheme, the king could only appoint to the bishoprics. See Cary-Elwes, *China and the Cross*, 129; Mungello, *The Spirit and the Flesh in Shandong*, 106–7; and Standaert, *Handbook of Christianity*, 576–78. *Handbook of Christianity* notes that during the period of proscription, these nine vicariates operated as a de facto three.

68. Society for the Propagation of the Faith, *Annals of the Propagation of the Faith*, 1844, 229, 325.

69. Ibid., 261.

70. Ibid., 1846, 193.

71. Ibid., 1848, 26.

72. Ibid., 1850, 14.

73. Ibid., 1843, 172–74.

74. *Treaties, Conventions, Etc., Between China and Foreign States*. The relevant article for the American treaty appears in English and Chinese (683); the article for the treaty between France and China appears in French and Chinese (782).

75. Morse, *The International Relations of the Chinese Empire*, 332; Latourette, *A History of Christian Missions in China*, 230.

76. *Chouban yiwu shimo*. This collection of documents, composed of memorials and edicts related to foreign relations with the West, was the work of Qing officials, produced under imperial command. The volumes include material from the Daoguang (r. 1821–50) through the Tongzhi (r. 1862–74) reigns. However, the

Daoguang material begins only in 1836, some fifteen years into the reign, and focuses mainly on matters related to the struggle over the opium trade.

77. Ibid., Daoguang, *zhuan* 73, 1a-3a. In the discussion of Qiying in this chapter, I reproduce the substance and, in many cases, the exact wording of Qiying's report.

78. Ibid., 2b.

2 / THE PROTESTANT BIBLE AND THE BIRTH OF THE TAIPING CHRISTIAN MOVEMENT

1. This religious movement is sometimes referred to as the Evangelical Awakening in Britain and as the Great Awakening in America. The leaders associated with the movement in England were men like John Wesley (1703–1791), who, along with his brother Charles, was the founder of Methodism, and George Whitefield (1714–1770), who had a greater impact on the Calvinist dissenting churches in England and America. In the American colonies, the most influential man in the early stages of the movement was Jonathan Edwards (1703–1758).

2. Neill, *A History of Christian Missions*, 261. The London Missionary Society was originally intended to serve as an interdenominational organization, but developed into a society for missionaries connected to Congregational churches.

3. The Protestant missionary enterprise in China was overwhelmingly Anglo-American, so the connection to British imperial expansion cannot be denied. What I want to correct is the assumption that the missionary movement sprang from the same motives as those of the trading empire. The missionaries had a different idea about the worth of empire, and they were often at cross-purposes with the merchants. The merchants were generally opposed to the missionary enterprise, as was demonstrated in the East India Company policy.

Some statistics will demonstrate the national character of the early mission movement. At the first conference of Protestant missionaries in China convened in 1877, seventy years after the first Protestant missionary arrived, there were 222 British, 210 American, and 26 continental missionaries resident in China. These missionaries were sent out by no less than 72 different American societies, 49 different English societies, 1 German society, and 4 "unconnected" societies. *Records of the General Conference of the Protestant Missionaries of China* (1878), 1–10, 486–87.

4. Stanley develops this perspective on the origins of the missionary movement in his *The Bible and the Flag;* see especially 60–61. The quotation, a missionary favorite, comes from Jesus' teaching on the signs of the end of the age; see Matthew 24:14.

5. The policy, referred to earlier, was not changed until 1813, when that part of the charter was struck. Of course, for China, the policy would have been rendered irrelevant anyway since the company's monopoly over the China trade was broken in the same year. See Lloyd, *The British Empire,* 136.

6. Morrison had finished his translation of the New Testament as early as 1813. The Morrison New Testament, which I examined in Hong Kong, was published in 1813; the Harvard-Yenching Library's Morrison manuscript was also published in 1813. Morrison was not the only missionary working on Bible translation. Another missionary, Joshua Marshman, resident in India, published a translation of the New Testament later than Morrison, but published the entire Chinese Bible a year before Morrison published his own translation of the entire Bible. Morrison's version, however, was regarded as the superior translation. See MacGillivray, *A Century of Protestant Missions in China,* 13. Also see Hykes, *List of Translations of the Scriptures into the Chinese Language,* 2–3.

7. Hill, *The English Bible and the Seventeenth-Century Revolution,* 7, 20.

8. Standaert, *Handbook of Christianity,* 344–45, provides the details of Basset's life given here. Strandenaes, "The Sloane MS #3599," 61–62, provides information about the Sloane manuscript, a copy of Basset's translation donated to the British Museum by Sir Hans Sloane Bart. Strandenaes says little about Basset himself, mentioning the date of his death (1707) and little more.

9. Strandenaes, "The Sloane MS #3599," 61. Morrison's copy of Basset became part of the library of Hong Kong University in 1924, where it is presently housed. I examined it there.

I have not examined the original Sloane manuscript copy of Basset housed in the British Museum, the copy from which Morrison made this copy. Strandenaes has studied several different copies of the Basset translation, and he does not mention any discrepancies in the various copies.

10. Basset died in 1707, and the papal bull which forbade the use of Shangdi and Tian (Heaven) was issued in 1715 (the 1715 decree actually reiterated the decision of 1704).

11. See Standaert, *Handbook of Christianity,* 344, on the Missions Étrangères de Paris policy. In *The Bible in China,* Zetzsche refers to a comment made by A. C.

Moule that Basset may have used Shen as his translation rather than Shangdi or Tianzhu to avoid becoming embroiled in the conflict over the terms. See his note 27 on page 30, where he refers to an article published by Moule on the Basset manuscript.

12. *The Morrison Transcript of the Basset Version of the New Testament*, vol. 1, chap. 1, "Gospel Harmony." Morrison's transcript does not have pagination or verse numbering.

13. Ibid., chap. 1.

14. Ibid., chap. 2.

15. The changes he makes are minor. Morrison uses the more colloquial *ni* instead of the classically influenced *er* for translating "you"; he also substitutes the transliteration Xifa for Basset's Sefa in rendering the name Stephen.

16. Morrison, *Yesu Jilishidu wozhu jiuzhe xinyi zhaoshu*; Luke 1:35. Verses are numbered in all Protestant Bibles produced in Chinese. While Morrison intended to convey the idea of a testament in his use of the term *zhaoshu*, its primary meaning is a royal or imperial proclamation or declaration. This same term was used in the title of the Taiping's New Testament.

17. Zetzsche, *The Bible in China*, 37.

18. McNeur, *China's First Preacher, Liang A-fa*, 40–41.

19. Boardman, *Christian Influence upon the Ideology of the Taiping Rebellion*, 52. This characterization is a bit anachronistic, since fundamentalism arose only in the 1920s.

20. In the January 1847 issue of *The Chinese Repository*, a list of Protestant missionaries to the Chinese until that point numbered eighty-six men. Of this number, fully sixty were from the Calvinistic-influenced boards of the London Missionary Society, the American Board of Commissioners for Foreign Missions (these were Congregationalists), and the American Presbyterian Board of Foreign Missions. Methodist missionaries, for example, do not appear on these lists until a few years later.

21. Wagner, *Reenacting the Heavenly Vision*, 13.

22. Congregationalist and Presbyterian churches had different associations in different nations. To be Congregationalist in America meant that you were part of the establishment; to be Congregationalist in Britain meant you were a dissenter or nonconformist. Nonetheless, a British Congregationalist would still be a part of a fairly steady and staid social group.

23. See Lutz and Lutz, "Karl Gützlaff's Approach to Indigenization," 268–91. I have relied on their research for most of what I say here about Gützlaff.

24. Lutz and Lutz use this latter Chinese term when talking about the Chinese Union.

25. For "blitz baptism," see Wagner, *Reenacting the Heavenly Vision*, 13. Gützlaff's distribution of Bibles from opium ships is decried by his partner in Bible translation, W. H. Medhurst, in his book *China: Its State and Prospects* (361–80).

26. Wylie, *Memorials of Protestant Missionaries to the Chinese*, 4–7. Wylie provides short biographical accounts of the early Protestant missionaries along with an annotated listing of their publications.

27. Ibid., 56–63.

28. It has even been argued that this understanding of the relationship of the physical and spiritual worlds is intrinsic to Protestantism and that its roots have been a part especially of Reformed Protestantism since Calvin's Reformation. For example, in his *War Against the Idols*, Eire argues that this distinction between the spiritual and the material, driven by an emphasis on the transcendence of God, was a necessary precondition for the unleashing of Reformation iconoclasm.

That view of things is expressed most vividly in the Swiss reformer Ulrich Zwingli's understanding of the eucharist as memorial, not sacrament. But too much can be made of this. For most early Calvinists, the sense of a seamless sacredness was more characteristic of their thought that all of life was sacred. Thus, at least for the early Reformers, there was no division between sacred and secular: the baker's calling was as sacred as the pastor's.

29. Liang, *Quanshi liangyan*. I use the pagination provided by the reprint. The version of the Morrison Old Testament that I use as the basis for the following comparisons is his *Shentian shengshu;* for the New Testament passages, I have relied on his *Yesu Jilishidu wo jiuzhu zhaoshu*. These copies are housed at the Harvard-Yenching Library. The University of Hong Kong also has an early version of Morrison's New Testament.

It would not be exaggerating to say that Liang's book of pamphlets is nothing more than a compilation of passages from Morrison's Bible, so massive is the borrowing. Further, that which he borrowed from Morrison, he altered little. For example, in the account of creation as recorded in Genesis, Liang's translation is exactly the same as Morrison's, save for Liang's tendency to remove some of the literary language's filler characters such as *ye* and *zhe* (cf. Morrison's Genesis 1–3 with Liang,

174–78). He does add a character here and there to make Morrison's meaning clearer. Liang indulges in this latter habit more in the New Testament passages than in the Old Testament. For example, in the Sermon on the Mount, while Morrison writes that Jesus saw the crowds, Liang has it that the Lord of Salvation saw the crowds (cf. Morrison's Matthew 5–7 with Liang, 51). In the Lord's Prayer, Liang adds that it is "our Heavenly Father who is in Heaven," clearing up Morrison's rendering, "our Father who is in Heaven" (Liang 59). At Revelation 22, Liang makes a few more substantial changes, including describing the river of the water of life as flowing "from the throne of God and of the Lord of Salvation" (Liang 321), instead of, as Morrison has it, "from the throne of God and of the Lamb," apparently fearing his Chinese audience will read this too literally and think Christians worship sheep. Liang also is not too enamored with the image of the church as the bride of Christ (Revelation 22:17), so he changes the word "bride" to read "God's son" (323), the first of his changes that actually distorts the meaning of a passage. He apparently is unsatisfied even with the transliteration of Christ, Jilishidu, changing the two middle characters of Morrison's transliteration to achieve a more learned effect (324), which was different yet from the Catholic transliteration. When Catholics and Protestants used the shortened term, Jidu, they all used the same exact characters for their transliteration.

30. Liang, *Quanshi liangyan*, 31–32.

31. Ibid., 69.

32. Ibid., 223; 304–9.

33. Ibid., 321.

34. MacGillivray, *A Century of Protestant Missions in China*, 13. In his *God's Chinese Son*, Spence talks about how the Chinese Union followed this same practice. He fails to mention, however, that this practice was initiated by Liang Afa.

35. Spence, following Bohr, who follows Jen, theorizes that the missionary who gave Hong a copy was a Rev. Edwin Stevens. Spence, however, does not propose this theory too dogmatically; see *God's Chinese Son*, 30–31.

36. Hamberg, *The Visions of Hung-Siu-Tshuen*, 31. See also Michael, *The Taiping Rebellion*, 2:70.

37. The term "Taiping" can be translated as either "Great Peace" or "Great Equality."

38. Hamberg, *The Visions of Hung-Siu-Tshuen*, 11.

39. Michael, *The Taiping Rebellion*, 2:63. The Son of Heaven is a title assumed by the emperor.

40. Most of the time I will refer to these as idols, as this is how the Taiping viewed them.

41. But not all. Hong Rengan recounts how one of his first actions upon making his profession was to remove the statues of Confucius and the god of literature from his home. Yet many of the most celebrated of the Society of God Worshippers' early iconoclastic forays targeted idols and temples that would not have been approved by Confucian authorities, as they were regarded by Confucians and Taiping alike as "licentious."

42. In his "Origins of the Taiping Vision," Kuhn takes a different approach. He sees Liang's tract as "overflowing with political and apocalyptic overtones." Hong, however, does not at first perceive these overtones, but only recognizes them in the charged social context of Guangxi (357). Liang's tract, however, was not enough by itself, even in combination with the changed social conditions of Guangxi, to enable Hong to see the political implications of his message. The tract's apocalyptic tone is evident, given Liang's concern with individual salvation, while its political tone is not. What really changed things for Hong was his reading of the Bible.

43. Gützlaff sent most of his evangelists to provinces in southeastern China, but he also claimed that he had representatives of the Chinese Union in twelve different provinces throughout China. See Lutz and Lutz, "Karl Gützlaff's Approach to Indigenization," 273.

Catholic missionaries had labored in Guangxi province prior to the imperial ban on Christianity. They had even erected a church in the provincial capital of Guilin. But little remained of that work when the missionaries returned after the Opium War. Launay, *Histoire des Missions de la Chine, Mission du Kouang-si*, 21–23.

44. Clarke, "The Coming of God to Kwangsi," 154. The numbers of members given here are the accounting of Gützlaff and so may have been exaggerated to a certain extent. Missionaries accused Gützlaff of inflating both the quantity and quality of the men he sent out.

45. Lutz and Lutz, *Hakka Chinese Confront Protestant Christianity*, features the biographies of two Chinese Union alumni: Zhang Fuxing (32 ff.) and Dai Wenguang (55 ff.).

46. Gützlaff, *Journal of Three Voyages Along the Coast of China*, 19.

47. Canton, *History of the British and Foreign Bible Society*, 402.

48. Michael, *The Taiping Rebellion*, 2:6.

49. Lutz and Lutz, *Hakka Chinese Confront Protestant Christianity*; see note 30 on page 53.

50. Clarke, "The Coming of God to Kwangsi," 172.

51. Clarke goes so far as to suggest that while Liang Afa's booklets probably introduced Hong to Christianity, members of the Chinese Union may have played a part in introducing some other Taiping followers to the faith. See Clarke, "The Coming of God to Kwangsi," 166–67. With respect to Hong himself, that suggestion is not supported either by the explicit reference to *Good Words* in "Hung Hsiu-chuan's Background" (Michael, *The Taiping Rebellion*, 2:3–4) or in the *Taiping Heavenly Chronicle*, which attributes Hong's introduction to Christianity solely to Liang's booklets and also assigns him the principal responsibility for converting his first followers (ibid., 2:63).

52. Michael, *The Taiping Rebellion*, 2:38, 39, 41. For the Chinese, see *Taiping Tianguo yinshu*, 393, 395.

53. Liang refers to the Old Testament as the *jiujing*; see *Quanshi liangyan*, 144.

54. Michael, *The Taiping Rebellion*, 2:57, 70.

55. Roberts, "Tae Ping Wang," 382.

56. Hamberg, *The Visions of Hung-Siu-Tshuen*, 45.

57. Lindley [Linle], *Ti-Ping Tien-Kwoh*, 46.

58. Fishbourne, *Impressions of China and the Present Revolution*, 224.

59. Clarke and Gregory, *Western Reports on the Taiping*, 149.

60. Hykes, *List of Translations of the Scriptures into the Chinese Language*, 5; Forrest, "The Christianity of Hong Tsiu Tsuen, A Review of Taeping Books," 190; Canton, *History of the British and Foreign Bible Society*, 405; Boardman, *Christian Influence upon the Ideology of the Taiping Rebellion*, 47–48.

61. Medhurst, *China: Its State and Prospects*, 558.

62. Hykes, *List of Translations of the Scriptures into the Chinese Language*, 5.

63. Ibid., 4–5; Wylie, *Memorials of Protestant Missionaries to the Chinese*, 62–63. Gützlaff produced several different revisions of the New Testament.

64. Meadows, *The Chinese and Their Rebellions*, 420.

65. Fishbourne, *Impressions of China and the Present Revolution*, 391.

66. Ibid., vii. The copy of the Taiping New Testament in the British Library does not, for some reason, contain the Gospel of John. All contemporary witnesses speak of the Taiping New Testament as being complete.

67. Except for Forrest, "The Christianity of Hong Tsiu Tsuen, A Review of Taeping Books," 200, there was no mention of the annotations in any of the accounts of Western observers I consulted.

Michael, *The Taiping Rebellion*, 2:223, persuasively argues for a date between September 1860, when the listing of the Old and New Testaments accompanying the release of the Taiping's "Gospel Jointly Witnessed" still carried their 1853 titles, *Jiuyizhao shengshu* and *Xinyizhao shengshu*, and August 1861, when Forrest received his copy of the annotated Old and New Testaments from the Shield King, with the titles *Qinding jiuyizhao shengshu* and *Qinding qianyizhao shengshu*.

The change in the title of the New Testament from "Xinyizhao" to "Qianyizhao" probably reflects the intention of the Taiping to elevate the status of the "Tianming zhaozhi shu" to the most recent of the authoritative scriptures. This is the text that the Taiping referred to as the "True Testament."

68. Wu and Luo, "Taiping Tianguo yinshu jiaokan ji," 266–82. These two scholars have examined all the passages in the two Taiping Bibles, comparing the early version with Hong's annotated and edited version.

69. In this last type of change, fewer alterations seem to have been made in the Old Testament than in the New Testament. Below are examples of the rectification of names and addresses taken from Matthew 5:16–28:

Matthew 5:20—the imperial *zhen* (I) replaces the common *yu* (I).
Matthew 5:16, 20, 26—the imperial *yu* (decree) replaces the common *gao* (tell).
Matthew 5:25—the imperial *zhen yu* (I decree) replaces the common *wo yu* (I say).

Jiuyizhao shengshu and *Xinyizhao shengshu; Qinding jiuyizhao shengshu;* and *Qinding qianyizhao shengshu*. The *Qinding* Old Testament contains the books of Genesis through Joshua; the New Testament includes all the New Testament books except the Gospel of John.

70. Wagner, *Reenacting the Heavenly Vision*, 59–60.

71. From one of the earliest lists of works approved by the Taiping kings, issued in 1853, there were fourteen different titles of publications. Of these fourteen, one is the Taiping edition of the Old Testament, and a second is an edition of the New Testament. Liang Afa's *Quanshi liangyan* does not appear on this list or on later lists. One of the final lists of official publications, issued in 1861, contains twenty-

nine different publications. Again, the Old and New Testaments appear on the list, and the *Quanshi liangyan* does not. Neither does *Pilgrim's Progress*. See *Taiping Tianguo yinshu*, 2–3, 126.

72. Michael, *The Taiping Rebellion*, 2:56–57. Hong identifies more specifically the three classes of books later in the same document (70).

3 / THE TAIPING CHALLENGE TO EMPIRE

1. Rowbotham, *Missionary and Mandarin*, 165–66. Standaert, *Handbook of Christianity*, gives an overview of the Rites Controversy, and the decisions pertaining to it (682–85).

2. Liang's opus, as I showed in chapter 2, is largely just that: a compilation of passages from the Morrison Bible.

3. For example, see Liang, *Quanshi liangyan:* Shentian Shangdi, 44; Tian Shangdi, 38; Shen, 237. The term Shangdi—used alone—appears in two places (456 and 495); along with the one reference to Shangdi on p. 456, there are four other references to Shentian Shangdi on the same page.

4. *Jiuyizhao shengshu, Xinyizhao shengshu, Qinding jiuyizhao shengshu, Qinding qianyizhao shengshu*. As mentioned earlier, *zhaoshu* could be translated as "Imperial Declaration" rather than "Testament." Both of these versions of the two testaments were published by the Taiping, but only the latter features Hong's annotations.

5. A history of the committee is featured in *The Chinese Repository*, 19:544–49. See also Spelman, "Christianity in Chinese," 27. Spelman deals almost exclusively with the religious issues of the debate, and only those dealing with the term Shangdi. He does at one point touch on the political implications of the term, but this is not the focus of his study.

6. In the most intense year of the debate, 1848, over 350 pages of *The Chinese Repository*'s total 650 pages were devoted to the controversy; at the climax of the debate in 1850, no less than nineteen different articles appeared on the controversy in the one year. See *The Chinese Repository*, 1848, 1850. While the number of pages is a testimony to the intensity of the debate, the fact that this term question produced a similar number of pages of discussion every time a new translation was taken up testifies to the duration of the debate.

7. This again was actually the decision of the Jewish translators who first translated the Hebrew scriptures into Greek during the third to the first centuries B.C.E.

See the article on this translation in *The Anchor Bible Dictionary* (New York: Doubleday, 1992), 5:1093–1103.

In the Septuagint version of the Book of Genesis, the words for God are mostly *kurios ò theos* (the Lord God) and, simply, *ò theos* (God).

8. *The Chinese Repository*, January 1848, 19–20. Note in Boone's comments how he relies on a cue to signify that the name of God is not a reference to the generic variety: he capitalizes the name. In the Greek, the apostles relied on a similar cue, referring to God in the singular nominative case. One device that was used by the advocates of a generic name for the deity in Chinese was to precede a reference to the name with a space, denoting a special reverence for the term. Of course, in Chinese documents, the emperor was accorded even greater respect—every reference to the emperor's name would require the forming of a new line and the elevation of his name above the body of the text.

9. Ibid., January 1847, 35. Part of the debate focused on finding a term which, like the Greek term *theos*, could signify both a generic sense of god and the majestic sense of the high God. Medhurst stumbled at one point in trying to argue that only the term Di satisfied both these requirements. In my view, he won the debate only when he argued that the Chinese language did not have one single term that supplied both these meanings.

10. Ibid., October 1848, 490. Ralph Cudworth, though cited by Medhurst here for his work in the Greek language, apparently was even more skilled in the Hebrew language, as he served as Regius Professor of Hebrew at Cambridge from 1645 until his death in 1688. For more information on his life and scholarship, see Leslie Stephen and Sidney Lee, eds., *Dictionary of National Biography* (New York: The Macmillan Company, 1908), 5:271–72.

11. It was noted that Morrison, Milne, and Marshman had primarily used *shen* in their translations, but others pointed out that Morrison and Milne had both changed their views on the proper name of God toward the end of their careers. See *The Chinese Repository*, February 1847, 102; March 1847, 123.

12. Ibid., April 1848, 162–63.

13. Ibid., March 1848, 130.

14. Ibid., May 1845, 201–29. This contains the full Chinese text of the monument. The Nestorian Church was an independent branch of early Christianity characterized by the belief that the divine and human aspects of Jesus existed as two

separate persons. The church was further characterized by the fact that the center of its faith was the city of Baghdad rather than Rome or Constantinople.

Nestorian missionaries operated in China during the Tang dynasty. The stele that the Tang emperor erected commemorating their work in the Chinese empire can still be seen in the city of Xi'an today.

15. Ibid., December 1846, 578–601. This is not as far-fetched a suggestion as Medhurst implies. After all, the Buddhists did this, as did the Catholics and Protestants in one unique case, that of the title of Christ. In the Chinese context, transliteration involves finding characters, not letters, to represent the sounds of the foreign word. The fact that it is a transliteration is often indicated by adding a mouth symbol to the left of each of the characters used in representing the sound.

16. Ibid., February 1848, 87.

17. Ibid. The word Elohim is interesting in itself. Elohim is one of the Hebrew names for the one God. The -im suffix, however, denotes plurality. This anomaly is explained by describing the -im suffix as serving to evoke the fullness of deity, the plurality of majesty. This explanation aside, the term does seem to reflect something of a polytheistic origin.

18. Ibid., May 1848, 221.

19. Ibid.

20. *The Chinese Repository*, May 1848, 230.

21. Ibid., April 1848, 174.

22. Ibid., July 1848, 329.

23. This was a point Ricci strongly advocated. In his catechism, *Tianzhu shiyi*, Ricci identifies the Lord of Heaven with Shangdi and then explains that the Chinese at one time worshipped the same God as the Europeans (123).

24. *The Chinese Repository*, March 1848, 109.

25. As we shall see, it was the American Episcopalian who adopted the more severe stance. It probably would be fruitless to try to untangle how much of the animus expressed in this debate was tied to national, denominational (Medhurst was a representative of British dissent; Boone represented the American branch of the Anglican establishment), cultural, social, or just personal differences. The hostility between them is, nonetheless, palpable.

26. *The Chinese Repository*, July 1848, 359.

27. Ibid., January 1848, 50.

28. Ibid., September 1848, 460–61.

29. Michael, *The Taiping Rebellion*, 2:107–8. I have used this source for all Taiping documents whenever these are available, indicating any differences I have with his translations here. *The Taiping Rebellion* includes most of the documents with the understandable exception of the Taiping Bibles. I have relied on Xiang's eight-volume collection of documents for the Chinese versions of these same documents. The document I refer to here is found in Xiang, *Taiping Tianguo*, 1:67.

30. Michael, *The Taiping Rebellion*, 2:157; Xiang, *Taiping Tianguo*, 1:226.

31. Michael, *The Taiping Rebellion*, 2:44.

32. Ibid., 2:46. This translation has God's son where I have inserted God's Crown Prince; Xiang, *Taiping Tianguo*, 1:97.

33. In the introduction to the *Taiping zhaoshu* (Taiping imperial declaration), Michael refers to two different dates for the composition of this statement: *Taiping tianri* (Taiping heavenly chronicle) suggests a date between 1844 and 1845, and Hamberg suggests a date between 1845 and 1846. See Michael, *The Taiping Rebellion*, 2:24. All of these dates fall before Hong visited Canton.

34. Wang Qingcheng, *Tianfu Tianxiong shengzhi*, 9–10.

35. Jen argues that it was this extreme monotheism, expressed in these incidents of iconoclasm, which was the most distinctive characteristic of the Taiping. See his *Taiping Tianguo dianzhi tongkao*, 3:1670–71, 1745. I agree with his statement, but I think that Jen should have gone one step further and showed how this iconoclasm supported the Taiping's rebellious inclinations. What leads Hong Xuiquan to go from smashing idols to attacking the emperor is the blasphemy of the imperial title.

36. Michael, *The Taiping Rebellion*, 2:74; Xiang, *Taiping Tianguo*, 2:649.

37. Clarke and Gregory, *Western Reports on the Taiping*, 388.

38. Wagner discusses this passage in *Reenacting the Heavenly Vision*, 38.

39. Michael, *The Taiping Rebellion*, 2:41; Xiang, *Taiping Tianguo*, 1:95.

40. Michael, *The Taiping Rebellion*, 2:45; Xiang, *Taiping Tianguo*, 1:97.

41. Jen, *Taiping Tianguo dianzhi tongkao*, 3:1660. Jen refers to these as the *Tiantiao*. I believe that the commandments Hong possessed in 1844 are not the full listing that he possessed in 1847. In Hong's earliest writings, he refers to the *Tiantiao* (Heavenly Commandments), yet he seems to be referring to the abbreviated version of the decalogue provided by Liang Afa and not to the full listing Hong obtained

later. The full listing is important, as it would contain the first three commandments, which focus on the name and position of Shangdi.

42. Fishbourne, *Impressions of China and the Present Revolution*, 180.

43. Liang's indirect mention comes when he quotes from Jesus' own summary of the decalogue in his conversation with the rich young ruler from Matthew 19:18–19. Jesus replied to the man's query about what he must do to gain eternal life by saying, "Do not murder, do not commit adultery, do not steal, do not give false testimony, honor your father and mother, and love your neighbor as yourself." The last commandment is a summary of the decalogue, rather than a part of the ten. See Liang, *Quanshi liangyan*, 88.

44. Michael, *The Taiping Rebellion*, 2:5.

45. Jen, *The Taiping Revolutionary Movement*, 161. Jen describes Hong's securing a copy of the commandments as the "single most important piece of literature Hong acquired during his stay with Roberts." I would differ with Jen on this point. I believe the Gützlaff Bible was the single most important piece of literature Hong obtained in Canton. I also wonder whether Hong had earlier obtained a copy of the Ten Commandments from the Chinese Union.

46. The Calvinist branch of Protestantism, following Jewish tradition, organized the Ten Commandments differently from the Catholics and the Lutherans. In Calvinist versions, the first three commandments concern God's place before other gods, His image, and His name. In Catholic and Lutheran versions, the first two of these are subsumed into one commandment.

47. *Jiuyizhao shengshu, Qinding jiuyizhao shengshu*; Exodus 20:1–7.

48. Michael, *The Taiping Rebellion*, 2:119–120; Xiang, *Taiping Tianguo*, 1:78.

49. The Catholic transliteration of Christ differed from the Protestant version in only a minor fashion. The characters of the transliteration are exactly alike except for the character representing *si*; the Protestants used the character for scholar, which is transliterated *shi*. For the Catholic transliteration, see especially Buglio's ritual guide *Shengshi lidian*, discussed in chapter 1. Buglio used the transliteration Jilisidu for the title of Christ throughout, including in his translation of the sign of the cross and in the Apostles' Creed. Buglio translated many major pieces of Catholic literature in the seventeenth century. In addition to the ritual guide, he also translated the missal and the breviary.

The Catholic and Protestant transliterations usually appear in a shortened form as Jidu.

50. I have found only one line in *The Chinese Repository* where the title of Christ was discussed. In that line, embedded in a footnote, Medhurst states that Morrison, in one of his tracts, had employed "Son of Heaven" (Tianzi) for the title, a term which, Medhurst remarks, is "solely appropriated to the Emperor of China." See *The Chinese Repository*, July 1848, 342.

51. See, for example, Liang, *Quanshi liangyan:* Jiuzhu, 51; Jiushizhu, 75.

52. Ibid., 142.

53. Ibid., 364, 263.

54. This is similar, as I note earlier, to that most resilient of the early church heresies: Arianism.

55. Taizi as a title given to Jesus is not used as frequently as the title of Taixiong. However, it appears in some highly significant contexts. For example, it is used in annotations at Matthew 17 and I John 5, both passages critical to the identity of Jesus. Here Hong states very directly that Jidu is Shangdi's Crown Prince (Taizi), and this title is used in the *Sanzijing*. See Xiang, *Taiping Tianguo*, 1:226. It also appears in this line from the *Taiping Imperial Declaration:* "Jiushizhu Yesu Huang Shangdi Taizi ye" (The World's Salvation Lord, Jesus, is the Supreme Shangdi's Crown Prince). See Xiang, *Taiping Tianguo*, 1:97.

Tianxiong (Heavenly Elder Brother) is the most frequently used title in the Taiping version of the Ten Commandments; see ibid., 1:75–77.

The *Taiping Heavenly Chronicle* contains one of the more complete and definitive summaries of the titles for Jesus in this line: "Jiushizhu Tianxiong Jidu shi Huang Shangdi Taizi" (The World's Salvation Lord, the Heavenly Elder Brother Christ, is the Supreme Shangdi's Crown Prince). See ibid., 2:631.

56. *Qinding qianyizhao shengshu*, Matthew 10. Since Hong used the title Taizi and the title Taixiong interchangeably, I have chosen to translate the latter term as "Eldest Prince."

57. Ibid.; Michael, *The Taiping Rebellion*, 2:229.

58. *Qinding qianyizhao shengshu*; Michael, *The Taiping Rebellion*, 2:234–235.

59. *The Chinese Repository*, May 1848, 222–23.

60. Liang, *Quanshi liangyan*, 52.

61. Ibid., 53. Morrison is the exception to this translation. He even parted company with his predecessor Bassett.

62. Ibid., 59. For Gützlaff's rendering, see *Xinyizhao shengshu*, Matthew 6:10.

63. *The Chinese Classics, Volume V: The Ch'un Tsew with The Tso Chuen*, translated by James Legge (reprint, Taipei: SMC Publishing, 1991). This is Legge's translation; I have changed his translation of Tianwang from "King [by] Heaven's [grace]" to the more natural "Heavenly King."

64. A title with a White Lotus sectarian provenance is the Shun Tian Wang (the King who is obedient to Heaven), which became popular among the Nian rebels during the time of the Taiping. Even before the Taiping Rebellion, this was a common title for the Nian; see, for example, *Gongzhong dang*, Nian Army Category, #5–21, Daoguang 28/12/10. For the Nian's use of the same title during the Taiping Rebellion, see *Gongzhong dang*, Nian Army Category, #9–10, Xianfeng 4/3/17.

65. Liu, *Qingchao xu wenxian tongkao*, zhuan 148, p. 9079.

66. Ibid., 9079.

67. According to Loewe, the worship of Heaven was established as the emperor's first duty only in 5 C.E., during the rule of Wang Mang. See Loewe, "The Religious and Intellectual Background," 664.

68. Liang, *Quanshi liangyan*, 150.

69. Michael, *The Taiping Rebellion*, 2:113. I have changed the translation of Great God to Supreme God; Xiang, *Taiping Tianguo*, 1:73.

70. Millenarianism in its Buddhist form has been linked to rebellion throughout early modern Chinese history. It has also been linked to revolution in China and in Europe. In his classic work, *Social Bandits and Primitive Rebels*, Hobsbawm declared that millenarian movements were the only primitive form of social protest that could legitimately be called revolutionary. He emphasized the characteristic shared by millenarian and revolutionary movements: the hope of a complete and radical change in the world. See, for example, p. 57.

71. Liang, *Quanshi liangyan*, 321. I did not find any reference in Liang to the Heavenly City, which is described in Revelation 21 and after which Hong named his capital.

72. Ibid., 495–502.

73. *Xinyizhao shengshu; Qinding qianyizhao shengshu:* Matthew 4:17.

74. *Qinding qianyizhao shengshu*, Revelation 21; Michael, *The Taiping Rebellion*, 2:237.

75. Boardman, *Christian Influence Upon the Ideology of the Taiping Rebellion*, 108.

76. Two Liberation theologies that have helped my own understanding of the import of these millenarian teachings are Miranda, *Communism in the Bible*, and Boff and Boff, *Salvation and Liberation*.

77. *Qinding qianyizhao shengshu*, Matthew 5; see also Michael, *The Taiping Rebellion*, 2:227.

78. In his study *Social Bandits and Primitive Rebels*, Hobsbawm, in discussing the connections between millenarianism and revolution, ruled out the possibility of religions such as Hinduism and Buddhism as being capable of inspiring revolutionary movements (57–58). He could not conceive of a religious tradition that sees the world as a constant flux as having the wherewithal to inspire a movement that would radically change the nature of that world.

79. *Qinding qianyizhao shengshu*, Matthew 24 and 25; Michael, *The Taiping Rebellion*, 2:229.

80. *Qinding qianyizhao shengshu*, Revelation 19, 20; Michael, *The Taiping Rebellion*, 2:237.

81. Michael, *The Taiping Rebellion, Tianming zhaozhishu* (The Book of Heavenly Decrees and Proclamations), 2:106; Xiang, *Taiping Tianguo*, 1:65.

4 / WORSHIP AND WITNESS IN THE TAIPING HEAVENLY KINGDOM

1. Zhang Dejian's account is also the most authoritative in terms of its inclusion of primary documents and is the most complete in terms of detail. It was issued in 1855, and so deals entirely with the early stages of the movement. Zhang seems to have been well suited for his espionage career: he kept his identity hidden. He is not listed in any of the major biographical dictionaries.

All the Qing loyalist accounts, along with Zhang Dejian's report, are published in Xiang, *Taiping Tianguo*.

2. Clarke and Gregory, *Western Reports on the Taiping*, 296. The date is not given in the selection. But it was noted in the original report to the London Missionary Society; see the Archives of the Council for World Mission, Set #2140, Box #1, Fiche #50.

In a letter to the *North China Herald* describing his travels through Taiping China, Rev. E. C. Bridgman notes that at Wuhu (safely below Anjing and not targeted by the Qing), there were few troops, that at Nanjing the troops had commandeered full sections of the city, and that Jinjiang "for the time being . . . is made one vast camp." Clarke and Gregory, *Western Reports on the Taiping*, 148. The effectual phrase is "for the time being."

3. Lindley [Linle], *Ti-Ping Tien-Kwoh*, 70.

4. Withers, "The Heavenly Capital." See chapter 3 for a complete description of life in the Heavenly Capital. In this chapter, he describes how all the residents of Nanjing were divided up and assigned to different institutes (*guan*), separated by sex and occupation (the separation of the sexes ended in 1855). This was a hybrid system, being an amalgam of the Taiping military organization, which was based on twenty-five-member units, and the Taiping Heavenly Land System, which established a twenty-five-member family unit for civilian administration.

It is Withers's argument that the Taiping were too successful at implementing their ideal order, which led to disaffection among the subjects. The problem with his argument is that he relies almost totally on the views of the gentry. As he admits in the final pages, "we cannot therefore be sure how the bulk of the populace reacted to many of the major aspects of the Taiping program" (218).

5. Xiang, *Taiping Tianguo*, "Zeiqing huizuan," 3:251.

6. Ibid., 261.

7. Ibid., "Jinling guijia jishi lue," 4:652.

8. Ibid., "Dunbi suiwen lu," 4:355.

9. Ibid., "Zeiqing huizuan," 3:267.

10. Clarke and Gregory, *Western Reports on the Taiping*, 30.

11. Ibid., 70.

12. Xiang, *Taiping Tianguo*, "Jiande zhai suibi," 6:757.

13. Ibid., "Zeiqing huizuan," 3:249; "Jinling zaji," 4:612; "Mengnan shuchao," 5:43; "Dunbi suiwen lu," 4:354.

14. Ibid., "Jinling zaji," 4:621.

15. Ibid., "Jinling beinan ji," 4:749.

16. Clarke and Gregory, *Western Reports on the Taiping*, 285.

17. Xiang, *Taiping Tianguo*, "Jinling guijia jishi lue," 4:666–80. This list forms an appendix to the account, and it supplies a rather extensive biography for each of the leaders. In addition to the information on the kings, this list provides a biographical listing of some hundred Taiping leaders. This account is an early one, 1853–54. The provincial composition of the upper offices did change as the movement developed, but the very top positions still went to Guangxi men.

18. Ibid., 655.

19. Ibid., "Zhang Jigeng yigao," 4:764.

20. Ibid., "Zeiqing huizuan," 3:124–25. A copy of this list in an English translation can also be found in Michael, *The Taiping Rebellion*, 2:566–69.

21. Michael, *The Taiping Rebellion*, 3:1271–355. Wang Qingcheng, *Taiping Tianguo de wenxian he lishi*, 593–604, contains photographic reproductions of a portion of these lists.

22. Xiang, *Taiping Tianguo*, "Jinling guijia jishi lue," 4:652. Another observer records that on the flag were written the words "Mingri Tianfu Jiangfan, Ge Yi Gongjing" ("Tomorrow, the Heavenly Father will descend into the world, everyone should reverently worship"), indicating the Taiping understanding of the dynamic presence of the Heavenly Father. This would suggest that the purpose of worship was to gather to worship the Heavenly Father in person, as it were. The Taiping sabbath was Saturday. Ibid., "Dunbi suiwen lu," 4:392.

23. Ibid., "Zeiqing huizuan," 3:227.

24. Ibid., 230.

25. Ibid., 261–62. Zhang does not include the fact that the Taipings delivered a sermon or teaching (*jiang daoli*) in his description here. But he includes it elsewhere, and this part of the service is included in the accounts of other observers. Hamberg describes the Taiping worship service in a similar manner. See Hamberg, *The Visions of Hung-Siu-Tshuen* (reprint), 35.

26. Xiang, *Taiping Tianguo*, "Zeiqing huizuan," 3:231.

27. Two eyewitness accounts in Suzhou and one account from Zhejiang offer descriptions similar to Zhang's. All three are from the 1860s. See Ibid.: on Suzhou, "Sutai milu ji," 5:290, and "Jieyu zashi," 5:313; on Zhejiang, "Huxue shenghuan ji," 6:737–38.

28. Michael, *The Taiping Rebellion*, 2:315; Xiang, *Taiping Tianguo*, 1:322. The Taipings did not have a separate institution that they designated as "church," i.e., an institution organized independent of the state and governed separately from the state; rather, they had a meeting place for worship, or, as it is called in this passage, the *libaitang* (worship hall).

29. One observer states that Taiping soldiers were whipped if they did not offer prayer at mealtime. This is suspicious, though, since this observer is the only one to mention such a punishment. Xiang, *Taiping Tianguo*, "Jinling zaji," 4:612. A similarly cynical remark is made by Zhang Dejian, who implies that the faith of the

Taiping rank and file was only as fervent as the regularity of the meals they prayed over. See ibid., "Zeiqing huizuan," 3:263.

30. Ibid., "Jinling guijia jishi lue," 4:652.

31. *North China Herald,* June 30, 1860. The report includes a Chinese and English version of the prayer.

32. Xiang, *Taiping Tianguo,* "Wuchang jishi," 4:601. This observer characterizes such activities as "ridiculous." I suppose the observer thought that the fact that they were to be executed showed how ineffective and powerless their religion was.

33. Ibid., "Jinling guijia jishi lue," 4:658.

34. Ibid., "Zeiqing huizuan," 3:228.

35. Clarke and Gregory, *Western Reports on the Taiping,* 236.

36. Xiang, *Taiping Tianguo,* "Jinling guijia jishi lue," 4:652.

37. Clarke and Gregory, *Western Reports on the Taiping,* 66–67.

38. Xiang, *Taiping Tianguo,* "Dunbi suiwen lu," 4:392. "Jiangnan chunmeng'an biji" features a doxology with a few more stanzas added, including the reference to Jesus as the Crown Prince (4:437–38).

39. Ibid., "Sutai milu ji," 5:290.

40. Ibid., "Wuchang jishi," 4:595.

41. Ibid., "Yangzhou yukou lu," 5:104.

42. Ibid., "Zeiqing huizuan," 3:266.

43. Michael, *The Taiping Rebellion,* 66; *Taiping Tianguo yinshu,* vol. 1, 43.

44. See Joseph Edkins's interview with the Shield King in Clarke and Gregory, *Western Reports on the Taiping,* 243.

45. Hamberg, *The Visions of Hung-Siu-Tshuen,* 35.

46. Clarke and Gregory, *Western Reports on the Taiping,* 242.

47. *North China Herald,* August 11, 1860.

48. Xiang, *Taiping Tianguo,* "Huxue shenghuan ji," 6:737–38.

49. Clarke and Gregory, *Western Reports on the Taiping,* 249. Xiang, *Taiping Tianguo,* "Sutai milu ji" (5:280), provides a description of an incident where those who violated the Ten Commandments were paraded through the streets, a poster carried before them detailing their sins or crimes. "Jieyu zashi" (5:313) describes a worship setting in Su-fu province.

50. Lindley [Linle], *Ti-Ping Tien-Kwoh,* 73.

51. Clarke and Gregory, *Western Reports on the Taiping,* 236.

52. Ibid., 289.

53. Fishbourne, *Impressions of China and the Present Revolution*, 138; Meadows, *The Chinese and Their Rebellions*, 259.

54. Xiang, *Taiping Tianguo*, "Zeiqing huizuan," 3:229.

55. Michael, *The Taiping Rebellion*, 2:41; Xiang, *Taiping Tianguo*, 1:95.

56. While the evangelical tide had washed over Anglo-American Protestantism in the late 1700s and early 1800s, it did not result in the wholesale abandonment of Calvinist traditions and doctrines among the dissenting churches. The main missionary organs in China up until the 1850s were all affiliated with Calvinistic or Reformed churches. I mentioned this in chapter 3, noting how the first Protestant missionary society in China was the London Missionary Society, whose members came from Calvinistic churches. Likewise, the first American missionary organization was the American Board. Even the Baptists during this era would have been considered Calvinistic Baptists. The founder of modern Protestant missions, William Carey, was an English Baptist, and the very title he selected for his call to missionary action demonstrates this orientation of the dissenting churches. The title of his work was *An Enquiry into the Obligations of Christians to Use Means for the Conversion of the Heathen* (1792), and his argument was directed against a hyper-Calvinist view. That is, since God had predestined men to be saved, He Himself would convert the non-Christian world, if it so pleased Him. He did not need the service of mere mortals.

57. Calvinists parted company with the Catholics and Lutherans in the very numbering of the Ten Commandments, which I mention earlier. The effect is that the Calvinists' first three commandments concern idolatry, whereas the Catholics and Lutherans divide up the commandments so that only the first two concern idolatry. The Calvinists then compensate at the end by combining the commandments involving coveting. Thus the Calvinists have three commandments at the beginning concerning idolatry (the first through third commandments) and one at the end concerning coveting (the tenth), whereas the Catholics and Lutherans have two commands concerning idolatry and two concerning coveting. Numbering in between is likewise affected. The net result for the Calvinist version is a greater emphasis on the sin of idolatry. The Taiping listing of the Ten Commandments follows the Calvinist model.

58. Eire, *War Against the Idols*, 151.

59. Ibid., 112–13; 118.

60. Ibid., 128, 136.
61. Ibid., 157.
62. Clarke and Gregory, *Western Reports on the Taiping*, 57.
63. Ibid., 89.
64. Ibid., 203.
65. Ibid., 219–20.
66. Ibid., 234.
67. Xiang, *Taiping Tianguo*, "Dunbi suiwen lu," 4:398.
68. Ibid., "Wuchang jishi," 4:601.
69. Ibid., "Zeiqing huizuan," 3:232.
70. Ibid., "Jinling guijia xin yuefu, wushi shou," 4:735.
71. This is a contradiction only for those outside the Taiping movement; in their iconoclastic activity, the Taiping believed they were saving Chinese civilization.
72. The Taiping favored style was long, flowing tresses; they are regularly referred to in accounts as "long-hairs."
73. Xiang, *Taiping Tianguo*, "Sutai milu ji," 5:279.
74. Clarke and Gregory, *Western Reports on the Taiping*, 381.
75. Xiang, *Taiping Tianguo*, "Jingshan yeshi," 3:6.
76. Ibid., "Mengnan shuchao," 5:61.
77. In his *Soulstealers*, Kuhn discusses the links between queue cutting, sorcery, and anti-Manchu sentiment.
78. Xiang, *Taiping Tianguo*, "Jinling shengnan zhilue," 4:715.
79. Ibid., "Zeiqing huizuan," 3:180.
80. Michael, *The Taiping Rebellion*, 2:314. *The Land System of the Heavenly Dynasty* was usually included on all the lists of "false documents" drawn up by Qing observers, which suggests a fairly wide distribution, since if they could get their hands on copies of the document, many others could as well. Zhang Dejian compiled one such list; see Xiang, *Taiping Tianguo*, "Zeiqing huizuan," 3:260.
81. Xiang, *Taiping Tianguo*, "Wuchang jishi," 4:593.
82. Clarke and Gregory, *Western Reports on the Taiping*, 267.
83. Xiang, *Taiping Tianguo*, "Kouding jilue," 6:811.
84. Ibid., "Zeiqing huizuan," 3:229.
85. Bernhardt, *Rents, Taxes and Peasant Resistance*. The introduction and chapter 3, entitled "The Taiping Occupation of Jiangnan," are most directly relevant to this question.

86. Wagner, "Operating in the Chinese Public Sphere," 115.

87. Xiang, *Taiping Tianguo*, "Jinling zaji," 4:612.

88. Ibid., "Zeiqing huizuan," 3:191. According to Zhong Jingwen, *Yu Hai* (An encyclopedia of Chinese folk language), vol. 1 (Shanghai: Wenshu Publishing Company, 1994), the phrase "snow in the midst of the cloud" refers to execution with a flying knife (i.e., a knife that is thrown). The *Yu Hai* states that the locus classicus for this word is found in this very Taiping-era document, the "Zeiqing huizuan." Michael has a somewhat different explanation: this "snow in the midst of the clouds" was the name of a sword given Hong Xiuquan by Shangdi; the phrase later came to refer to execution by beheading. Michael, *The Taiping Rebellion*, 2:57–58.

89. Xiang, *Taiping Tianguo*, "Zeiqing huizuan," 3:193–99.

90. Ibid., 218. This is given as typical of declarations issued, not surprisingly, by Yang Xiuqing, the Eastern King.

91. Ibid., 217.

92. Ibid., "Jinling shengnan jilue," 4:690.

93. Ibid., "Sutai milu ji," 5:280.

94. Ibid., "Wuqing riji," 5:340.

95. For the warning about the Heavenly Father's wrath, see ibid., "Jinling shengnan jilue," 4:694.

96. Ibid., 695.

97. For the third year of the kingdom, see Michael, *The Taiping Rebellion*, 2:323–24; for the calendar from the fourth year of the kingdom, see ibid., 334–35. The Chinese version of these calendars is included in the collection *Taiping Tianguo yinshu*; see p. 127 for the 1853 calendar and p. 487 for the 1854 calendar.

98. Luo, *Taiping Tianguo wenwu*, 12, 15, 31, 50, 60.

99. Ibid., 64–67, offers examples of these coins.

100. Xiang, *Taiping Tianguo*, "Zeiqing huizuan," 3:252–53.

101. A distinct advantage of the collection of materials assembled in the two volumes of *Taiping Tianguo yinshu* is that the editors have attached the list of authorized publications the Taiping had appended to the documents they produced. These lists are dominated by the specifically Christian documents the Taiping published, ranging from one list published early in the rebellion that includes the titles of thirteen documents (see p. 58 for one of the earliest lists), most of which are also mentioned by Zhang Dejian here, to one attached to the Taiping calendar issued in eleventh year of the kingdom, which had expanded to twenty-nine titles (718).

102. Xiang, *Taiping Tianguo*, "Dunbi suiwen," 4:391, 393.

103. Ibid., "Jinling zaji," 4:611.

104. Ibid., "Jiangnan chunmeng'an biji," 4:436. "Jinling shengnan jilue" even enumerates the commandments and quotes from the *Three Character Classic;* see 4:717.

105. Guo Yisheng, *Taiping Tianguo lishi ditu ji*, 9–10.

106. Xiang, *Taiping Tianguo*, "Jinling zaji," 4:621. Griffith John also reported that he visited a Taiping school for younger boys; see Clarke and Gregory, *Western Reports on the Taiping*, 297. We know the Taiping set up schools in the Heavenly Capital, but there is no other comment on this from the descriptions of other cities. Because the Taiping had begun to conduct their own version of the bureaucratic exam, schools were probably set up in other Taiping-occupied cities as well.

107. Ibid., "Kouding Jilue" (6:809–12), describes the practices of the Taiping in Fujian, including maintaining the sacred treasury, chanting the doxology, and smashing idols.

108. Lindley [Linle], *Ti-Ping Tien-Kwoh*, 148.

109. Clarke and Gregory, *Western Reports on the Taiping*, 282.

5 / THE TAIPING LEGACY AND MISSIONARY CHRISTIANITY

1. Wuchang: Xiang, *Taiping Tianguo*, "Dunbi suiwen lu," 4: 392; Nanjing: ibid., "Sitong ji," 4: 479; Yangzhou: ibid., "Yangzhou yukou lu," 5:104; Suzhou: ibid., "Sutai milu ji," 5:290.

2. Ibid., "Sutai milu ji," 5:290.

3. Ibid., "Wuchang bingxian jilue," 4:571.

4. Ibid., "Yangzhou yukou lu," 5:104; ibid., "Yuezhou jilue," 6:768.

5. Ibid., "Wuchang jishi," 4:599; ibid., "Hukou riji," 6:790.

6. *Junjichu dang*, #2836–5, Xianfeng 3/2/24.

7. Xiang, *Taiping Tianguo*, "Zeiqing huizuan," 3: 249.

8. Ibid., "Dunbi suiwen lu," 4:392.

9. Society for the Propagation of the Faith, *Annals of the Propagation of the Faith*, 220–21.

10. Ibid., 1855, 84.

11. Clarke and Gregory, *Western Reports on the Taiping*, 58–59.

12. Ibid., 110, 113.

13. Ibid., 201.

14. Zhu and Guo, *Yuanni baofa*. The authors of this tract were probably native Chinese Catholics, since they are using "Christian names." Ximan is the transliterated form of Simon, Baolu is the form of Paul. (It is ironic that the Chinese names European missionaries adopted were more indigenously Chinese than the names their converts adopted.) I would assume that either one, or both, of the authors is also a native priest, but I could not find their names on the rolls of priests provided by Van Den Brandt's *Les Lazaristes en Chine*.

15. Society for the Propagation of the Faith, *Annals of the Propagation of the Faith*, 1844, 261.

16. Ibid., 1867, 58–61.

17. Zhu and Guo, *Yuanni baofa*, 9A.

18. In his *China and Christianity*, Cohen provides a highly informative analysis of the provenance of *A Record of Facts to Ward Off Heterodoxy*. See the appendix, 277–81. An English translation of the tract *Death Blow to Corrupt Doctrines* is similar to *A Record of Facts*. There is an overlap in the contents; both contain Yang Guangxian's tract *Bixie lun*, for example, as well as a chapter titled "Miscellaneous Quotations." They are different publications, though, as *A Record of Facts* includes chapters *Death Blow* does not. Even in the chapters they do share, such as the "Miscellaneous Quotations," *A Record of Facts* includes many more quotations than *Death Blow*. The latter work does include one chapter which the *A Record of Facts* does not, that carrying the provocative title "Petition from Hunan for the Expulsion of the Non-Human Species."

19. *Bixie jishi*, "Tianzhu xiejiao jishuo," 1a.

20. Ibid., 3a.

21. For the slanders concerning eyeballs used in magical potions, see, e.g., ibid., "Tianzhu xiejiao jishuo," 4a; on the menstrual discharge used in worship, see ibid., "Zayin," 3b; for charges of the father and son's relations, see ibid., "Anzheng," 11b. These accusations and variations on them are repeated several times throughout the pages of *Bixie jishi*.

22. Ibid., "Pibo xieshuo," 20b-21a.

23. Ibid., appendix. The term Tianxiong appears twice (1b and 3a). The title for Jesus, Jidu, is never mentioned in this song or, for that matter, in the entire book.

24. Ibid., 3b.

25. Ibid., 4b.
26. Ibid., 7b.
27. Ibid.
28. Ibid., 8b-9a.
29. Pan Guoguang, *Tianzhu sheng jiao shijie quanlun sheng ji*. The 1869 edition is a reprint first published in 1650. The author's Western name is Francesco Brancati (1607–1671). See Pfister, *Notices Biographiques et Bibliographiques sur Les Jésuites de L'Ancienne Mission de Chine*, 228; Standaert, *Handbook of Christianity*, 429.
30. Liang, *Zhendao wenda qianjie*, 3b.
31. Milne, *Youxue qianjie wenda*, 4b.
32. Milne, *Zhendao rumen*, p. 4a.
33. Blodgett, *Zhenli wenda*, 16b.
34. The Taiping version is available in the Chinese in Xiang, *Taiping Tianguo*, 1:225–27; and in English in Michael, *The Taiping Rebellion*, 2:152–61. I used a traditional Chinese version originally edited during the Song dynasty by Wang Yinlin bearing the simple title *Sanzi jing*. The missionary version I used was first composed and published by Walter Medhurst in 1823. The earliest edition I had access to was published in Hong Kong in 1843, and it, too, bore the simple title *Sanzi jing*. Medhurst's version seems to have been a popular one, at least in missionary circles. I ran across several editions and revisions. It was revised in 1870 at Fuzhou, and the resulting work makes for a smoother reading; the chapter headings and topics remain the same. The only significant difference is that this revision, published after the rebellion, changes the name of God from *shen* and *zhen Shenzhu* (the true divine Lord) to Shangdi. While I would like to think that this resulted from the missionaries having learned from the appeal of the Taiping message, there is no indication of this in the preface. Indeed, as seen in my discussion above, the Taiping experience was ignored in all other aspects. Still, there is something strange about the use of *shen* in even the earlier version of this text, for it was Medhurst who had been the main proponent of using Shangdi as God's name. He was the missionary who advocated the use of Shangdi in the debate I covered in chapter 3.
35. It is somewhat strange that Medhurst ignores the historical context, since it was Medhurst, in the Shangdi vs. *shen* debate, who endorsed the view of Chinese history that the Taiping espoused. Early Catholic missionaries held the same view about Chinese history but did not always present it in their literature either. It could very well be that this view was considered offensive to the reigning monarch. The

Ming dynasty convert, Yang Tingyun, adhered to this view. In a preface to a missionary treatise, he wrote that Heaven was once worshipped in classical times; "However, after the Ch'in Dynasty, the worship of Heaven began to decrease, and since the Han it has gone down." Cited in Zürcher, "A Complement to Confucianism," 77.

36. Protestants were initially referred to as the Yesu Jiao (Jesus Sect); later they are referred to as the Jidu (i.e., Christ) Jiao.

Glossary

Bai Shangdi Hui　拜上帝會　Society of God Worshippers
buru yifo　補儒易佛　complete Confucianism and displace Buddhism

chuguijing　出鬼經　exorcism classic, manual

Di　帝　God; god; emperor
diyu　地獄　hell
du　瀆　blaspheme

Er wang jiu zhi　爾王就至　Your reign would come

fanzui　犯罪　commit a sin; commit a crime
Fu Han Hui　福漢會　Chinese Union
futou　浮頭　floating head
futu　浮圖　floating map

Huang Shangdi　皇上帝　Supreme Sovereign on High

huangdi　皇帝　emperor; god. Traditionally translated into English as "emperor," but could literally be translated as "glorious or supreme ruler" or "glorious or supreme god"

Jidu　基督　Shortened form of the transliteration for "Christ"
jiebai　結拜　to swear brotherhood
Jilishidu　基利士督　Protestant transliteration of "Christ"
Jilisidu　基利斯督　Catholic transliteration of "Christ"
jiu　咎　sin; crime
Jiushizhu　救世主　World's Salvation Lord
Jiuyi Zhaoshu　舊遺詔書　Old Testament

kong　空　emptiness

Glossary

mogui 魔鬼 devil

Shangdi 上帝 Sovereign on High; (Protestant) Christian God
Shangzhu 上主 High Lord
shen 神 god; spirit
sheng 聖 sagely wisdom; moral holiness; imperial
shengshen 聖神 holy spirit; holy god; angel
shengshi 聖使 imperial messenger; angel
shengyu 聖諭 sacred words; imperial decree
Shengzhu 聖主 Holy Lord
shengzuo 聖座 sacred throne; imperial throne
shenpin 神品 spirit utensils
shenshi 神使 divine messenger; godly messenger; angel
Shentian 神天 Heavenly God; God, or gods, of Heaven
Shentian Shangdi 神天上帝 God of Heaven, Shangdi
songjing 誦經 chant scripture; chant liturgy

Taiji 太極 The Supreme Ultimate
Taixiong 太兄 Elder Prince
Taizi 太子 Crown Prince; Heir Apparent; anointed prince
Tian Shangdi 天上帝 Shangdi of Heaven; Heavenly Sovereign on High
tianbing 天兵 heavenly soldiers; imperial soldiers
Tiandi 天帝 Sovereign of Heaven; Heavenly Emperor
Tiandi Hui 添弟會 Increasing Brothers Society
Tiandihui 天帝會 Heavenly Emperor Society
tian'en 天恩 heavenly grace; imperial grace
Tianguo 天國 Heavenly Kingdom; Kingdom of Heaven
Tianguo jinyi 天國近矣 The Heavenly Kingdom draws near
Tianshen 天神 Heavenly Spirit; Heavenly God; angel
tianshi 天使 heavenly or imperial messenger; angel
Tiantan 天壇 Altar of Heaven; Temple of Heaven
Tiantang 天堂 Heaven
Tianwang 天王 Heavenly King; used by Liang Afa as "Heavenly Reign"
tianwei 天位 heavenly throne; imperial throne
Tianxiong 天兄 Heavenly Elder Brother
Tianzhu 天主 Lord of Heaven; the (Catholic) Christian God
Tianzhu jiao 天主教

Heavenly Lord teaching or sect; Catholicism
Tianzi 天子 Son of Heaven
tuanfangfa 團防法 methods of militia defense

wu 無 non-being
Wu ducheng ru Shangzhu Huang Shangdi zhiming 無瀆稱汝上主皇上帝之名 Do not blaspheme Supreme High Lord Shangdi's name
wuwei 無為 daoist: non-activity; Buddhist: nirvana

xieshen 邪神 evil spirits; evil gods

yu 閾 threshold
yu 諭 decree

zhaoshu 詔書 imperial declaration; also, translation of "Bible"
Zhen Shenzhu 真神主 True Divine Lord
zhenren 真人 Daoist: immortal; Buddhist: enlightened one
Zhenyu 朕諭 I (the emperor) decree
Zhenzhu 真主 True Lord

Bibliography

Ahern, Emily. *Chinese Ritual and Politics.* Cambridge: Cambridge University Press, 1981.
Archives of the Council for World Mission. "London Missionary Society: Central China." Set #2140, Boxes 1–26. Yale Divinity School, Day Mission Library.
Bai Yingli. *Tianzhu sheng jiao bai wenda* (A catechism of the holy religion of the Lord of Heaven). N.p., n.d.
Baller, F.W. *The Sacred Edict.* Shanghai: American Presbyterian Mission Press, 1892.
Bartlett, Beatrice. *Monarchs and Ministers.* Berkeley: University of California Press, 1991.
Bays, Daniel. "Christianity and Chinese Sects: Religious Tracts in the Late Nineteenth Century." In *Christianity in China: Early Protestant Missionary Writings,* edited by Suzanne Barnett and J. K. Fairbank. Cambridge: Harvard University Press, 1985.
———, ed. *Christianity in China: From the Eighteenth Century to the Present.* Stanford: Stanford University Press, 1996.
Bell, Catherine. "Religion and Chinese Culture: Toward an Assessment of 'Popular Religion.'" *History of Religions* 29, no. 1 (1989): 35–57.
———. *Ritual Theory, Ritual Practice.* New York: Oxford University Press, 1992.
Bernhardt, Kathryn. *Rents, Taxes and Peasant Resistance.* Stanford: Stanford University Press, 1992.
Bixie jishi (A record of facts to ward off heterodoxy). N.p.: n.p., 1871.
Blodgett, Henry. *Zhenli wenda* (A catechism of the truth). Peking: n.p., 1873.

Boardman, Eugene. *Christian Influence upon the Ideology of the Taiping Rebellion, 1851–1864.* Madison: University of Wisconsin Press, 1952.

Bodde, Derk, and Clarence Morris. *Law in Imperial China.* Philadelphia: University of Pennsylvania Press, 1973.

Boff, Leonardo, and Clodovis Boff. *Salvation and Liberation.* Maryknoll, N.Y.: Orbis Books, 1984.

Bohr, P. Richard. "The Politics of Eschatology: Hung Hsiu-ch'uan and the Rise of the Taipings, 1837–1853." Ph.D. diss., University of California, Davis, 1978.

Buglio, Ludovico, trans. *Shengshi lidian* (A manual of ritual holy matters). Pekin: n.p., 1675.

Canton, William. *History of the British and Foreign Bible Society.* Vol. 2. London: John Murray, 1904.

Carey, William. *An Enquiry into the Obligations of Christians to Use Means for the Conversion of the Heathen.* Leicester, 1792; facsimile edition: London, 1961.

Cary-Elwes, Columba. *China and the Cross: A Survey of Missionary History.* New York: P. J. Kennedy, 1957.

Chen, Kenneth. *Buddhism in China.* Princeton: Princeton University Press, 1964.

Chesneaux, Jean, ed. *Popular Movements and Secret Societies in China, 1840–1950.* Stanford: Stanford University Press, 1972.

Chiang Siang-tseh. *The Nien Rebellion.* Seattle: University of Washington Press, 1954.

The Chinese Recorder and Missionary Journal. Foochow, 1868–72; Shanghai, 1874–1900.

The Chinese Repository. Canton, 1845–51.

Chouban yiwu shimo (A complete account of our management of barbarian affairs). Peking: n.p., 1930.

Clarke, P. "The Coming of God to Kwangsi." *Papers on Far Eastern History* 7 (March 1973): 145–81.

Clarke, Prescott, and J. S. Gregory. *Western Reports on the Taiping.* Honolulu: The University Press of Hawaii, 1982.

Cohen, Paul. *China and Christianity: The Missionary Movement and the Growth of Chinese Anti-Foreignism, 1860–1870.* Cambridge: Harvard University Press, 1963.

Daqing lüli huiji beilan (The Great Qing statutes and sub-statutes, collected and classified). N.p.: n.p., 1877.

Daqing lüli huitong xinzuan (A comprehensive new edition of the statutes and sub-statutes of the Great Qing). Edited by Yao Yuxiang. Peking: n.p., 1873. Reprint, Taipei: n.p., 1964.

Death Blow to Corrupt Doctrines. Shanghai: n.p., 1870.

DeGroot, J. J. M. *Sectarianism and Religious Persecution in China.* Amsterdam: Johannes Muller, 1904.

Dehergne, Joseph. *Répertoire des Jésuites de Chine.* Rome: Institutum Historicum, 1973.

Eire, Carlos. *War Against the Idols: The Reformation of Worship from Erasmus to Calvin.* Cambridge: Cambridge University Press, 1986.

Entenmann, Robert E. "Catholics and Society in Eighteenth-Century Sichuan." In *Christianity in China: From the Eighteenth Century to the Present,* edited by Daniel Bays. Stanford: Stanford University Press, 1996.

Esherick, Joseph. *Reform and Revolution in China: The 1911 Revolution in Hunan and Hubei.* Berkeley and Los Angeles: University of California Press, 1976.

Feng Bingzheng. *Shengshi churao* (A grass cutter in a prosperous age). N.p: n.p. Reprint, 1796.

Feuchtwang, Stephan. *The Imperial Metaphor: Popular Religion in China.* London and New York: Routledge, 1992.

Fishbourne, E. G. *Impressions of China and the Present Revolution.* London: Seeley, Jackson, and Halliday, 1855.

Forrest, Robert James. "The Christianity of Hung Tsiu Tsuen, A Review of Taeping Books." *Journal of the North China Branch of the Royal Asiatic Society* 4 (December 1867): 187–208.

Gernet, Jacques. *China and the Christian Impact: A Conflict of Cultures.* Translated by Janet Lloyd. Cambridge: Cambridge University Press, 1985.

Gongzhong dang (Palace Memorial Archive). Peasant Uprising and Nian Army Categories. Beijing: Ming-Qing Archives.

Gregory, Peter. *Tsung-mi and the Sinification of Buddhism.* Princeton: Princeton University Press, 1991.

Guo Tingyi. *Taiping Tianguo shishi rizhi* (Historical facts and calendrical record of the Taiping Heavenly Kingdom). Shanghai: Shanghai Bookstore Publishers, 1986.

Guo Yisheng, ed. *Taiping Tianguo lishi dituji* (A historical atlas of the Taiping Heavenly Kingdom). Beijing: China Maps Publishing, 1989.

Gützlaff, Charles. *Journal of Three Voyages Along the Coast of China in 1831, 1832, and 1833*. London: Frederick Westley and A. H. Davis, 1834. Reprint, Taipei: Ch'eng-wen Publishing Company, 1968.

Guy, R. Kent. *The Emperor's Four Treasuries: Scholars and the State in the Late Ch'ien-lung Era*. Cambridge: Harvard University Press, 1987.

Hamberg, Theodore. *The Visions of Hung-Siu-Tshuen, and Origin of the Kwang-si Insurrection*. Hong Kong: China Mail Office, 1854. Reprint, Peking: Yenching University Library, 1935.

Hill, Christopher. *The English Bible and the Seventeenth-Century Revolution*. London: The Penguin Press, 1993.

Hobsbawm, E. J. *Social Bandits and Primitive Rebels*. Glencoe, Ill.: The Free Press, 1959.

Huang Yubian. *Poxie xiangbian* (A detailed refutation of heterodoxy). N.p.: n.p., 1883.

Hykes, John R. *List of Translations of the Scriptures into the Chinese Language*. Yokohama: Fukyin Printing Company, 1915.

Jen Yu-wen. *Taiping Tianguo dianzhi tongkao* (Studies on the institutions of the Taiping Heavenly Kingdom). 3 vol. Hong Kong: n.p., 1958.

———. *The Taiping Revolutionary Movement*. New Haven: Yale University Press, 1973.

Jiuyizhao shengshu (The Old Testament). Gützlaff version. N.p.: n.p., 1853.

Johnson, David, Andrew Nathan, and Evelyn Rawski, eds. *Popular Culture in Late Imperial China*. Berkeley and Los Angeles: University of California Press, 1985.

Jones, William C., trans. *The Great Qing Code*. Oxford: Clarendon Press, 1994.

Jordan, David. *Gods, Ghosts, and Ancestors*. Berkeley: University of California Press, 1972.

Junjichu dang (Grand Council archive). Peasant Uprising and Nien Army Categories. Beijing: Ming-Qing Archives.

Kuhn, Philip. "Origins of the Taiping Vision: Cross-Cultural Dimensions of a Chinese Rebellion." *Comparative Studies in Society and History* 19 (1977): 350–66.

———. "The Taiping Rebellion." In *The Cambridge History of China*, edited

Bibliography   217

by Denis Twitchett and John K. Fairbank. Pt. 1 of vol. 10, *Late Ch'ing, 1800–1911*. Cambridge: Cambridge University Press, 1978.

———. *Soulstealers: The Chinese Sorcery Scare of 1768*. Cambridge: Harvard University Press, 1990.

Latourette, Kenneth Scott. *A History of Christian Missions in China*. London: Society for Promoting Christian Knowledge, 1929.

Launay, Adrien. *Histoire des Missions de la Chine, Mission du Kouang-si*. Paris: n.p., 1903.

Lettres Édifantes et Curieuses. Nouvelle edition. Vols. 16–20. Toulouse: n.p., 1810–11.

Liang Afa. *Zhendao wenda qianjie* (The true way catechism simply explained). Malacca, 1829.

———. *Quanshi liangyan* (Good words to admonish the age). Canton: Religious Tract Society, 1832. Reprint, Taipei: Taiwan Xuesheng shuju, 1965.

Liang jiang zhongyi lü (A record of martyrs from Jiangsu and Jiangxi). 1877 and 1893.

Lindley [Linle], Augustus F. *Ti-Ping Tien-Kwoh, The History of the Ti-Ping Revolution*. Vol. 1. London: Day and Son, 1866.

Liu Cheng-yun. "The Ko-Lao Hui in Late Imperial China." Ph.D. diss., University of Pittsburgh, 1983.

Liu Jinzao, ed. *Qingchao xu wenxian tongkao* (Encyclopedia of source materials for the Qing dynasty). Shanghai: Commercial Press, 1935.

Liu Kwang-ching, ed. *Orthodoxy in Late Imperial China*. Berkeley: University of California Press, 1990.

Lloyd, Trevor. *The British Empire*. New York: Oxford University Press, 1984.

Loewe, Michael. "The Religious and Intellectual Background." In *The Cambridge History of China*, edited by Denis Twitchett and Michael Loewe. Vol. 1, *The Ch'in and Han Empires*. Cambridge: Cambridge University Press, 1986.

Lundbæk, Knud. "Joseph De Prémare and the Name of God in China." In *The Chinese Rites Controversy: Its History and Meaning*, edited by D. E. Mungello. Nettetal: Steylar Verlag, 1994.

Luo Ergang, ed. *Taiping Tianguo wenwu* (Relics of the Taiping Heavenly Kingdom). Nanjing: Jiangsu Publishing House, 1992.

Lutz, Jessie G., and R. Ray Lutz. "Karl Gützlaff's Approach to Indigenization:

The Chinese Union." In *Christianity in China: From the Eighteenth Century to the Present,* edited by Daniel Bays. Stanford: Stanford University Press, 1996.

———. *Hakka Chinese Confront Protestant Christianity, 1850–1900.* Armonk, N.Y.: M. E. Sharpe, 1998.

MacGillivray, D. *A Century of Protestant Missions in China (1807–1907).* Shanghai: American Presbyterian Mission Press, 1907. Reprint, San Francisco: Chinese Materials Center, 1979.

McNeur, George H. *China's First Preacher, Liang A-fa.* Shanghai: Kwang Hsueh Publishing House, 1934.

Meadows, Thomas T. *The Chinese and Their Rebellions.* London: Smith Elder, 1856. Reprint, Stanford: Stanford University Reprints, 1953.

Medhurst, W. H. *China: Its State and Prospects.* London: John Snow, 1840.

———. *Sanzi jing* (The three character classic). Hong Kong: n.p., 1843.

Michael, Franz. *The Taiping Rebellion: History and Documents.* In collaboration with Chung-li Chang. 3 vols. Seattle: University of Washington Press, 1971.

Milne, William. *Youxue qianjie wenda* (An elementary scholar's catechism simply explained). Malacca: n.p., 1817.

Milne, William C. *Zhendao rumen* (The entrance to the true way). Amoy, 1855.

Minamiki, George. *The Chinese Rites Controversy from Its Beginning to Modern Times.* Chicago: Loyola University Press, 1985.

Miranda, Jose. *Communism in the Bible.* Maryknoll, N.Y.: Orbis Books, 1982.

Morrison, Robert, trans. *Yesu Jilishidu wozhu jiuzhe xinyi zhaoshu* (The New Testament; lit., Jesus Christ, my lord and savior, newly transmitted imperial declaration). N.p.: n.p., 1813.

———. *Yesu Jilishidu wo jiuzhu zhaoshu* (The New Testament; lit., The imperial declaration of Jesus Christ, my salvation lord). Canton: n.p., 1813–14.

———. *Shentian shengshu* (The holy book of the God of Heaven). Malacca: n.p., 1823.

The Morrison Transcript of the Basset Version of the New Testament. N.p.: n.p., 1806.

Morse, Hosea B. *The International Relations of the Chinese Empire.* London: Longmans, Green, and Company, 1910.

Mungello, David. *The Forgotten Christians of Hangzhou.* Honolulu: University of Hawaii Press, 1994.

———. *The Spirit and the Flesh in Shandong, 1650–1785.* Lanham, Md.: Rowman and Littlefield, 2001.

Naquin, Susan. *Millenarian Rebellion in China: The Eight Trigrams Uprising of 1813.* New Haven: Yale University Press, 1976.
Neill, Stephen. *A History of Christian Missions.* Vol. 6 of *The Pelican History of the Church*, edited by Owen Chadwick. Middlesex: Penguin Books, 1964.
North China Herald. Shanghai, 1853–1900.
Overmyer, Daniel. "Attitudes Toward the Ruler and State in Chinese Popular Religious Literature: Sixteenth and Seventeenth Century *Pao-chüan*." *Harvard Journal of Asian Studies* 44, no. 2 (1984): 347–79.
———. *Folk Buddhist Religion.* Cambridge: Harvard University Press, 1976.
———. *Precious Volumes: An Introduction to Sectarian Scriptures from the Sixteenth and Seventeenth Centuries.* Cambridge: Harvard University Press, 1999.
Ownby, David. "The Heaven and Earth Society as Popular Religion." *The Journal of Asian Studies* 54, no. 4 (November 1995): 1023–46.
Ownby, David, and Mary Somers Heidhues. *"Secret Societies" Reconsidered.* Armonk, N.Y.: M. E. Sharpe, 1993.
Pan Guoguang. *Tianzhu Shijie quanlun sheng ji* (A discussion of the holy record of the ten prohibitions of the Heavenly Lord). 1650. Reprint, n.p.: n.p., 1869.
Perry, Elizabeth. *Rebels and Revolutionaries in North China, 1845–1945.* Stanford: Stanford University Press, 1980.
———. "Taipings and Triads: The Role of Religion in Inter-Rebel Relations." In *Religion and Rural Revolt*, edited by J. Bak and G. Benecke. Manchester: Manchester University Press, 1984.
———, ed. *Chinese Perspectives on the Nien.* Armonk, N.Y.: M. E. Sharpe, 1981.
Pfister, Le P. Louis. *Notices Biographiques et Bibliographiques sur Les Jésuites de L'Ancienne Mission de Chine.* Shanghai: Catholic Mission, 1934.
Qin Baoqi and Dian Murray. *The Origins of the Tiandi Hui: The Chinese Triads in Legend and History.* Stanford: Stanford University Press, 1994.
Qinding Jiuyizhao Shengshu (The [Taiping] royally authorized Old Testament). N.p.: n.p. [1860?]. British Museum Microfilm.
Qinding qianyizhao Shengshu (The [Taiping] royally authorized New Testament). N.p.: n.p. [1860?]. British Museum Microfilm.
Records of the General Conference of the Protestant Missionaries of China. Shanghai: American Presbyterian Mission Press, 1878, 1890.
Ricci, Matteo. *Tianzhu shiyi* (The true meaning of the Lord of Heaven).

Translated with an introduction by Douglas Lancashire and Peter Hu Kuo-chen; edited by Edward J. Malatesta. Taipei: Ricci Institute, 1985.

Roberts, Issachar J. "Tae Ping Wang." *Putnam's Magazine* (October 1856): 380–83.

Rowbotham, Arnold. *Missionary and Mandarin: The Jesuits at the Court of China.* Berkeley and Los Angeles: University of California Press, 1942.

Sanzijing (Three character classic). 1852. In *The Taiping Rebellion: History and Documents* by Franz Michael, 3 vols., Seattle: University of Washington Press, 1971, and in *Taiping Tianguo* (Taiping Heavenly Kingdom), ed. Xiang Da et al., 8 vols., Shanghai: Shenzhou guoguang she, 1952.

Seidel, Anna K. "The Image of the Perfect Ruler in Early Taoist Messianism: Lao-Tzu and Li Hung." *History of Religions* 9, no. 2/3 (1969–70): 216–47.

Shih, Vincent Y. C. *The Taiping Ideology: Its Sources, Interpretations and Influences.* 1967. Reprint, Seattle: University of Washington Press, 1972.

Society for the Propagation of the Faith. *Annals of the Propagation of the Faith.* Paris, 1838–39; London and Baltimore, 1840–1900.

Soothill, William E., and Lewis Hodous. *A Dictionary of Chinese Buddhist Terms.* London, 1937. Reprint, Delhi: Motilal Banarsidass, 1977.

Spelman, Douglas G. "Christianity in Chinese: The Protestant Term Question." (Harvard) *Papers on China* 22A (1969): 25–52.

Spence, Jonathan. *God's Chinese Son: The Taiping Heavenly Kingdom of Hong Xiuquan.* New York: W.W. Norton, 1996.

Standaert, Nicolas. *The Fascinating God: A Challenge to Modern Chinese Theology Presented by a Text on the Name of God.* Rome: Pontifical Gregorian University, 1995.

———. "The Bible in Early Seventeenth-Century China." In *Bible in Modern China: The Literary and Intellectual Impact,* edited by Irene Ebert et al. Sankt Augustin: Institut Monumentica Serica, 1999.

———, ed. *Handbook of Christianity in China.* Vol. 1, *635–1800.* Leiden: Brill, 2001.

Stanley, Brian. *The Bible and the Flag: Protestant Missions and British Imperialism.* Leicester, England: Appolos, 1990.

Strandenaes, Thor. "The Sloane MS #3599: An Early Manuscript of an Incomplete Chinese Version of the New Testament." *Theology and Life,* no. 6 (December 1983): 61–76.

Taiping Tianguo yinshu (Published documents of the Taiping Heavenly Kingdom). 2 vols. Jiangsu Publishing House, 1979.
Taiping tianri (Taiping heavenly chronicle). 1848. In *The Taiping Rebellion: History and Documents* by Franz Michael, 3 vols., Seattle: University of Washington Press, 1971, and in *Taiping Tianguo* (Taiping Heavenly Kingdom), ed. Xiang Da et al., 8 vols., Shanghai: Shenzhou guoguang she, 1952.
Taiping zhaoshu (Taiping imperial declaration). In *The Taiping Rebellion: History and Documents* by Franz Michael, 3 vols., Seattle: University of Washington Press, 1971, and in *Taiping Tianguo* (Taiping Heavenly Kingdom), ed. Xiang Da et al., 8 vols., Shanghai: Shenzhou guoguang she, 1952.
Taylor, Rodney. *The Religious Dimensions of Confucianism*. Albany: SUNY Press, 1990.
Ter Haar, Barend J. "China's Inner Demons: The Political Impact of the Demonological Paradigm." *China Information* 11, no. 3/4 (1996): 54–88.
———. *Ritual and Mythology of the Chinese Triads: Creating an Identity*. Leiden: Brill, 1998.
———. *The White Lotus Teachings in Chinese Religious History*. Honolulu: University of Hawaii Press, 1999.
Tianchao tianmou zhidu (The land system of the Heavenly Dynasty). 1853. In *The Taiping Rebellion: History and Documents* by Franz Michael, 3 vols., Seattle: University of Washington Press, 1971, and in *Taiping Tianguo* (Taiping Heavenly Kingdom), ed. Xiang Da et al., 8 vols., Shanghai: Shenzhou guoguang she, 1952.
Tiantiao shu (The book of heavenly commandments). 1847(?) In *The Taiping Rebellion: History and Documents* by Franz Michael, 3 vols., Seattle: University of Washington Press, 1971, and in *Taiping Tianguo* (Taiping Heavenly Kingdom), ed. Xiang Da et al., 8 vols., Shanghai: Shenzhou guoguang she, 1952.
Tiedemann, R.G. "Christianity and Chinese 'Heterodox Sects': Mass Conversion and Syncretism in Shandong Province in the Early Eighteenth Century." *Monumentica Serica* 44 (1996): 339–82.
Treaties, Conventions, Etc., Between China and Foreign States. Shanghai: Inspectorate General of Customs, 1917.
Van Den Brandt, J. *Les Lazaristes en Chine, 1697–1935: Notes Biographiques et Mises À Jour*. Pei-p'ing: Imprimerie des Lazaristes, 1936.

Wagner, Rudolf. *Reenacting the Heavenly Vision: The Role of Religion in the Taiping Rebellion.* 1982. Reprint, Berkeley: University of California Press, 1987.

———. "Operating in the Chinese Public Sphere: Theology and Technique of Taiping Propaganda." In *Norms and the State in China*, edited by Chun-chieh Huang and Erik Zürcher. Leiden: Brill, 1993.

Wang Qingcheng. *Tianfu Tianxiong shengzhi* (The holy decrees of the Heavenly Father and the Heavenly Elder Brother). Liaoning: Liaoning People's Press, 1986.

———. *Taiping Tianguo de wenxian he lishi* (Documents and history of the Taiping Heavenly Kingdom). Beijing: Social Science Publications, 1993.

Wang Yinlin. *Sanzi jing* (Three character classic). Collated by Chen Xuguo. Changsha: n.p., 1986.

Weller, Robert P. "Historians and Consciousness: The Modern Politics of the Taiping Heavenly Kingdom." *Social Research* 54, no.4 (1987): 731–55.

———. *Resistance, Chaos and Control in China: Taiping Rebels, Taiwanese Ghosts and Tiananmen.* Seattle: University of Washington Press, 1994.

Withers, John L. "The Heavenly Capital: Nanjing Under the Taiping, 1853–1864." Ph.D. diss., Yale University, 1983.

Wright, Arthur F. *Buddhism in Chinese History.* Stanford: Stanford University Press, 1959.

———. *Studies in Chinese Buddhism.* Edited by Robert M. Somers. New Haven: Yale University Press, 1990.

Wu Liangzuo and Luo Wenqi. "Taiping Tianguo yinshu jiaokan ji" (A list of alterations in Taiping printed literature). *Taiping Tianguo xuekan* 3 (1987): 266–82.

Wylie, A. *Memorials of Protestant Missionaries to the Chinese.* Shanghai: American Presbyterian Press, 1867. Reprint, Taipei: Ch'eng-wen Publishing Company, 1967.

Xia Chuntao. *Taiping Tianguo zongjiao* (The religion of the Taiping Heavenly Kingdom). Nanjing: Nanjing University Press, 1992.

Xiang Da et al., eds. *Taiping Tianguo* (Taiping Heavenly Kingdom). 8 vols. Zhongguo jindaishi ziliao congkan. Shanghai: Shenzhou guoguang she, 1952.

Xinyizhao shengshu (The New Testament). Gützlaff version. N.p.: n.p., 1853.

Young, J. D. *Confucianism and Christianity: The First Encounter.* Hong Kong: Hong Kong University Press, 1983.

Zelin, Madeline. *The Magistrate's Tael.* Berkeley: University of California Press, 1985.

Zetzsche, Jost Oliver. *The Bible in China: The History of the Union Version.* Monumentica Serica Monograph Series. Nettetal: Steyler Verlag, 1999.

Zhongguo renming da cidian (The Chinese biographical dictionary). Shanghai: n.p., 1984.

Zhu Ximan and Guo Baolu. *Yuanni baofa* (A treasured raft which rescues the drowning). N.p.: n.p., 1860.

Zhuang Jifa. *Qingdai mimi huidangshi yanjiu* (Research on the history of Qing era secret societies). Taipei: Wenshizhe Publishing House, 1994.

Zürcher, Erik. *The Buddhist Conquest of China.* Leiden: E. J. Brill, 1972.

———. "The Lord of Heaven and the Demons: Strange Stories from a Late Ming Christian Manuscript." In *Religion und Philosophie in Ostasien.* Würzburg: Königshausen und Neumann, 1985.

———. "A Complement to Confucianism: Christianity and Orthodoxy in Late Imperial China." In *Norms and the State in China,* edited by Chun-chieh Huang and Erik Zürcher. Leiden: Brill, 1993.

Index

angel(s): terms for, 32, 35, 59–61
Anhui, 122–24, 132, 139
Annals of the Propagation of the Faith, 46
Anqing, 121, 147
"anti-foreignism," 157–58
apocalyptic doctrines, 12, 56, 111, 113–16. *See also* millenarian teachings
Apostles' Creed, 36, 160, 195n49

baptism, 160; "blitz baptism," 63, 186n25; as Catholic rite, 34–36; as practiced by Taiping, 128–29
Baptist Missionary Society, 55
Basset, Jean, 58–60, 184n10; and influence on Morrison, 60–61, 80, 101
Beijing Convention of 1860, 49–50
Bernhardt, Kathryn, 141–42
Bible: Catholic translations of, 57–58; distribution in China, 69, 73; influence on Taiping, 57, 68–69, 71–78, 188n42; Protestant translations of, 57–60, 73–74, 81, 95; Taiping version of, 73–75, 78, 81, 95, 190n67. *See also* New Testament; Old Testament; Ten Commandments
blasphemy: as charged to Chinese rulers, 15, 87–88, 136; as reason for Taiping Rebellion, 13, 88, 92–94, 98–99, 104, 143–44, 164–65, 194n35; as viewed by missionaries, 68, 165–67
Blue Lotus sect, 52
Boardman, Eugene, 6–8
Bohr, P. Richard, 8, 12
Book of Declarations of the Divine Will Made During the Heavenly Father's Descent to Earth, 9
Book of Heavenly Commandments, 11, 99
Book of Heavenly Decrees and Proclamations, 75–76, 115–16
Book of History, 106
Boone, William, 81–83, 86–88, 90, 192n8; and Medhurst, 90–91, 193n25
Bridgman, E. C., 73, 119, 198n2

Britain, British; and hostilities with China, 46, 49; and ideas of empire, 55, 90, 183n3; merchants' views of Taiping, 118

Buddhism, 31–32, 173n2; and Catholicism, 14, 19–21, 25–31, 34–38, 41–42, 165, 175n1; and millenarianism, 114–15, 197n70, 198n78; sectarians, 158, 161, 173n2; and Taiping, 136; and translation of religious terms, 27–30, 178n31, 193n15

Buglio, Ludovico, 34, 195n49

Calvinism, 55, 62, 134–36, 139, 183n1, 186n28, 202nn55–56

Canton (Guangzhou), 65–66, 81; and Hong Xiuquan, 70–73, 92, 95, 98

Canton, William, 69

Carey, William, 54–56, 202n56

A Catechism of the Holy Religion of the Lord of Heaven, 31–33

Catholicism, Catholic(s), 14–15; 20, 47, 157–58, 182n67; and Buddhism, 15, 20–23, 30–38, 40, 43; and links to Taiping rebels, 153–54, 170–71; sacramental rites of, 34–38, 160; statistics on, 46–49, 54, 156, 181n63. *See also* Catholic missionaries; Christianity; Heavenly Lord sect

Catholic missionaries, 14–15, 19–22, 54; and Confucianism, 19–27, 33, 38, 40, 100, 175n1, 207n35; impact of, 22, 24–25, 39–40; and translation of Christian terms, 21–34, 40, 86, 101, 193n15, 195n49; and view of Taiping, 154–56, 165–66. *See also* Dominicans; Franciscans; Jesuits; *names of individuals*

Changsha, 144

Chinese classical religious tradition, 5, 14, 89, 113, 171; and Catholicism, 14–15, 19–25, 42; and Taiping, 4–6, 15–17, 78–79, 99–100, 116, 168–69

The Chinese Repository, 99–101, 196n50; debate over name of God, 81, 86, 90–91, 191nn5–6

Chinese Union, 63, 65, 69, 74, 187n34; influence on Taiping, 69–71, 92, 189n51

Christ. *See* Jesus, title of Christ

Christianity, 17, 42, 49, 91; Chinese hostility, suspicion of, 17, 39, 150–51, 157–60, 174n11; Chinese persecution of, 43, 47–48, 161–63; as completing Confucianism, 14–17, 19–25, 39, 100; doctrine and teachings of, 11, 20, 31; European style of, 7, 101, 165–66; proscription of, 20, 43–49, 175n3; relationship to Chinese religions, 14–15, 164–65; and Taiping religion, 117–19, 170–71. *See also* Catholic missionaries; Catholics; Protestant missionaries; Protestants; Taiping Christianity

churches, establishment of, 49, 53

Clement XI (pope), 22–23, 27, 34, 80, 179n47

Cohen, Paul, 157–58, 174n11, 206n18

Confucian, Confucianism, 14–16, 33, 173n2; and Catholicism, 19–27,

38–39; literati, 19, 24–25, 38–40, 42, 143, 179nn49–50; and Taiping Christianity, 18, 95, 100, 114, 137–38, 140, 168, 171
Couplet, Philippe, 31–33, 178n32

Daoguang period, 44, 49, 159, 161, 182n76
Daoism, 14, 19, 22, 173n2; and Buddhism, 29–31; and Christianity, 25, 29, 41–42
Death Blow to Corrupt Doctrines, 159, 206n18
DeGroot, J. J. M., 43
de Lagrene, Theodose, 51
demon(s), devil, 10, 29, 37–38, 96
A Detailed Refutation of Heterodoxy, 160–61
Dominicans, 38

East India Company, 55–56, 183n3, 184n5
Edkins, Joseph, 122, 130–32, 149, 201n44
Eight Trigram sect, 4, 11, 44, 51–52, 152
Eire, Carlos, 135–36
emperor: authority of, 4, 46, 149; deification of, 4, 13, 16–17, 33, 79, 87–88, 93, 106, 139, 166–67, 192n8
Enlightenment, 7, 64
Enquiry into the Obligation of Christians to Use Means for the Conversion of the Heathen, 54
Evangelical Awakening, 54–55, 183n1

evangelicalism, evangelicals, 61–62, 64, 115, 202n56. *See also* Protestants
exorcism, 37–38, 41

Feng Yunshan (The Southern King), 66–67, 73, 128, 130
Fishbourne, E. G., 70, 73–74, 136, 155
Five Classics, 19, 23, 27
France, French, 50–52, 56
Franciscans, 38, 120, 154
Fujian, 148, 205n106

gentry: and view of Heavenly Lord sect, 16, 54, 150–53, 156–60, 170–71; and view of Taiping Rebellion, 16, 149, 169–71, 199n4. *See also* Qing loyalists
Gernet, Jacques, 40–42, 174n11
Good Words to Admonish the Age, 62–65, 98, 111, 147, 186n29; and influence on Hong Xiuquan, 8–9, 66, 92, 134, 188n42; and influence on Taiping, 65, 71, 78–79; and name for God, 80, 191n3
Guangdong, 66, 78, 122–23, 148, 152, 161
Guangxi, 9, 66–67, 70, 78, 148, 152; and Taiping leadership, 122, 124, 199n17; and Taiping rebels, 121, 123, 131–32, 157
Gützlaff, Karl, 55, 62–63, 186n25; Bible translation of, 73–75, 78–80, 92, 102, 104, 106, 195n45; evangelistic method, 69–71, 188nn43–44; and influence on Taiping, 78–79, 94, 99; and name for God, 78–80, 92, 94

Hamberg, Theodore, 69, 194n33
Hangzhou, 147
Heaven: in Catholic doctrine, 19, 25, 41; classical view of, 29, 160–62; importance to Taiping, 104, 126, 144, 146; terms for, 29, 90, 175n3, 105–6. *See also* "kingdom of Heaven"
Heavenly Kingdom. *See* Taiping Heavenly Kingdom
Heavenly Lord sect, 14–15, 20–21, 175n2; as foreign religion, 50–51, 150; as heterodox sect, 15–16, 20–21, 38, 43–46, 52, 150–51, 157–64, 175n2; impact of Taiping Rebellion on, 150–58, 164, 169; proscription of, 43–46, 150, 159, 163, 180n59; and Taiping Christianity, 16, 43, 47, 53–54, 158–64; toleration of, 43–49, 52–53, 164; as viewed by Chinese gentry, officials, 54, 150–53, 156–60, 170–71
hell, 29, 41, 160
Hill, Christopher, 57
Hobsbawm, E. J., 197n70, 198n78
holy: terms for, 29–30
Holy Spirit: terms for, 32, 35–36, 59–61
Hong Rengan (Shield King), 7–8, 70, 72, 178n32, 190n67, 201n44; conversion of, 66, 128, 188n41; in later years, 130–31
Hong Xiuquan (Heavenly King), 3, 12, 15, 159, 161; and annotations to Bible, 75, 103–4, 112–13, 190nn68–69; background, 66–67; and belief in "kingdom of Heaven," 107, 110–16; and belief in Shangdi, 5, 15, 89, 91–92, 104; as brother of Jesus, 13, 94–95, 102–4, 115; conversion of, 66, 128–30; and creation of new paradigm, 4, 13–15, 17–18, 168–69; and declaration as Heavenly King, 3, 13, 67, 93–96, 100, 107, 169, 174n10, 204n88; and desire to remake culture, 5, 13–15, 100, 107, 151, 168–69; and evangelicalism, 62, 64, 115; and name for God, 91–95; and Old Testament, 96–98, 194n35; and opposition to emperor, imperial culture, 13–17, 79, 88, 92–96, 110, 116, 194n35; political ambitions of, 68, 107, 110; and shaping of Taiping religion, 4–5, 9, 15–17, 78–79, 134; and title of Christ, 13, 100, 103, 196nn55–56; and vision of journey to heaven, 8–9, 66, 68, 76, 138–39, 169, 174n10; Huangdi, 4–5, 87–88, 93, 143
Hubei, 9, 120–24, 131–32, 154, 156
Huc, L'Abbe, 49
Hunan, 9, 48, 120–24, 131, 154, 156–57

iconoclasm, 96–97, 170–71; in Hong's early actions, 68, 95, 136; in Protestant teachings, 15, 134–39; in Taiping Christianity, 13–16, 96–99, 134–40, 144, 149, 151, 165, 194n35, 203n71 idolatry: as defined by Hong, 68, 96–97; as opposed by Taiping, 94–96, 98, 133, 136–40, 149; as viewed by Protestants, 136

imperial office, system of, 17–18, 33, 93, 177n29; Taiping attacks on, 4–6, 12–13, 99, 117, 144, 149, 170–71

imperial title, 86–89; as condemned by Taiping, 4–6, 15, 92, 94, 97, 110

Innocent XI (pope), 34

Jen Yu-wen, 12, 194n35, 194n41, 195n45

Jesuits, 14, 19; failures and successes of mission, 39–40, 42; role as missionaries, 21–22, 25, 31, 175n3, 175n7; and translations of religious terms, 26–30, 34–36. *See also* Ricci, Matteo

Jesus: Catholic teachings about, 32–33, 36; Chinese conceptions of, 36, 160, 163; Protestant teachings about, 64–65; and relation to imperial office, 32–33; Taiping ideas of, 94–96, 103; terms for, 21–22, 32, 36, 100–103, 195n49. *See also* title of Christ

Jiangnan, 48–49, 123, 141–42

Jiangsu, 122–24

Jiangxi, 49, 156

Jiaqing, Emperor, 44, 167

Jiuyao (Nine Demons) Temple, 174nn10

John, Griffith, 119, 127, 132, 137, 141, 205n106

"kingdom of Heaven": Protestant views of 112–13; as understood by Taiping, 79, 104–5, 113–14; various translations of, 112–13, 160

Kuhn, Philip, 173n1, 188n42, 203n77

Land System of the Heavenly Dynasty, 5, 11, 126, 128, 146, 199n4, 203n80

Legge, James, 89, 197n63

Liang Afa, 8, 12, 57, 65, 102, 166, 187n34; conversion of, 61–62; as evangelist, 65–66, 68; and influence on Hong Xiuquan, 68, 92, 188n42, 189n51, 192n71; and influence on Taiping, 61, 64, 71, 76–79, 97, 134; and "kingdom of Heaven," 106–7, 110; and millenarian teachings, 110–11; and Morrison, 186n29; and Old Testament, 97–98, 195n43

Lindley, Augustus, 72, 119, 132, 148

Li Xiucheng (Loyal King), 124, 132

London Missionary Society, 7, 55–57, 73, 183n2, 198n2, 202n56; representatives of, 62, 80, 119, 122

Lundbæk, Knud, 29, 176n11

Lutz, Jessie, 63, 69

Lutz, Ray, 63, 69

Manchus, 3, 99, 114; attacks against, 139–40; as vilified by Taiping, 10, 120, 127, 133, 136, 138–39, 149, 203n77

Marshman, Joshua, 80, 192n11

Meadows, Thomas T., 74, 133

Medhurst, Walter H., 73–74, 99–100, 169, 196n50, 207n34; and Boone, 91, 193n25; and debate over God's name, 80–90, 192nn9–10, 193n15, 207n35; and Hong Xiuquan, 91, 94; and "kingdom of Heaven," 105–6; and Taiping, 136–37

Methods of Militia Defense, 162–63

Michael, Franz, 9, 103, 114, 124, 173n3, 190n67, 194n29, 194n33, 204n88, 207n34

millenarian teachings, 56, 110–11, 197n70, 198n76–77; and influence on Taiping, 110–15

Milne, William, 61, 166–67, 192n11

Missions Étrangères de Paris, 58–59

monotheism, 103–4, 194n35

Morrison, Robert, 56–57, 61–64, 166; as influenced by Bassett, 60–61, 80, 101, 185n15; and title of Christ, 101, 196n50; and translation of Bible, 57–58, 60–61, 73, 80, 106, 184n6, 185n16, 186n29, 192n11

Mungello, David, 22, 174n11, 176n7

names for God, 21–22, 58–59, 80–81, 193n17; associations with imperial title, 81, 167; Catholic controversy about, 22–23, 27, 30, 80, 154, 158, 175n3; political implications of, 86–89, 91–92, 99, 167; used by Chinese Christians, 24–25, 166; used by Jesuits, 23–27, 59, 80, 84, 176n9, 176n11; used by Protestants, 15, 61, 80–91, 191nn5–6, 192n9, 193n25. *See also* Shangdi; *shen*; Tianzhu

Nanjing, 48, 121, 132, 151; controlled by Taiping, 119, 134, 137, 141, 155, 198n2; during siege, 142, 144–45; fall of, 126, 149, 169–70; as Heavenly Capital, 67, 107, 122–24, 198n4

Nestorians, 86, 192n14

New Testament, 10–11, 146–48; Catholic translations of, 57–58; Protestant translations of, 73–74; Taiping version of, 74, 189n66, 190n67, 190n71, 191n4

Nian rebels, 148

1911 Revolution, 17

Old Testament, 11, 65, 71, 147–48; influence on Taiping, 71–72, 74, 77, 146, 190n67, 190n71; Protestant translations, 73–74; Taiping version, 74, 190n67, 190n71

Opium War, 21, 44, 46; and effect on Christianity, 46, 48–50, 53, 150

polytheism, 31–33, 84

Proclamation by Imperial Sanction, 5

Protestant missionaries, 15; arrival in China, 54–57, 183n3, 202n56; and debate over name for God, 15, 81–91, 160, 166–67; and evangelical ideas, 62, 64–65, 78, 90; and impact of Taiping Rebellion on, 150, 159, 166–71; methods of, 63–64, 74; title of Christ, 100–101, 167–68, 195n49; and translation of Bible, religious

terms, 57–61, 73–74, 81–91; and view of Taiping, 117–18, 122, 126, 132, 134, 137, 164–67. *See also* London Missionary Society; *names of individuals*
Protestants, Protestantism, 12, 14, 208n36; Anglo-American, 4, 6, 7, 10, 13; 183n3; influence on Taiping, 54, 56, 134, 166; statistics on, 54, 69, 185n20. *See also* evangelicalism, evangelicals

Qin dynasty, 4–5, 87, 93, 168
Qing dynasty, 3, 94, 120, 158, 160, 180n59, 182n76; campaign against Taiping and Heavenly Lord sect, 157–64, 170; fear of Taiping, 140, 142; law code, 50, 164; and mandate to rule, 107–110; propaganda, 148–49, 158–63; victory over Taiping, 3, 150
Qing loyalists, 149, 156, 203n80; discussion of Taiping documents, 146–47; and view of Heavenly Lord sect, 152–53, 157–61, 170; and view of Taiping, 117–18, 120–28, 134, 137, 170
Qiying, 49–52, 183n77

A Record of Facts to Ward Off Heterodoxy, 157–61, 170, 206n18, 206n21
religious publications, 12, 63, 76; authorized list, sanctioned by Taiping, 11–12, 76, 147, 174n8, 190n71, 204n101

Ricci, Matteo, 22, 151–52; and Buddhism, Confucianism, 23–27; missionary method, 14–15, 19–25, 42; and name for God, 80, 89, 193n23; and teachings about Jesus, 32–33; and translations of religious terms, 23–29, 176n9, 176n11
Rites Controversy, 14, 22, 34, 43, 158, 175n1, 175n3, 179n47
Roberts, I. J., 63–66; and Hong Xiuquan, 67, 69, 71–72, 76, 92, 95, 98, 195n45

sacraments of Catholic church, 34–38
The Sacred Decree of the Heavenly Brother, 10
The Sacred Decree of the Heavenly Father, 9–10
The Sacred Edict, 20, 158
secret societies, 44–45, 144–45, 148, 153, 158
sectarianism, 5, 21; and Heavenly Lord religion, 42, 45, 150, 163–64; and Taiping, 161–64
secularization, 30, 177nn29–30
Shangdi (Sovereign on High), 3, 10; as God of Taiping, 4, 8, 10–11, 98, 104, 114, 138–39, 141, 158, 170; Hong Xiuquan's view of, 4–5, 92–94, 115; as name of Christian God, 14–15, 21–29, 80, 85–90, 158, 160, 175n3, 193n23; as title of Chinese ruler, 86–88, 94; used by Protes-

Shangdi *(continued)*
    tants, 80–81, 83–84, 87, 91, 166–67, 169, 207nn34–35. *See also* names for God; *shen*; Tianzhu
Shanghai, 148
shen: as name for Christian God, 58–59, 90; term for god, spirit, 32, 35, 89; as used by Protestants, 80–83, 91, 169, 207nn34–35. *See also* names for God; Shangdi; Tianzhu
Shi Dakai (Wing King), 148
Shih, Vincent, 6–7
Small Sword Society, 148
Society of God Worshippers, 9, 11, 92, 152; early practices, 128–31, 143; founding of, 67, 69, 153; transformation to political rebellion, 67–68, 76, 79, 86, 99, 104. *See also* Taiping Christianity; Taiping Rebellion; Taiping religious practices
Spence, Jonathan, 12
spirit possession, 9–11
Standaert, Nicolas, 24, 43, 174n11, 178n37
Suzhou, 48, 119, 123, 126–27, 132, 137, 144–45, 148–49, 151, 200n27

Taiping Christianity: and devotion of followers, 130–33; doctrines of, 3–10, 15–17, 79–80, 99, 117, 132–33, 141, 144, 169; distinctiveness of, 7–8, 12, 15, 17–18, 93, 116; and Heavenly Lord sect, 16, 53–54, 117, 154–55, 158–64, 170; and ideas of economic equality, 141–42; impact of, 147–49, 161–68; literature, 142–47, 204n97; and local, indigenous connections, 8–11, 79, 116–17, 164, 168–69; and name for God, 13, 80, 88, 92, 158; as new Chinese religion, 4–18, 78, 93, 116, 133, 171, 174n9; and opposition to imperial culture, 4–6, 12–14, 17–18, 79, 88, 92–93, 116–17, 165; proselytizing campaigns, 133–34, 142–49; Qing view of, 117–18, 120, 131, 143–44, 160–62, 198n1; as restoration of classical religion, 4–6, 78–79, 93, 100, 105, 116, 168–69; scholarly view of, 6–11, 130, 141, 146–47; and Ten Commandments, 65, 92, 96–97, 119, 132–34, 140–41, 146, 165; and translated Bible, 57, 73; and views of Heaven, 110–11, 161–62; and views of Jesus, 103–4, 158; Westerners' views of, 6–8, 12, 117–18, 120, 126, 137, 149, 164–68. *See also* Society of God Worshippers; Taiping Heavenly Kingdom; Taiping religious practices
Taiping Heavenly Chronicle, 69, 71, 76, 114, 189n51, 196n55; and history of Hong Xiuquan, 95–96, 128
Taiping Heavenly Kingdom, 14; and calendar, coins, 146, 204n97, 204n101; and commitment to social

justice, 141; establishment of, 67, 104, 117, 133, 187n37; fall of, 150, 164; organization of, 119, 147–48; strengthening of, 140–41, 147; and support of peasants, 120, 142. *See also* Society of God Worshippers; Taiping Christianity; Taiping legacy; Taiping Rebellion

Taiping Imperial Declaration, 71, 93, 96, 134

Taiping legacy, 3–8, 17–18, 150; as ignored by Christian missionaries, 164–71; on imperial order, 17, 170–71

Taiping Rebellion, 3, 53; as attack on blasphemy, 13–14, 92, 99, 143; as attack on imperial culture, 4–6, 13–14, 79, 99, 133; and causes for failure, 3–4; impact of, 142, 148–49, 170–71; as a mission, 133, 140, 142, 146–48; popular appeal of, 3–4, 79, 116, 120, 123–24, 131, 148–49, 169–71, 199n4; as religious war, 4–7, 12–14, 17–18, 93–99, 115–17, 162–64; as seen by gentry, 16, 149, 169–71, 199n4; suppression of, 3–4, 149, 157–63. *See also* Taiping Heavenly Kingdom

Taiping rebels: and ability to recruit, 4, 120–23, 131; and attacks on Manchus, 139–40, 203n77; and attacks against religious statuary, 11, 68, 95–96, 136–39, 149, 154, 171, 188n40–41; and banditry, 120–21; and faith in Shangdi, 4–5, 11–12, 115, 134, 146; geographic diversity of, 9, 121–24, 130; hairstyle of, 138, 203n72; numbers of, 121–24; organization of, 119, 121, 199n4; prayers of, 126–27, 200n29, 201n32; and religious motives, beliefs, 4–6, 10, 12–13, 80, 92–93, 99, 104, 132, 173n1; and religious requirements, 10–11, 118–21, 124–27, 132–34, 141, 200n29; and spirit possession, 9, 10; and treatment of Catholics, 154–56. *See also* Taiping Heavenly Kingdom; Taiping Rebellion; Taiping religious practices

Taiping religious practices, 117–19, 124, 133, 201n49, 205n107; for city dwellers, peasants, 118–20; communion, 130; daily Sabbath worship services, 124–27, 133, 200n22, 200n25, 200nn27–28; decline of, 130–32; familial labels, 140–41; meals, 119, 124; prayers, 119, 125–27, 132, 200n29, 201n32; preaching, 119, 128; sharing of goods, 119, 141–42; separation of genders, 140; singing, chanting, 119, 124–25, 127, 131–33, 201n38. *See also* Society of God Worshippers; Taiping Christianity; Ten Commandments

Taixiong (Eldest Prince), 103, 196nn55–56

Taizi (Crown Prince), 103, 127, 132, 167, 196nn55–56

Taylor, Charles, 74, 120, 127
Temple of Heaven, 107–9
Ten Commandments, 65, 92, 99, 147; and Catholics, 165–66; and Hong Xiuquan, 96–97, 110, 134, 194n41, 194n45; and importance to Taiping, 97, 119, 132–34, 140–41, 146; and Protestants, 135–36, 166–67, 195n46, 202n56
ter Haar, Barend, 10–11, 173n2
Thistle Mountain, 67, 72
Three Character Classic, 93, 132, 146–48, 207nn34–35; Taiping version of, 168–69
Three Teachings, 14, 15
Tianxiong (Heavenly Elder Brother), 103, 158, 160, 196nn55–56, 206n23
Tianzhu (Lord of Heaven), 23, 29, 59, 175n3; as used by Catholics, 15, 29, 59, 80. *See also* names for God; Shangdi; *shen*
Tianzi (Son of Heaven), 167
title of Christ, 79, 167, 193n15; debates about translation of, 100–101, 195n49, 196n50; as viewed by Taiping, 79, 94, 158. *See also* Jesus
Tongzhi, Emperor, 43; reign of, 157
translation of religious language: by Buddhists, 27–30, 178n31; by Catholics, 21–35, 38, 101, 178n37; by Protestants, 60–61, 101; and revolutionary nature of, 79. *See also* Bible; names for God; title of Christ; *specific terms*

A Treasured Raft which Rescues the Drowning, 156–57, 206n1
Treaty of Nanjing, 48, 50, 53
Treaty of Tianjin, 43, 50, 150, 164
Triad sects, 44–45
Trinity, 31–33, 36, 104
The True Meaning of the Lord of Heaven, 23, 25–26, 32, 176nn9–11

Wagner, Rudolf, 8–10, 62, 76, 116, 142
Wang Qingcheng, 9, 12, 94, 147
Wei Changhui (Northern King), 133–34
Weller, Robert, 9–11
Wesley, John, 55, 183n1
Wesleyan religious groups, 54, 62
White Lotus sect, 4, 10–11, 51–53, 121, 197n64; and millenarianism, 114; and rebellions, 152, 161, 164
Wright, Arthur F., 27–29, 30, 178n31
Wuchang, 121, 128, 141, 147, 151–52
Wylie, Alexander, 137

Xianfeng, Emperor, 95, 107–110, 156
Xiao Chaogui (Western King), 10, 92, 94
Xu Guangqi, 24

Yang Guangxian, 159, 206n18
Yang Tingyun, 24, 208n35
Yang Xiuqing (Eastern King), 10, 67, 138, 159, 161, 204n90

Yangzhou, 148, 151
Yangzi River Valley, 49, 53, 67, 147, 149
Yan Mo, 24
Yongan, 121, 143–44, 148
Yongzheng, Emperor, 20, 38–39, 180n55; proscription of Heavenly Lord sect, 42, 44, 50

Zeng Guofan, 116, 152, 156, 158
Zetzsche, Jost, 61, 184n11

Zhang Dejian, 118, 123, 198n1; on Heavenly Lord sect, 152–53; and Taiping documents, 143–44, 146, 103n80, 104n101; on Taiping practices, 119–20, 125, 128, 134, 140, 200n25, 200n29
Zhou dynasty, 19
Zhu Xi, 22, 24
Zürcher, Erik, 24–25, 28, 175n1, 179n50

www.ingramcontent.com/pod-product-compliance
Lightning Source LLC
Chambersburg PA
CBHW030619230426
43661CB00053B/2071